Players of Shakespeare 6

This sixth volume of essays by members of the Royal Shakespeare Company and the National Theatre is the first to be devoted to a single group of Shakespeare's plays. To celebrate the arrival of the new millennium the RSC presented productions of all the history plays of Shakespeare's two Lancastrian tetralogies, and the chance to see all eight in sequence in the spring of 2001 seems to have been the first such opportunity in English theatrical history. Half of the twelve essays in this volume accordingly come from this important and historic cycle. Of the other six essays, from later productions, three are from the rarely performed *King John*, one from the even more rarely performed *Edward III* and the remaining two deal with the best-known title roles among the history plays, in two major recent independent productions of *Henry V* and *Richard III*. The contributors to this volume are Guy Henry, Kelly Hunter, Jo Stone-Fewings, David Rintoul, Samuel West, David Troughton, Nancy Carroll, Desmond Barrit, Adrian Lester, Fiona Bell, Richard Cordery, and Henry Goodman. A brief biographical note is provided for each of the contributors, there is a list of performance credits for all the productions covered and an Introduction places the performances which the essays record in the overall context of the productions for which they were created.

ROBERT SMALLWOOD is Honorary Fellow of the Shakespeare Institute, Stratford-upon-Avon and was, until his retirement in 2001, Head of Education at the Shakespeare Centre, Stratford-upon-Avon. He has edited or co-edited the previous volumes in the *Players of Shakespeare* series. He is also the general editor of *Shakespeare at Stratford* and is the author of the book on *As You Like It* in that series.

Players of Shakespeare 6

Essays in the Performance of Shakespeare's History Plays

edited by
Robert Smallwood

CAMBRIDGE
UNIVERSITY PRESS

PUBLISHED BY THE PRESS SYNDICATE OF THE UNIVERSITY OF CAMBRIDGE
The Pitt Building, Trumpington Street, Cambridge CB2 1RP, United Kingdom

CAMBRIDGE UNIVERSITY PRESS
The Edinburgh Building, Cambridge, CB2 2RU, UK
40 West 20th Street, New York, NY 10011–4211, USA
477 Williamstown Road, Port Melbourne, VIC 3207, Australia
Ruiz de Alarcón 13, 28014 Madrid, Spain
Dock House, The Waterfront, Cape Town 8001, South Africa

http://www.cambridge.org

First published 2004

Printed in the United Kingdom at the University Press, Cambridge

Typeface Plantin 10.25/13 pt.   *System* LaTeX 2$_\varepsilon$ [TB]

A catalogue record for this book is available from the British Library

ISBN 0 521 840880 hardback

To

Sonja Dosanjh

RSC Company Manager throughout almost the entire period of Stratford theatre covered by the six volumes in the *Players of Shakespeare* series, who arranged, with unerring reliability and care, many hundreds of question-and-answer sessions with RSC actors for my visiting university groups, including those that lie behind virtually every one of the seventy-four essays in the *Players* series, and who has done so much to bring Stratford's academic and theatrical Shakespearians together, this volume is dedicated in friendship and affection.

Contents

Illustrations

Sources

Preface

This sixth volume in the *Players of Shakespeare* series, with its twelve essays, by twelve actors, on fourteen roles, in ten plays, is the first to devote itself to a single group of Shakespeare's plays. To celebrate the arrival of the new millennium the RSC mounted productions of all eight of the history plays of the first and second Lancastrian tetralogies and in London in the spring of 2001 played them in sequence together, something that appears never to have been achieved before in the British theatre. From that 'This England' millennium project come six of the essays in this volume, on eight roles that together cover all eight plays of the octet. Of the other six essays, from later productions, three are from an important production of the rarely performed (the *too* rarely performed, surely) *King John*, and one from the even more rarely performed *Edward III*, that apocryphal play increasingly finding a place in complete editions of Shakespeare (among them that of the publishers of the current volume). The other two essays deal with the two best-known title roles among the history plays, in two major recent independent (that is, non-cyclical) productions of *Henry V* and *Richard III*. The only absentee among the history plays of the 1623 Folio is the later, collaborative *Henry VIII*; essays on its leading roles may be found in the fourth volume of this series. Four of the plays – *Edward III*, *Richard II*, and the two parts of *Henry IV* – are new to the *Players of Shakespeare* series, as are no less than ten of the fourteen roles here considered. Once again I find myself regretting the fact that so few of the dramatic characters here discussed are women, though, in the history plays, four out of fourteen is, perhaps, about the best sort of ratio one could expect.

The essays in the volume are arranged in the Folio order of plays which, for the history plays, of course, means that they appear in the chronological order of their historical subject matter. (I have placed *Edward III*, therefore, where the Folio editors would certainly have put it, had they decided to include it.) Quotations and references are, as ever in this series, to the New Penguin Shakespeare, the edition still most likely to be issued to RSC actors in rehearsal. For *Edward III*, which is not included in the Penguin edition, I have used the edition specifically produced (by Roger Warren) for the RSC production (London, Hern, 2002). There is, as usual, at the head of each essay, a biographical note on its writer with emphasis on Shakespearian work, and at the end of the volume a list of credits for the eight productions (some of multiple plays) that are discussed in the book.

I acknowledge with gratitude a generous grant by the Shakespeare Birthplace Trust from its Jubilee Education Fund towards the reproduction fees for photographs; this has made it possible to maintain the number of illustrations in this volume at the same level as in previous volumes in the series. I am grateful to Susan Brock and Helen Hargest at the Shakespeare Centre Library for their unfailingly kind and meticulous help with photographs of Stratford productions and with many other questions and requests for information; nowhere could one find librarians more generous with their time and knowledge. I am grateful also to Pia de Souza at the National Theatre's press office for generous assistance with photographs of the National's production of *Henry V*, and to Nada Zakula of the RSC Press Office and David Howells, RSC Curator, for their patience and help in tracking down photographs of RSC productions from outside the Shakespeare Centre's collections. Most of the essays here began in question-and-answer sessions for groups of visiting students from universities around the world on the courses that, before my recent retirement, I used to organize for the Shakespeare Centre and the Shakespeare Institute; I am grateful to colleagues in both organizations for their friendship and support, and in particular to Rebecca Brown at the Shakespeare Centre for sharing memories of productions with me. Victoria Cooper and Sarah Stanton of Cambridge University Press remain as generous as ever in their support for this series, in spite of the sometimes rather large space of time between the proposal and planning of a volume and the final gathering-in of the latest of the contributions; to both of them I am grateful. I offer my sincere thanks also to all the players of Shakespeare in this volume, and in its predecessors, who have somehow managed, in their busy professional lives as actors, to find the time to display also their insights and skills as writers.

My most enduring debt, as editor of this volume and of this series, is acknowledged in the book's dedication to the closest of several good friends at the RSC whose careers there were ended by the devastating reorganization that hit the company in 2001, to which Kelly Hunter refers in her essay, and whose after-effects continue to be felt. This débacle, which included the closure of The Other Place studio theatre that had just staged the remarkable *Richard II* of which Sam West and David Troughton write so memorably in this volume, was known as 'Project Fleet' and was directed against the priceless ensemble repertoire tradition, and the company structures that supported it, that had been built up over the forty years of the RSC's existence and which provides the only possible basis from which to attempt productions of the great cycle of history plays with which this book is concerned. To all those (at the RSC and elsewhere) who, as a direct or indirect result of those lamentable events, have, like me, moved beyond our once close-knit Shakespearian Stratford community, I offer my warmest good wishes for the future – and the reassurance of my own discovery, already shared by many of them, that 'there is a world elsewhere'.

CHAMPAGNAC, CANTAL, FRANCE

Introduction

ROBERT SMALLWOOD

'Master William Shakespeare's Comedies, Histories, and Tragedies' the compilers of the first collected edition of Shakespeare's plays called their great folio of 1623, conferring in the process a distinctness of generic identity on the history play that it had perhaps never quite enjoyed before; for in earlier, individual (quarto) printings of some of what we now so readily refer to as 'the histories', 'tragedy', or 'true tragedy', or, perhaps, 'tragical history' had been the genre-identifying labels that title-pages offered. There was more, however, to the Folio's formal initiation of this third dramatic genre to add to the two classically recognized categories: while the comedies and the tragedies appear in the book in an order which offers little immediate sense of logical arrangement, either in terms of subject matter or of what we now believe about the plays' order of composition, the ten histories line up in meticulous chronological order of subject matter, with *King John* and *Henry VIII* as slightly outlying flankers at either end, and in between an octet of plays, from *Richard II* to *Richard III*, that covers a more or less continuous period of English history from 1398 to 1485. Whether these plays were originally conceived as in some sense an epic serialization of English history used to be the subject of much academic critical debate; that they came retrospectively to be seen as that is clear, however, not just from the Folio's arrangement, with its two-part and three-part division of certain reigns (in the case of *Henry VI* a division probably created for the Folio publication), but also from the epilogues attached to the second part of *Henry IV*, with its promise that the author 'will continue the story', and to *Henry V* with its solemn warning of future disintegration 'which oft our stage hath shown'. Indeed, the very nature of the historical source material that lies behind the plays, which makes the question 'What happened next?' askable (and, in a sense, answerable) at the end of *Richard II* in a way that it is not at the end of *Hamlet*, say, or *Othello*, makes the urge to treat these plays as a cycle almost inevitable.

Not that their performance history offers many examples of cyclical treatment. Those of Shakespeare's history plays that have held the stage over the last four centuries have, for the most part, done so as independent, individual pieces, *Richard III*, for example, providing in its title role the sort of star vehicle (ratchetted up a little in Cibber's rearranged version) that has made the reputations of actors from Burbage's day to our own. The patriotic energies which Olivier found in *Henry V* for his wartime film, or the note of elegiac tragedy that Gielgud so eloquently exploited in *Richard II*, the propagandist (anti-papal and later anti-French) slant that gave *King John* a lively performance history in the eighteenth and early nineteenth centuries, or the enormous theatrical generosity to actors from Will Kemp to Des Barrit of the role of Falstaff, are all witnesses to the much larger truth that the theatrical realization of these texts has no necessary connexion with their supposed cyclical inter-relationship. Nevertheless, to present some, or all, of these plays as a cycle has become, in the last century or so of professional theatre in this country, something of a defining symbol of the coherence and corporate strength of a theatre company and to tackle the *Henry VI* plays, in particular, has seemed increasingly to offer a sure sign of company self-confidence.

The collection of essays that follows comes, appropriately enough, from both sides of these contrasting theatrical traditions, six of them deriving from individual productions of separate plays and six from what was probably the most ambitious production of a history cycle ever attempted. In endeavouring to offer, as it is the business of the introductions to these volumes to do, some general sense of the productions within which the performances discussed by the essayists were to be seen, I want to deal first with the history cycle that provides the context for the essays by Samuel West, David Troughton, Nancy Carroll, Desmond Barrit, Fiona Bell, and Richard Cordery, the cycle that prompted the idea of focusing, for the first time, a *Players of Shakespeare* volume on a single group of plays.

When, in the spring of 2001, the Royal Shakespeare Company presented, at three theatres in London, the Pit Theatre at the Barbican, the Barbican Theatre itself, and the Young Vic, the chance to see, in sequence, in less than a week, all eight plays of Shakespeare's two Lancastrian tetralogies (with a rehearsed reading of the apocryphal *Edward III* thrown in for good measure), they were achieving what no other theatre company in Britain had achieved before. The 'This

England' millennium project had begun in Stratford in the preceding spring and summer, with *Richard II* at The Other Place studio theatre, the two parts of *Henry IV* at the Swan, and *Henry V* at the Royal Shakespeare Theatre, and these productions arrived in London (*Richard II* at the Pit, the others at the Barbican Theatre) by way of the traditional RSC autumn residence in Newcastle. The rest of the project, the three parts of *Henry VI* and *Richard III*, began life in the winter of 2000–2001 at the Swan in Stratford, but came to London (to the Young Vic) by way of a season at the Power Centre for the Performing Arts in Ann Arbor, Michigan, whence significant financial support had made possible a project more ambitious than could otherwise have been realized.

This enormous enterprise, involving around a hundred actors, in two companies, in eight plays, in three spaces, supported by massive sponsorship, public and private, and inconceivable outside the structure of a large and permanent theatre company, may be thought of as in many ways epitomizing the sort of ambitious work that the development through the twentieth century of publicly subsidized national theatre companies had made possible. It went much further than Anthony Quayle's valiant achievement, with the then one-season repertory company system at Stratford's Shakespeare Memorial Theatre, for the Festival of Britain in 1951, of producing the four plays of the second tetralogy in sequence; it went further even than the great flagship declaration of the RSC's arrival on the national theatrical scene, the seven-play cycle of 'The Wars of the Roses' directed by Peter Hall and John Barton for the quatercentenary of Shakespeare's birth in 1963–4, two years after the founding of the company, for that had reduced the three *Henry VI* plays to two. The same had been done with Michael Bogdanov's and Michael Pennington's seven-part adaptation which marked the English Shakespeare Company's arrival at the height of its strength in the 1980s, and would be repeated by Adrian Noble in his RSC trilogy 'The Plantagents' (*Henry VI*, reduced to two plays, and *Richard III*) in 1988. The 2000–1 'This England' project was, in fact, only the fourth time in modern British theatre history that all three parts of *Henry VI* had been produced together. At Stratford in 1906, and after years of building up the repertoire with his permanent (and mostly touring) company, Frank Benson did a seven-play history cycle (omitting *Henry V* which he had frequently performed); Douglas Seale achieved productions of all three parts of *Henry VI* in the heyday of the company at Birmingham Repertory Theatre in 1951 (and those productions later came to the Old Vic to make possible that theatre's five-year completion of the Shakespeare canon); and Terry Hands directed the trilogy with the RSC at Stratford in 1976, and, over adjacent seasons, the rest of the octet of histories, with Alan Howard playing all the kings except Henry IV (in whose plays he appeared as Prince Hal). But to get all eight plays in repertoire together was the unprecedented achievement of the 'This England' project, and the moment marked, as one century gave way to the next, what Michael Dobson described in his annual essay on British Shakespeare productions for *Shakespeare Survey*, 'the last flowering of the RSC as we thought we knew it' (volume 55, page 286).

For, only a matter of weeks later, a massive reorganization of the Royal Shakespeare Company was announced, under the title of 'Project Fleet', that would dismantle the ensemble company tradition so painstakingly built up over the forty years of the RSC's existence, replacing it with much shorter contracts for actors and considerably more independent productions outside the main company repertoire, and thus making a repetition of the 'This England' project inconceivable in the foreseeable future; and in spite of many resignations, and some appointments, and much talk (and even a little evidence) of movement back in the direction of an ensemble system, since that devastating announcement, the RSC remains a very long way from its position of confidence and strength of a few years ago. Much has been written, most of it fiercely hostile, about 'Project Fleet' and this is not the appropriate place to re-examine the issues it raised, but its timing needs here to be recorded, for response to it breaks surface in some of the essays that follow, and the model of company structure that it replaced, and the model it heralded, are of central relevance to the two contrasting theatrical approaches, cyclical and independent, to the performance of Shakespeare's history plays.

Ironically, a by-product of 'Project Fleet' was the closure of The Other Place, that studio theatre in Stratford where, during the almost thirty years of its existence, the RSC had achieved some of its most notable successes and where, in the spring of 2000, the entire 'This England' enterprise began. What distinguished the cycle from all other attempts on the octet was that the RSC used four directors and three theatre spaces (Steven Pimlott in The Other Place for *Richard II*, Michael Attenborough in the Swan for the two parts of *Henry IV*, Edward Hall in the Royal Shakespeare Theatre for *Henry V*, and Michael Boyd in the Swan for the three parts of *Henry VI* and

Richard III), and two companies of actors, one for the first tetralogy and one for the second. In a sense, therefore, the project combined the independent and the cyclical approaches to the plays, allowing, in spite of continuity of casting where characters survive from play to play, a heterogeneousness of approach, at least in the second tetralogy, that some thought inimical to the whole principle of cyclical presentation and some (including David Troughton in his essay on Bolingbroke) found relevant and illuminating.

It all began in The Other Place with Steven Pimlott's remarkable *Richard II*, a production that cut away, with surgical precision, the traditional theatrical presentation of this play as a poetic lament for a doomed king, a medieval pageant with a plangently self-elegizing tragic monarch at its centre. Under unforgiving fluorescent lighting that shone with equally searching clarity on audience and actors alike, and in the laboratory of a white box to which The Other Place had been transformed, the play became a cool, unromantic, clinical examination of political infighting, of rival factions struggling for supremacy, of power changing hands and the causes and the consequences of that phenomenon. It was in modern dress – designer chic with occasional state-opening-of-parliament fustian touches for scenes of particular formality – but it never had the slightest intention of simply re-presenting a late sixteenth-century play about late fourteenth-century England in a naturalistic, self-contained, illusionistic modern world. The performance was in-the-moment immediate, actors and audience simultaneously and presently aware of their mutual participation in the recreation of this story. It began with the central participant in that story locking the doors to ensure everyone's concentration on this particular re-examination of it – and then beginning at the end, with lines from Richard's soliloquy in prison. It was a prison to which we had all been confined, so that our concentration on the immediate issues, our attention to the present moment, should not be diverted by any trivial wondering about how it would all end.

In that unrelenting white box any properties brought on stage would, as Samuel West says in his essay, have quotation marks around them – and be set in bold capitals too, one felt. A golden chair was just a chair, identical to the dozen or so white chairs around the walls on which actors not currently participating in the story-telling would sit; and yet it wasn't, for getting to sit on the golden chair meant that you had achieved ultimate power. A mound of soil, sullying the white floor, was

5

Gloucester's grave; and yet it was also the earth of England to which, for their own political purposes, most of the play's principal characters pay homage. A rough wooden ammunition box made its first appearance as the cupboard in which were kept the great axes with which Bolingbroke and Mowbray seemed about to fight; but it would later do service as the looking-glass that Richard demands in the deposition scene, as the prison in which he stood hammering out his intellectual search for the ease of being nothing, and as the coffin in which his corpse was presented to his successor, the search for nothingness finally rewarded. The brilliantly suggestive economy of it all was in the impressive tradition of Shakespeare at The Other Place over the thirty or so years before that remarkable theatre's lamentable demise.

This mercilessly clear, forensic examination of political behaviour presented a struggle between the conservative old guard, of Gaunt, York, and Bolingbroke and their supporters, grimly determined to regain control of the country, and the callow, elegantly fashionable group of young men around Samuel West's intelligent, wry, self-regarding Richard. What is 'This England', the production opened the cycle by asking, who owns it, who speaks for it? Gaunt's famous speech on the sceptred isle became, not the usual patriotic celebration, but an urgently spoken, angry statement of a reactionary political position that provoked such a fury in Richard that he was restrained only with difficulty from knocking the old man out of his wheelchair – a wheelchair in which Richard later whizzed round the stage organizing the confiscation of his deceased uncle's estate. Nor was there any point, since Richard was here so determined to alienate one's sympathy, in seeking to invest it instead in Bolingbroke, for in David Troughton's performance, Bolingbroke seemed unstoppable in his need for power. The threat of violence was always latent behind his cool, energetic efficiency, his emotions carefully concealed by his political astuteness – except, perhaps, his contemptuous loathing for the Bushys and Greens of Richard's world, in whose execution (with silenced revolvers) he personally participated. The essays by Samuel West and David Troughton chart the journeys of these two cousins, Richard's from that early, rather laid-back petulance, through a smilingly self-mocking, ironic sense of betrayal (far indeed from the lyrical self-pity to which most performances of the role incline and frequently devastating in its shrewdly witty self-awareness), and finally to the successful search for ease in being nothing; Bolingbroke's from that early, driving, self-righteous ambition, and tactical canniness, to a growing sense of unease, and isolation, and loss of self that possessing power, and being possessed by power, brought with it, and thence to that long and bitter struggle with conscience that would oppress his mind in the *Henry IV* plays.

For Michael Attenborough's production of the two parts of *Henry IV* the 'This England' project moved from white box studio to thrust-stage, semi-Elizabethan Swan Theatre and to an altogether different theatrical register – and, as David Troughton's essay makes clear, a rather different directorial method of working too. This was a much more traditional production than its predecessor, its costumes more or less medieval (in an unspecific sort of way) and in a range of hues that suggested the autumnal, as did its atmospheric, mostly subdued lighting – as far as possible, in fact, from the white-lit post-modernism of *Richard II*. The set had a steep rake at the back, thrust through with sharpened stakes, spear-like and alarming, for the Battle of Shrewsbury scenes, the king and his followers silhouetted atop the bank in misty-morning light. From the same slope later sprouted the branches of Gaultree Forest where, in a foggy dawn, a prissily puritanical John of Lancaster would secure the surrender of the northern rebels. The same branches, in warmer lighting, shades of green faded into its sunlight, took us economically to the mellow afternoon of Shallow's orchard, where Falstaff's recruits, diseased, absurd, and misshapen – fugitives, it seemed, from a Brueghel painting – lined up to buy themselves out of the war. The surface of the stage was crusty, earth-like, and from beneath it fires glowed for the battle scenes, civil war seeming to burn the very land itself.

From this earth Falstaff was born, struggling, old-mole-like, through its floor at the beginning of the second scene of Part One, just as Hal was materializing apparently from somewhere under his father's throne – a moment that Desmond Barrit discusses in his essay. At the beginning of the preceding scene, to the accompaniment of plainsong, we had met David Troughton's King Henry, in monkish robe, on his knees and penitentially clutching a great wooden crucifix, while his courtiers stood priest-like around him. 'Wan with care' he was indeed, but in his defiance and determination recognizably the man who had seized the crown in the preceding play, only to find himself now in that prison of regal responsibility from which death is the only escape. The crown never left him: to wear it on his head was to inflict piercing pain upon himself; to be parted from it was to lose his reason for living; mostly he

7

clutched it possessively to him, his prize, his burden, his destroyer. The unswerving determination beneath the care-worn exhaustion, the latent possibility of violence, the fiercely possessive love for his son, the need to show that love and the awful inhibitions about doing so, are the subjects of David Troughton's essay.

At the beginning of the play's second scene Falstaff and King Henry were seen briefly together on stage, father and surrogate father on either side of William Houston's enigmatic, watchful Prince Hal, an unreadable smile so often on his lips (though rarely in his eyes), accepting with easy tolerance Falstaff's need to demonstrate his affection in hugs and hair-rufflings, but always, meticulously, maintaining that slight sense of separateness, that care never entirely to commit. Desmond Barrit's essay takes us through that relationship, from this early, easy physicality to what he sees as the mortal blow of the final rejection, on the way drawing attention to the fierceness of Falstaff's love of life and to his profound need for companionship, both of which emerged vividly in the performance. This was a Falstaff haunted by his fear of mortality, terrified of loneliness, desperate for attention, and for love – qualities even more apparent in the ageing, silver-haired, limping, pock-marked figure of Part Two.

Nancy Carroll's essay records the production's important re-examination of the Percy marriage. Adam Levy's youthful, rather vulnerable Hotspur was far from the through-and-through military man of tradition and the flowing, silvery cloak that he frequently wore rather suggested the aesthete than the soldier. His energy, emotional openness, and impetuosity were matched by the ardour of Kate's aching love for him, so that beneath the surface quarrelsomeness of their scenes together the depth of their mutual commitment was clear. Hotspur's decision to exclude his beloved Kate from knowledge of the conspiracy thus became something very serious and difficult, an expression of his love for the partner that he must not endanger rather than the usual carefree, vaguely misogynistic, thoughtlessness; and he went off to Shrewsbury, brave and determined, but desperately aware of the awful seriousness of what he was about. The effect of these decisions on the theatrical power of their scenes together, and on Kate's wonderful epitaph for her dead husband in Part Two, was profound and is described in Nancy Carroll's essay.

With the two parts of *Henry IV* up and running at the Swan, the saga of 'This England' then moved to Stratford's main stage at the Royal

Shakespeare Theatre and to Edward Hall's modern-dress production
of *Henry V*, which is not represented among the studies that follow.
(Not every invitation, sadly, to contribute to this series produces the
hoped-for essay.) In the autumn and winter of 2000–2001 the journey
was resumed, now back at the Swan but with a different company of
actors, in Michael Boyd's productions of all three parts of *Henry VI* (for
only the second time in the RSC's history) and *Richard III*. This was not
quite, however, the Swan as we had known it before. The thrust stage
was removed, an immense pair of battered bronze doors, much used
in crashing battle exits and entrances, was installed on the opposite
side of the building, with a balcony above for ceremonial (and often
ghostly) appearances, and the audience was seated round all sides of a
playing area that, viewed from above, roughly resembled the shape of
a corpse. And viewed from above it quite frequently was – by actors at
least, for an unusual credit in the programme was to Gavin Marshall
for 'Company Rope-work', and an extraordinary vertical dimension to
the production (reflecting, perhaps, the plays' depictions of hierarchies
overturned) frequently made for physically exciting theatre. Jack Cade
and his followers swung over the stage on trapezes; attacks on, and
flights from, battlements were made on swinging ropes; the embalmed
corpse of Henry V hung above the stage before Part One began, and
was lowered to it, then entombed beneath it, in the first scene; Joan
of Arc, suspended above the flames discernible in the centre-stage pit
(vertical exits could be downwards as well as upwards), was stabbed in
her genitals by York in savage mockery of her claims to virginity; the
ghost of Humphrey Duke of Gloucester returned to act as hangman to
the Bishop of Winchester, hoisting him, screaming and squirming, to
the flies (in more than one sense), where he hung on a chain like a side
of meat in a butcher's slaughter-house. (These last two examples of the
production's remarkable series of images of verticality are discussed in
the essays by Fiona Bell and Richard Cordery.)

Apart from those battered bronze doors the stage was basically without colour, providing a striking contrast to the vivid shades of the costumes (medieval in a timeless sort of way): King Henry's white robe
and golden cloak, the Dauphin's vivid blue, Beaufort's cardinal red,
Jack Cade's green, the cream-coloured tunic of Joan of Arc, the deep
red and gold of Margaret of Anjou's sumptuous court dresses, the white
of York, the black of Richard. At intervals, between or during scenes,
with an arbitrariness that seemed to reflect the arbitrariness of all the

killings their colours provoked, white and red feathers would flutter down from above, blown in the swirl of battle or drifting among the corpses. Bells and gongs, urgent, harsh, insistent, eerie chimes, and thunderous, terrifying drums for battle entrances, provided the musical accompaniment.

Except for David Oyelowo as Henry VI, the still, calm centre of these turbulent plays, his kingly graciousness poignantly irrelevant to the national turmoil, every actor in the company played two or more roles in a production of great pace and energy. Many of the doublings created significant links and coherences through the sequence. The actors who in Part One had played Talbot and his son – Talbot watching his boy's corpse being hoisted aloft as he lamented the death of his 'Icarus' (Part One, IV.vi.55) – returned in Part Three as the son who has killed his father and the father who has killed his son, and were there again at the end of *Richard III* as Derby and Richmond. Aidan McArdle, playing the Dauphin, external enemy to Henry VI, returned as Richard of Gloucester, mortal enemy to Henry VI at home. Fiona Bell, more than humanly dangerous to English rule in France as a driven, haunted Joan of Arc (with a Scots accent), returned – with impressive speed, as her essay describes – as Margaret of Anjou, elegant, cool, and ruthless (and now with an English accent), more than humanly dangerous to the peace of England; in *Richard III*, crazed with vengefulness and grief and in a ritual that fuelled the ferocity of her curses, she was to be seen solemnly arranging the skeleton of her dead son from the bones which she carried over her shoulder in an old sack. The apposition that the production explored between Henry Plantagenet and Richard Plantagenet, the sixth and third of those forenames to occupy the throne of England, continued even beyond the ample limits suggested in the text: both were still there, staring at each other in ghostly manifestation, as Richmond spoke his final victory speech. This symbiotic relationship was reflected in another notable double, the subject of Richard Cordery's essay. Henry's saintly benevolence and Richard's diabolical malice provoke (paradoxically) roughly equal levels of political chaos in England. The parallel is reflected in their principal servants, their 'protectors', Humphrey Duke of Gloucester, gracious, calm, and ineffective, and Henry Duke of Buckingham, suave, sanctimonious, and chilling – as Richard Cordery presented them in his performances of the two roles. Both imagine themselves capable of guiding and controlling their protégés – of wielding power over those who wield the ultimate power symbolized by throne and crown – and both find themselves hurled aside to violent death by the onward rush of events that will ultimately generate the violent deaths even of the kings they thought they could manipulate.

That return for a last ghostly reprise of the earlier polarity of Henry and Richard was part of the production's determination to bring the past into the present by a much more liberal use of ghosts than that provided for in the text's restriction of them to the scene of Richard's dream before Bosworth. There were spectral reappearances throughout the cycle and interwoven with the recurrent patterns of doubling they provided a series of connexions and equivalences, of cause and effect, that impressively bound the plays together. For his (interpolated) coronation procession Richard's way to the throne was past the shades of Margaret and York, Prince Edward and King Henry; the dead marched across battlefields, impeding their former enemies; Richmond's victory speech was watched, from the balcony above the battered doors, by the two little York princes; Talbot's ghost returned as Suffolk's executioner, Duke Humphrey's as Winchester's. The whole sequence insisted, indeed, upon the endless, mad futility of the cycle of vows made and broken, of prophecies fulfilled, of the past endlessly re-enacted in the present, of hatred answered with hatred, of ambitions achieved and lost, of killings and their revenges, of throne-lust and blood-feud, a cycle that revealed (as productions of the complete tetralogy seem always to do) the thrilling theatricality of the terrible vision of national chaos that these too-rarely performed plays present.

In the spring of the following year, 2001, another rarely performed play, *King John*, made its début on the Swan stage in a production by Gregory Doran, a sort of appendage or postscript, perhaps, to the huge 'This England' project of the previous year, but also the first of the four independent productions of history plays represented in this volume. Doran had had a considerable success at the Swan a few years earlier with his production of Shakespeare's (and Fletcher's) only other non-cyclical history play *Henry VIII* – there are essays on its two principal roles in *Players of Shakespeare, 4* – but the approach here, though similar in terms of a severely plain stage setting, was very different in terms of costume, for the meticulous mid-Tudor of the earlier production was here replaced by a deliberate avoidance of the temporally specific, with vaguely medieval robes and dresses mixing with more modern (or timeless) leather and woollen jerkins and jackets. The only prop on stage was a more or less unadorned high-backed chair in plain wood. On it John sat in the first scene to hear the French embassy and to determine the Faulconbridge property case, so we accepted it as a throne; whether it had reverted to being an ordinary wooden chair when, shortly afterwards, the bastard son of Coeur-de-lion sat on it to tie his boot-lace during his first soliloquy was more ambiguous. There were occasional bits of pageantry – banners were swirled and waved and swished, with dramatic side-lighting, to represent the battle scenes; an immensely long St George's flag descended startlingly from the flies as a backdrop to the throne-chair for John's second coronation (a pathetically under-attended event); an ornate altar appeared, with a nuns' chorus and much Catholic ritual for John's obeisance (naked but for a rather surprising pair of long flannel knickers) to Pandulph – but for the most part the production was content to allow the words of the text to take us into the world of the play.

It proved to be a curiously modern world in many ways. In the Angiers scenes, for example, the elaborate royal appeals for loyalty, those self-justifying public utterances thinly veiling naked greed and ambition, were spoken out to the auditorium where the representative citizen, Hubert (who is expected to vote for one side or the other), stood, detached and contemptuous, among the rest of us; in what was a British election year the episode offered an engagingly apposite comment on the politics of spin. The image of unscrupulous politicians, trading insults, then finding it convenient to make a treaty, then falling out again and making war, could hardly have seemed more relevant in its cynicism. At the centre of all this, the King John of Guy Henry was clearly only too aware (as his essay suggests) of the flimsiness of his own claim to power: his own mother had told him, after all, only a few seconds into the play (and in this production he was clearly much dashed by her forthrightness), that he ruled much more by 'possession' than by 'right' (1.i.40).

The production began with John scurrying in late for the French ambassador's audience with him and then needing a prompt for the ambassador's name; but whether this was a carefully stage-managed diplomatic insult or merely evidence of John's incompetence it was impossible to know. His crown was clearly uncomfortable, needing constant adjustment – or removal to hang on the top of the throne – but whether this was to be read symbolically, or just as evidence of John's general edginess and gangling awkwardness, was (as, again,

Guy Henry's essay makes clear) something that the production wasn't anxious to decide for us. This King John never knew whether or not to take himself seriously as a monarch; his petulance and anger were frequently funny in their childishness; and even his deathbed – or, as it was in this production, his death-chair – seemed to lack dignity, John rising from it to greet his cousin the Bastard and then falling to the floor to die, while the Bastard was in the middle of delivering the news of the war.

King John is an unsettling play, quite literally so in its leaving of audiences with nowhere to settle, uncertain where, if anywhere, to allow their sympathies to rest. This quality is perhaps encapsulated most tellingly in Arthur's death: John wants him dead and orders his execution, but the order seems to have been commuted to blinding (equally effective in incapacitating the boy for rule but – and just making the distinction draws attention to its obscene speciousness – falling short of the full sinfulness of murder); the order is then withdrawn by John, for reasons of sheer political advantage, though too late for the change of plan to reach Hubert, the executioner; Hubert then discovers that the poker that he has heated for the work has cooled preternaturally and uses this as an excuse to show mercy (and in this production the decision did seem to be based on superstition rather than compassion); Arthur is then killed trying to escape from prison on what may be a suicide mission but which in this production seemed a genuine accident, the boy scrambling precariously along the bannister of the Swan's high top balcony, only to slip and fall inwards, a dummy taking his place (in a clever bit of theatrical legerdemain) for a heart-stoppingly convincing crash to the floor; the rebellious barons, and the Bastard Faulconbridge, who find the corpse, then blame John, who may be innocent technically but is hardly so morally. It was to that sort of complexity that this production responded so astutely, even the immensely likeable, rather impish, Bastard Faulconbridge of Jo Stone-Fewings having to admit (as he describes in his essay), that his initial energetically cheerful, shoulder-shrugging cynicism proves to be an inadequate guide through the 'thorns and dangers of this world', where he himself finds it impossible not to 'lose his way' (IV.iii.140–1).

In this world of breathtaking male insincerity, where those in power one by one succumb to the suave, oily, manipulative persuasions of the papal legate, Cardinal Pandulph, it is the women who provide some sense of moral perspective: Eleanor of Aquitaine, fierce in loyalty to her family, to her son and to her newly discovered grandson; Blanche, the obedient pawn in this male hegemony, sacrificed to the ambition and pride of uncle and husband which 'whirl asunder and dismember' her hopes and commitments (III.i.330); and above all Constance, whose all-consuming maternal love for her child, and all-consuming, heart-rending grief at his loss, are analysed in Kelly Hunter's essay. Constance's response to the sneering brutality of King Philip's accusation, 'You are as fond of grief as of your child' has about it a fullness of commitment, a wholeness of emotional logic, that singles her out from everyone else in the play: 'Grief fills the room up of my absent child' (III.iv.92–3).

At the end of Gregory Doran's *King John*, with the women of the play dead, and the corpse of the king sprawled in all its unkingly indignity across the stage, there was a moment when the assembled barons, and the Bastard, eyed each other suspiciously to see who would make the first move, and what it would be. Then, as if at some invisible signal, and in unison, they scurried across to Prince Henry, now King Henry III, scrambling to be the first to kneel at his feet. And there, the production said very clearly, ending as cynically as it had begun, there mightest thou behold the great image of royal authority.

The reign of yet another medieval English king was presented to the perusal of audiences at the Swan Theatre in Stratford in the following season; the play on this occasion was an even greater theatrical rarity than *King John*. The anonymously published *Edward III* had been offered two years earlier in a rehearsed reading as part of the two remarkable weeks when the RSC's millennium 'This England' project brought all eight of the history plays of the two tetralogies together in London. Anthony Clark's production of the play was put together in difficult circumstances in the spring of 2002 when, in the aftermath of 'Project Fleet', resignations and turmoil were still continuing in Stratford. It was the first production of the play by the RSC and only the second professional production in Britain since the seventeenth century (the first was at Theatre Clwyd in 1987). It was rehearsed in some haste (as David Rintoul's essay reveals) and formed part of a Swan season of rarely performed Elizabethan and Jacobean plays.

Speculation about the possibility of Shakespeare's having had a hand in *Edward III* goes back to the mid-eighteenth century, and a belief in Shakespeare's involvement with the two seduction scenes between King Edward and the Countess of Salisbury had, during the twentieth century, become almost a critical orthodoxy. The publication of editions of the text with Shakespeare's name firmly on the title page, one of them in the New Cambridge Shakespeare from the publishers of this *Players of Shakespeare* series, was, nevertheless, a comparatively recent phenomenon when visitors to the Swan Theatre in 2002 found programmes (and an RSC text of the play published by Nick Hern from which the quotations and references in David Rintoul's essay are taken) stating, unequivocally and without qualification, Shakespeare's authorship. This is not the place to join the authorship controversy: if Shakespeare wrote *Edward III* some explanation has to be found for long stretches of writing so dull that there is nothing like them to be found elsewhere in his work ('iambic tosh' is a phrase that comes up in reviews of the production), and in providing such an explanation David Rintoul's proposal of an apprentice piece hastily revised for performance may be as plausible as any; it is the general characteristics of Anthony Clark's production that concern us here.

The play was offered on a more or less bare Swan stage, with the outline of a medieval castle on a gauze screen for the early scenes, high chairs (like those used by tennis umpires) for King John of France and King Edward to oversee the battles, a stylized upstage tree, ropes tautened across the stage to suggest armies encamped before battle, and a few canvas-covered bundles to represent the mounds of corpses at Crecy and Poitiers. Costumes were eclectic: Edward and his nobles wore modern military dress uniform in the formal early scenes, but there was an approximation to medieval armour, for the upper body at least, in the battle scenes – and a remarkable variation on this, described in David Rintoul's essay, for Queen Philippa; fleeing civilians crossed the stage before some of those battle scenes, carrying battered suitcases and looking much like the familiar images of refugees during the most recent military invasion of France (inviting a comparison, it seemed, between King Edward's army and Hitler's); Lodowick, Edward's bewildered secretary, had a reporter's notepad and ball-point pen in the amusing scene in which he took notes from his master towards the creation of a love poem; the not-quite-six burgesses of Calais (whose numbers David Rintoul explains in his essay) in their ragged shifts might have come from any century.

It was a clear, fast-moving, vigorous production, with excitingly choreographed battle scenes to a background of sound and music – including, at one point, the chillingly ominous cawing of ravens – that gave a vivid sense of primitive armies in combat, and if it didn't quite manage to demonstrate that the writing was of unvaryingly high quality, it did vindicate the play as a watchable, coherent, and challenging piece of theatre. David Rintoul made no attempt to disguise the self-regarding imperiousness of King Edward, the threat that his power, unless restrained and guided, represents to enemies and subjects alike. His two scenes with Caroline Faber's coolly beautiful, alluringly aloof Countess of Salisbury had something of the quality of the Angelo/Isabella encounters in *Measure for Measure*, not only in the confrontation between, on the one hand, political strength and moral degeneracy and, on the other, political weakness and passionate morality, but also in the sense that they gave of a profound mutual fascination operating dangerously beneath her fierce ethical repugnance and the self-knowing shamefulness of his abuse of power. Seen within the context of the production as a whole, the scenes – although, of course, theatrically and poetically striking – took their place in the play's ongoing examination of the workings of power, the significance of oaths, public and personal, the claims of conscience, the morality of war, the proper treatment of defeated enemies – all those areas in which Edward (as David Rintoul makes clear in his essay) is repeatedly, and narrowly, diverted from making the wrong choices, political and moral. Like all the other history plays in this volume, then, the play was asking urgent questions about kingship, about the way absolute power operates, and about the status, and the rights, and the possibilities for redress, of those who suffer, and suffer from, the use, and the misuse, of royal authority.

That these issues of personal and political morality should be raised by a play on the reign of a king famous principally for victory in France clearly looks forward to *Henry V*. Before discussing the National Theatre's production of that play, however, as background to Adrian Lester's essay on the title role, I want to remain in Stratford and to complete the discussion of the RSC productions represented in this volume. Sean Holmes's version of *Richard III* opened at the Royal Shakespeare Theatre in the summer of 2003 and saw the long-awaited, eagerly anticipated, return of Henry Goodman to Stratford after an absence of over fifteen years (a good deal of it spent, in fact, at the National Theatre). The production followed the long-established RSC tradition of moving later to Newcastle, but then provided yet another example of the destructive legacy of 'Project Fleet', which had included among its raft of regrettable decisions the withdrawal from the RSC's permanent London theatre at the Barbican before an alternative had been found. This meant that neither *Richard III*, nor most of the rest of the interesting and exciting work from the 2003 Stratford season, was seen in London, breaking a tradition that went back to the creation of the RSC at the beginning of the 1960s.

Henry Goodman's essay on the role of Richard makes clear the production's eagerness to explore the play's self-conscious theatricality and fully examines its principal metaphor in so doing, the red velvet curtain that was lowered to mark the division between the play's two worlds, the one in front of that curtain which Richard, in soliloquy, shares with the audience, and the one behind it, in which he is an actor in the events which he plans in advance, and retrospectively analyzes, with his fellow conspirators in the auditorium. The production began – a considerable rarity in theatrical annals, surely – when the curtain was lowered; through it, after a pause, peeped, and then stepped, Richard, an eager master of ceremonies, it seemed, in buff top hat and tails, to speak the famous opening soliloquy with sarcastic, parodic enthusiasm. He flaunted his summer suit on 'glorious summer' and cued the band for an appropriate tune to which he shimmied a little waltz on 'capers nimbly' (1.i.2, 12). He soon broke down with the futility and pain of the enterprise, however, and began stripping off the party finery to reveal, even as he said it, a body 'not shaped for sportive tricks' (1.i.14), a body bent and held together with black leather straps, a shocking purple birthmark on his face, his left leg twisted. The jack boots and the maroon shirt that were now revealed had more than a hint of fascism about them and the debonair figure we had momentarily thought was to be our guide through the evening was transformed into the leering, twisted monster, nipping off stage to stab a dog that barked at him, who now invited our collusion. And this was the pattern of the first half of the play, with Richard as it were introducing, and then revealing, behind the big red curtain, the scenes in which we were to watch his (or, rather, our) plans put into practice.

The world in which he invited us to watch him operate was a late Victorian or Edwardian one, all heavy armchairs and chaises-longues, with earls and dukes in pompous frock-coats, women in long, dark, heavily corsetted dresses, and children in Eton collars playing with rocking horses, a world oddly reminiscent of the one that had recently been made familiar to British television viewers in Stephen Poliakoff's

The Lost Prince. There were quietly spoken civil servants in bowler hats (one of them by the name of Tyrrel) and murderers who might have attracted the investigative attention of Sherlock Holmes. What seemed to be the rear wall (and would later prove to be a back-cloth) offered a representation of the London skyline, with Big Ben, and in front of it the suggestion of the river, flowing ever on, bearing Clarence, and the princes, away to the Tower. The staid and deliberate pace of this humourless Edwardian court, its King Edward in a big iron wheelchair (around which his crippled younger brother capered rather nimbly), provided an extraordinary contrast to the fierce, demonic energy of Richard, whether he was operating destructively within the court world or sharing with us, on the other side of the curtain, his reactions to it. With remarkable dexterity he moved, in the first half of the play, between these two worlds, and the contrast was highly theatrical.

As Henry Goodman shows in his essay, however, that freedom of movement begins to desert Richard as he nears and achieves his goal, a gleefully incredulous cackle all that there was time for him to share with the audience as he ascended the strange overgrown high chair that was the throne for which he had schemed so hard. In the later stages of the play, the history upon which it is based begins, ineluctably, to take over from the celebration of its own theatricality. In response to this, it seemed, the production moved back in time and we watched Richard, now in distinctly medieval armour, being pulled (by human horse-power), in a little cart that might have come out of the RSC's 1964 'Wars of the Roses', towards confrontation with his past at Bosworth. And there, before his final collusion in his own death, the last vestige of the theatrical pageant in which he had invited us to watch him operate, the London skyline on the false rear wall, was flown out and revealed the bare bricks of the back wall of the theatre building itself. In front of it Richard's past lined up to greet him, dominated by young Richard of York energetically riding his rocking horse in a terrible mockery of the famously despairing cry for a horse an older Richard of York would soon utter. The confrontation with his past, and its effect on Richard's psychological self-awareness – its effect, indeed, on the very idea of the genre 'history play' with which this introduction began, as Richard's history here arrives at the brink of tragedy – is analysed in Henry Goodman's essay.

It is a commonplace of sixteenth-century justifications for the writing of history books – a genre in which the period was prolific – and which such writers as Heywood and Nashe were quick to turn to the justification of history plays, and thence of theatre itself, that a study of the past is immensely beneficial to the contemplation and illumination of the present. The last of the four independent (that is, non-cyclical) productions of history plays to be dealt with in this introduction is clearly a case in point. Nicholas Hytner's inaugural production as the National Theatre's incoming Artistic Director was, surprisingly, the first time that *Henry V* had been staged there. It opened in the Olivier auditorium in the spring of 2003, just after the first phase of the Anglo-American war in Iraq had achieved its aim of toppling the incumbent régime. Adrian Lester's essay reveals that when the production was first contemplated, no decision had been made about period, but that international political events during the planning stages made a contemporary setting unavoidable – and, one might add, surely right too.

The production used what has sometimes seemed the daunting spaciousness of the Olivier stage to powerful and often exciting effect. For the scenes of the French campaign the stage was a cavernous black space – 'vasty fields' indeed – across which jeeps roared and squads of helmeted soldiers in combat uniform heaved and flung themselves through the smoke of battle, the flashes of exploding shells, and the deafening rattle of machine-gun fire. Another, more important, version of the war, however, was being fought further downstage, for on the production's only real bit of 'set', a partition that divided the playing space, was a large television screen that symbolically masked the actual war zone and dominated the theatre (and the minds of those in charge of the campaign), and provided a constant, and brilliantly apposite, connexion to the way audiences had just been experiencing the war in Iraq. At Southampton and at Harfleur, in the post-battle scenes at Agincourt, and at the final peace settlement, Henry, surrounded by the media circus, was always ready at a moment's notice to re-arrange his facial muscles and confront the cameras with an appropriate sound-bite for the nation. His broadcasts were to be seen in the pub where Nym and Bardolph, gloomily brooding over their pints, half watched him for a moment before flicking channels to the snooker; they were to be seen also, with French sub-titles, at the French (the Elysée) palace, with its Louis XIV furniture and elegant china, where they frightened Princess Katherine into a realization of the need to learn English and provoked her father into a televised message to the French nation on his war preparations (Act Three, Scenes Four and Five). At

Harfleur, demanding the surrender of the town through microphone and loudspeakers, Henry signalled for the newsreel cameras and sound to be cut as his threats grew more vicious. In the pub, the slick professionalism of Henry's screen presentation contrasted with the snippet of home video we had seen (as we learned of the death of Falstaff) of part of the tavern scene from the first part of *Henry IV*, with Hal in dreadlocks alongside Des Barrit's Falstaff (revived, in a rather elegant little in-joke, from Stratford a couple of years earlier). The smile of friendship and happiness on Hal's face was in vivid contrast, in its openness and generosity, to the watchful astuteness of Henry's manner now, in government.

We had first observed that watchfulness in the opening council scene, which was set as a cabinet meeting with everyone (men and women) in sharp suits, bottles of mineral water on the table, and dossiers on the Salic law handed out in advance. Henry (his mind, one thought, perhaps already made up, though it was impossible to be sure) sat scrutinizing his ministers to make sure they were all on board in this carefully guided discussion of the rights and wrongs of invading another country (France was the one they mentioned, Iraq was the one we thought of) – an invasion for which there was, perhaps, not altogether unquestionable justification. Henry's PA, somewhat donnish in long skirt and cardigan, eager, enthusiastic, and a little patronizing, had already presented the pro-war propaganda in the opening chorus and would continue to spin events to Henry's advantage between stages of the campaign. The sense of everything being under the tightest control was interestingly qualified, however, by Henry's reaction to the Dauphin's message, when his fury was held in check only through a tremendous effort of will. He ended the meeting, though, just as he had begun it, with suave, gracious, steely efficiency.

That mixture of charm and ruthlessness was evident in Henry throughout the play and is revealingly analyzed in Adrian Lester's essay. It gave him the energy to find a way of goading his soldiers, groaning with exhaustion before Harfleur, to fight their way back into the breach; it allowed him to shoot his former companion Bardolph in the head as an example to his troops – and also as a way of saving Bardolph from the firing squad; it inspired the quiet, understated yet charismatic, determination of the St Crispin's speech and the shocking decisiveness of the order to kill the prisoners of war; it produced his courteous but immovable insistence that the French king, broken and humiliated as he was, should surrender on every single point of the peace terms; and it kept him going through the wooing of a tense, hostile Princess Katherine, clearly shocked that she should be forced into marriage with her country's conqueror, in the play's final scene. With his soldiers Henry seemed entirely at home, marching alongside them, carrying a bigger pack than any of them, eager to justify himself in the highly charged discussion with Bates, Court, and Williams on the rights and wrongs of the war, and chagrined when they drifted away as the detail and obsessiveness of his argument lost their interest.

That moment was one of many when the production seemed accurately to catch the collective mood of soldiers in war: the groan of exhaustion and unwillingness when invited to renew the attack on Harfleur; the suggestion, in two jeering monosyllables, that it was time for the French herald to depart; the speed with which Bardolph's pockets were picked as soon as his corpse was left unattended; the stunned disbelief and grumbling murmur of refusal when the order to kill the POWs was given, so that it was left to a battle-crazed fanatic with a machine-gun, Llewellyn, to carry it out; the clumsy, rowdy celebration of victory and the cheers of aggression and relief as the names of the French dead were read out. In the lower ranks, as at the top, the production's contemporaneity was constantly telling, most of all, perhaps, in its presentation of a war leader desperately anxious that his decisions should be seen to be justified – by God, by history, and by the people, the voters. In a way that seemed peculiarly relevant to a national theatre and a national dramatist, the production debated issues of nationhood and nationalism, of invasion and conquest (and their aftermath), of political leadership and political expediency, that illuminated both the text of *Henry V* and the current national mood. Little more could be asked of a history play – at the end of the sixteenth century or at the beginning of the twenty-first.

King John

GUY HENRY

GUY HENRY played the title role in Gregory Doran's production of *King John* at the Swan Theatre in Stratford in the summer season of 2001 and afterwards at the Pit Theatre at the Barbican. His other part that year was Malvolio. Earlier roles for the RSC had included Sir Andrew Aguecheek, Longaville, the Lord Chamberlain in *Henry VIII*, Dr Caius, Cloten, Octavius Caesar in *Antony and Cleoptra*, Ananias in *The Alchemist*, and Mosca in *Volpone*. At the National Theatre a range of work includes roles in *Hamlet*, *The Changeling*, *Bartholomew Fair*, and *The School for Scandal* and among other theatre work he has played Feste (for Cheek by Jowl), Algernon in *The Importance of Being Earnest*, and Sergey in *Wild Honey*. Television credits include *Emma*, *Wings of Angels*, and *Peak Practice*, and among his films are *Lady Jane*, *England My England*, and *Family Ties*.

The baddie would-be king in the Robin Hood stories; Magna Carta; one of Peter O'Toole's sons in *The Lion in Winter* – the dribbly one; Runnymede; he lost his jewels in the Wash; a surfeit of lampreys (was that him?); he was 'not a good man', but he got a bouncy rubber ball for Christmas. Such are the few impressions that most of us have of King John. Not much, but not bad, I suppose: I mean, those of us who aren't historians do nevertheless have a scanty knowledge of some of our livelier monarchs, but know next to nothing of the duller, quieter ones. King John was succeeded by his son, who became Henry III, apparently. A.A. Milne, it appears, didn't know, or care, what *he* got for Christmas. John's predecessor was, of course, Richard I, the Lionheart, who crusaded a lot, and their father was Henry II (the Law-maker), otherwise known as Peter O'Toole in the films *Becket* and *The Lion in Winter*. But who the hell was Henry I? Did *he* mislay any jewellery? So King John was one of the colourful, loud ones; we know who he was. Except we don't, of course. What we non-historians 'know' of him is simply a tiny amount of historical fact, a splash of romantic folk-lore, and a rather charming poem by the man who created Winnie the Pooh. And some people might know that William Shakespeare wrote a play about him, but nobody ever does it; not even the Royal Shakespeare Company does it very often.

When we started rehearsing for the RSC's 2001 production of the play (the Company's first since 1988) our great fear was that we would find out rather painfully *why* it's so rarely performed: playing in a flop for a hundred and forty performances over sixteen months is a situation best avoided if possible. Our great hope was that people would ask why the play isn't done more often. I first worked for the RSC in the 1991–2 season, playing, amongst others, the wonderfully named Sir Formal Trifle in Shadwell's *The Virtuoso*, a foppish orator who (to quote Anne Barton) 'never uses one word when sixteen will do', and have worked very happily for the Company over quite a few seasons since. I've lost count of the number of reviews describing me as a 'beanpole' – I'm six foot three inches tall, and skinny – and a variation on the theme has recently been provided by the *Evening Standard*'s description of me as 'the RSC's booming skeleton'. Certainly my gangly physique, together with a natural propensity for comedy (partly inherited, I'm sure, from my father, who worked for years in variety as a 'straight man' to comedians such as Al Read, Arthur Haynes, and my godfather Charlie Drake), has led me to – and through! – a series of wonderful eccentrics for the RSC, of which Ananias in *The Alchemist*, Aguecheek in *Twelfth Night*, Cloten in *Cymbeline*, and Mosca in *Volpone* are a few of my favourites. But these qualities of comedy beanpole lead me very firmly away from many a title role and from most eponymous Shakespearian heroes.

For with the definite exception of Richard II – a part which, since auditioning successfully for RADA with bits of it twenty-five years ago, I have longed to play – and the possible exceptions of Richard III and maybe Hamlet (if you take the 'he's everyman' view of the part), there aren't many title roles in Shakespeare that I'm cut out to play. I can't really imagine myself as Coriolanus, Henry V, or Romeo – or Juliet, for that matter – so why should you have to? I think I could now play Berowne, and I'd love to play Benedick, but in the absence of a chance to play Richard II – Sam West had played it the season before (sod him!) – I had certainly got used to being sanguine about not yet having played a name-part in Shakespeare. And then along came director Gregory Doran with the offer of King John.

The title role – and a king to boot! 'I'm the fucking king', the cry I uttered if trifled with by lesser mortals in rehearsal, became the *King John* company catch-phrase. (I won't mention our other main catch-phrase, dealing as it did with private parts distinguished by their girth, and I recall it here only to provide a glow of nostalgia for any member of the 2001–2 company who may come across this essay.) So never mind the fact that (as usual) two more-famous-than-me actors had turned down the part of King John; it was mine if I wanted it, as was the challenge of Malvolio in the ever-beautiful *Twelfth Night* to be directed by my friend Lindsay Posner, with whom I'd recently had such a happy time on *Volpone*.

When having a look at a part before accepting it (or not), I tend to flick through it fairly swiftly, hoping that I'll get a feel, a 'bubble' for it; specifically I hope for a line or two that sing out at me, lines that I know I'll feel at home saying and that in some way define the character for me. When looking at Ananias, the anabaptist zealot in *The Alchemist*, for example, I knew I'd love pointing an accusatory finger at someone and shouting 'Thou look'st like Antichrist, in that lewd hat' (IV.vii.55). With King John I was delighted to find my 'touchstone' lines in the death scene when, burning with fever, he says:

> I am a scribbled form, drawn with a pen
> Upon a parchment, and against this fire
> Do I burn up.
>
> (v.vii.32–4)

So yes, thank you, I did want to try to play King John.

The late Paul Eddington, when asked what the best part of the acting job was for him, replied 'the phone call', and certainly there are occasions when it's all downhill after the offer to do the job has come in. Thankfully, for the great majority of the *King John* company, this was not the case. Casting a group of actors to put on a play is quite an art, hit and miss at best, but Greg Doran seems to be good at it. I suppose that ideally you need to assemble a cast of highly individual, gifted performers who will nevertheless be complementary enough, both on and off stage, to get the best out of each other and out of the play. Happily, with our *King John* team, it was much more hit than miss: the amalgam was a good one.

From the moment we started performing the show, a common response from the audience – particularly from those acquainted with the play only on the page, where much of it (notably the long rhetorical passages throughout Act Two) can seem dauntingly heavy going – was amazement that it wasn't boring at all and surprise that a deal of it was actually funny. So how was the tone of our production set; how did we find the tenor of the play?

If Greg Doran as the director, the 'common denominator', had cast *another* set of people to fulfil the very same hopes and aims he had for his production when he cast us, he would have ended up with a different show. That's a statement of the obvious, perhaps, but it's worth remembering. I think that, regardless of the skill and vision of the director, it is the professional, and specifically the *personal*, characteristics of the cast which that director has assembled that can make, or break, the heart of a production. I'm sure that, as a director with a love for the text and a sharp theatrical eye, Greg would have moulded any good company into a similar shape to ours, but as he also encourages the personal contribution of each of his actors, he would have allowed other actors to be their own king, their own Pandulph, Dauphin and so on, so that, while the story of Shakespeare's play would have remained pretty much identical with a different cast, the tone and tenor of that production would have been markedly different from ours.

It was an unusually exciting adventure for us all, approaching *King John* in rehearsal. Normally an RSC cast, designer, director, and stage management will already know quite a bit about the play they're working on: will probably have read it before, seen it, and are quite likely to have been in it if they are actors who've done a fair bit of classical work, whether at the RSC or elsewhere. For instance, although I was also about to play Malvolio for the first time, I'd played Feste for Cheek by Jowl in 1987 and Aguecheek for the RSC in 1996, as well as having seen several other productions of *Twelfth Night*, so it was hardly a stranger to me. But *King John* wasn't known to us at all. In a way it was like doing a new play – by William Shakespeare. The challenge of doing justice to most of Shakespeare's well-known plays is always daunting: again using *Twelfth Night* as an example, from both the very different productions of it that I'd experienced as an actor I knew it to be, in my view, one of the funniest, saddest, most beautiful plays ever written, so the great worry when approaching it again was that we – I! – would let it down, fail to live up to its proven delights. I really hate the thought of failing a great play, but, with the best will in the world, it's easily done.

But with *King John*, obviously, the challenge was rather the opposite one: it was for us all to get to know it, every syllable of it; to explore its strengths and weaknesses, to fulfil the story of each person in it, the characters who give substance and life to it; if possible to begin even to love it – in the hope that those audiences bold enough to risk seeing it might feel the same.

A word, then, about the rehearsal process under Greg Doran: I'd first worked with him as the Lord Chamberlain in his triumphant production of another little-known Shakespearian history play, *Henry VIII; or, All is True* in the Swan Theatre in 1997 and was happy to see that the rehearsal techniques that I'd enjoyed then were going to be employed on our *King John*. Basically the cast won't read the play through on the first day, as is often the case; they'll read it through slowly over the first couple of weeks, painstakingly examining, and paraphrasing into 'modern' English, every word and line of it, as a full company together, so that each and every member of the cast knows precisely what's being said at any time. The one rule in this process is that you never get to read your own part; but Victoria Duarri, for instance, cast as Blanche, will read King John when it gets round the table to her, the Dauphin will find himself as Pandulph for a while, and so on. This is a great way for the company to get to know, and hear, each other; it allows those cast in the smaller parts to be genuinely involved in the production from the outset, and it means that no-one feels any pressure to 'perform' their own part – nor get set in their ways with it! – at such an early stage.

Alongside this work, research projects are undertaken: we are, after all, dealing by and large with real people, and real historical happenings, even if they have been imaginatively wobbled about a bit by our author; and some embarrassing mental and physical games are played to loosen us all up a bit. (I was once squirming about on the floor with a new company at the RSC when I found myself in a position that would not have disgraced a sex manual with the actress Hilary Cromie, who managed to whisper to me: 'Well, I don't know', she said, 'I was quite happy doing pantomime'!)

With *King John* the cast was consulted about how the design should look – although I think Greg may have forgotten that he'd told me pretty much what the design would be like when offering me the part a couple of months earlier! Still, in this age of director-designer theatre, it was nice of him and the designer Stephen Brimson Lewis to make us feel that it was at least a little to do with us; and a splendid, uncomplicated design it was too. The costumes were simple – medieval in flavour but inspired greatly by far more recent Russian military wear. They were, I think, a great success of the production, as was the bare wooden floor dusted in chalky grey-white and the one piece of furniture, a pale, plain chair – sometimes just a chair, sometimes a throne.

Playing a king for the first time, I was childishly excited by the prospect of wearing a crown. Mine turned out to be a wonderful, tough, heavy, silvery-pewtery affair. I'm not sure how real monarchs manage with theirs, but my crown was a trifle unruly. It looked downright uncomfortable (and was); in moments of passion, it wobbled; and I was often fiddling with it, correcting it from the jaunty angle to which it had unceremoniously slipped to the place I thought it should be, right on the top of my head. Much comment was passed by audience members I spoke to about what a brilliantly symbolic masterstroke my wobbly crown was and how, in its wobbliness, it so perfectly suited such an imperfect king. I was more than happy to accept these plaudits for my crown, but the truth is that its wobbliness was more accident than symbol. Despite numerous 'crown fittings', it just didn't fit very well – perfect!

I find rehearsing difficult. Although no longer the deeply inhibited eighteen-year-old at RADA and now with many a rehearsal period and thousands of performances behind me, I still feel inadequate and incompetent in front of my peers. (John Hopkins, cast as the Dauphin, admitted to me later that he was relieved when he realized that I was the bloke he'd seen as Cloten, a performance he'd enjoyed, because up to that point he couldn't understand why they'd cast me as King John at all!) I find it hard to believe a word I'm saying in the early stages, when the 'bubble' isn't there. For me that bubble – the feeling you get when you know 'inside', without having to impose it, how the person you're pretending to be walks and talks, and *why* they say what they do – comes worryingly (for me and everyone else) late. Usually it's not until we're running scenes, or the whole play, that I get an inkling; and only when we get into the make-believe world of the theatre itself does it all begin to seem real to me. (It's a definite panic on the thankfully rare occasions when I still don't believe in it all even then!)

Adrian Noble told me when we were previewing *Cymbeline* that I was 'naughty' because I 'rehearse in front of the audience'. Certainly it's true that, like most actors, I learn a lot when putting the play

1 Guy Henry as King John with Alison Fiske as Queen Eleanor, *King John*,
Act I, Scene i: 'Our strong possession and our right for us.'

before the audience for the first time. And why not – what the hell are
'reduced-price previews' *for*? For me, especially in the case of old plays
with their soliloquies and asides, their rhetoric and debate, the audience
is the vital component, the one missing in rehearsal; I see them as the
other character in the drama, the other person in the room. Without
the audience there's a hole where the heart should be; they complete
the play. As an actor, or performer, my 'relationship' with the audience
is often remarked upon – not always favourably. My dear friend Edward
Petherbridge once accused me of being an 'end-of-the-pier comedian'
(which I thought was pushing it a bit – I'm not *that* good!), but I think
it's fair to say that in my almost innate belief in including the audience
in the play – and I'll be winking at them and throwing them sweets
in a minute – lies my strength, as well as many of my faults, as an
actor.

I happily admit to seeing humour in *King John*; most of the other
actors did too, I'm glad to say. It's there in the script, but getting
the balance of it right in performance was always a challenge. One
of the play's special characteristics, which can seem awkward or clumsy

until you begin to live up to it, is its switchback quality, its ability to change mood and emphasis, not just from scene to scene, but sometimes amazingly in one line. You could perform the play without recognizing its humour, but to do so would seem to me rather like missing the point. For instance, when John receives a welter of bad news, including the death of his mother (IV.ii.120–21), his confusion has a comic edge; but when left alone he has his only soliloquy of the play – three words: 'My mother dead!' (IV.ii.181). Not funny, that – but sharper, truer, perhaps, because some of the bits before it were. On a good night, exploring these shifts is part of the pleasure of this odd play, for actor and audience alike.

When we started to put the play on its feet it swiftly became clear that there was much in the playing of it to enjoy – and more than a little to fear, specifically how to make the lengthy rhetorical debates of Acts Two and Three invigorating and appealing to the modern ear. At a time when the art of rhetoric is no longer taught and the popular use of language revolves around e-mails and text-messages, speeches in a play that are over a page long are bound to be a bit tense-making, both for actor and audience. The answer seemed to be to embrace the emotional and intellectual passion the speaker has for his speech, embrace the Swan Theatre itself, which is a wonderful debating chamber where the audience could be addressed as the people of Angiers, summon up as much vocal dexterity as we could, and go for it!

To our delight and relief, as often as not the audience would go for it too, pointing to one reason why Shakespeare's savage satire on political spin (a key element in the play) is so relevant and accessible to us today. We know so much more now, more even than just a few years ago, mainly through the probing of the various media, about those who rule over us, that we can be certain that the great and the good are usually neither of those things. To see this demonstrated so wittily by Shakespeare was a huge pleasure – and it was certainly no hindrance that we opened the play in the run-up to a general election. Thucydides first pointed out that political battles are really about language; he would have relished *King John*.

Why, then, were speeches which at first seemed impenetrably dry so capable of amusing a modern audience? It's the sheer mounting hyperbole of each side's claims, I suppose, for one thing – and substantial quotations are essential to illustrate this. Thus King John addresses the citizens of Angiers:

29

All preparation for a bloody siege
And merciless proceeding by these French
Confronts your city's eyes, your winking gates;
And but for our approach those sleeping stones,
That as a waist doth girdle you about,
By the compulsion of their ordinance
By this time from their fixèd beds of lime
Had been dishabited, and wide havoc made
For bloody power to rush upon your peace.
But on the sight of us your lawful King,
Who painfully, with much expedient march,
Have brought a countercheck before your gates,
To save unscratched your city's threatened cheeks,
Behold, the French, amazed, vouchsafe a parle.

(II.i.214–27)

To which Philip of France's lengthy riposte concludes:

But if you fondly pass our proffered offer,
'Tis not the roundure of your old-faced walls
Can hide you from our messengers of war,
Though all these English and their discipline
Were harboured in their rude circumference.
Then tell us, shall your city call us lord
In that behalf which we have challenged it,
Or shall we give the signal to our rage
And stalk in blood to our possession?

(II.i.258–66)

But it's when the citizens' implacable spokesperson Hubert refuses to acknowledge *either* party as England's king that our two heroes rather lose their grip (with helpful analysis from the Bastard):

HUBERT In brief, we are the King of England's subjects;
    For him, and in his right, we hold the town.
KING JOHN Acknowledge then the King, and let me in.
HUBERT That can we not. But he that proves the King,
    To him will we prove loyal. Till that time
    Have we rammed up our gates against the world.
KING JOHN Doth not the crown of England prove the King?
    And if not that, I bring you witnesses,
    Twice fifteen thousand hearts of England's breed –
BASTARD (*aside*) Bastards and else!

30

KING JOHN – To verify our title with their lives.
KING PHILIP As many and as well-born bloods as those –
BASTARD (*aside*) Some bastards too!
KING PHILIP – Stand in his face to contradict his claim.

(II.i.267–80)

And when Hubert remains immovable, suddenly it's war – and, as in most wars, God seems to be on *both* sides:

KING JOHN Then God forgive the sins of all those souls
    That to their everlasting residence,
    Before the dew of evening fall, shall fleet,
    In dreadful trial of our kingdom's king.
KING PHILIP Amen, amen! Mount, chevaliers! To arms...
    Command the rest to stand. God and our right!

(IV.i.283–99)

It then only needs the heralds from either side both to claim that his party is the victor in the ensuing unseen battle – and Hubert to credit neither of them – for the Bastard to suggest the ultimate solution:

By heaven, these scroyles of Angiers flout you, Kings...
Be friends awhile, and both conjointly bend
Your sharpest deeds of malice on this town,
By east and west let France and England mount
Their battering cannon chargèd to the mouth...
Leave them as naked as the vulgar air.
That done, dissever your united strengths
And part your mingled colours once again;
Turn face to face and bloody point to point...
How like you this wild counsel, mighty states?
Smacks it not something of the policy?

(IV.i.373–96)

We always knew that if John's reply to this example of what I can only describe as sensible absurdity didn't get a pretty good laugh, our audience that day hadn't quite got the tone of it:

Now, by the sky that hangs above our heads,
I like it well! France, shall we knit our powers
And lay this Angiers even with the ground,
Then after fight who shall be king of it?

(IV.i.397–400)

31

In the midst of all the desperate wrangling it is, of course, the child prince, Arthur of Brittany, who sees with the clearest of eyes and the most honest of hearts:

> I would that I were low laid in my grave.
> I am not worth this coil that's made for me.
>
> (II.i.164–5)

I am often struck, incidentally, by how frequently one innocent figure can become a focus for the outrage – hypocritical or otherwise – of the world at large. I'm thinking, for instance, of the girl running, burnt and screaming, from the flames of an American attack in Vietnam, or the boy standing in front of the tanks in Tianenmen Square. Despite the hundreds – thousands, no doubt – of boy soldiers who would have been maimed or killed in the skirmishes between France and England that are depicted in *King John*, it is Arthur, the pawn in the middle of the political game, who is just such a focus of outrage in our play, as the Bastard so clearly sees:

> Go, bear him in thine arms.
> I am amazed, methinks, and lose my way
> Among the thorns and dangers of this world.
> How easy dost thou take all England up!
> From forth this morsel of dead royalty
> The life, the right and truth, of all this realm
> Is fled to heaven; and England now is left
> To tug and scamble and to part by th'teeth
> The unowed interest of proud-swelling state.
>
> (IV.iii.139–47)

We as actors, like our audiences, are probably almost entirely unaware of whatever prevailing mood there may be that shapes and informs our response to a play at any given time. After six months of performing *King John*, we were doing yet another matinée of it on 11 September 2001. As we were acting out war, violence, and aggression in Stratford, the twin towers of New York were falling; and as we prepared for the evening performance I remember there was a feeling almost of embarrassment amongst the company that we should be doing, on such a day, something as silly as a play, particularly one in which we should be required again to play-act violence and death. Maybe members of the audience wondered too, about their presence there. I remember

Jo Stone-Fewings, so excellent as the Bastard, saying to me that Greg Doran was always asking him to show more anger in the role, but that he didn't feel like being angry on that day.

Although obviously irrelevant in the great scheme of things, our performance that night of a play that examines, amongst other things, absurd territorial claims and the misuse of religious fervour, had a new, sadder resonance. The laughter was still there but, although we didn't actively, consciously change our performance of the play, I think it's fair to say that most of us were less glib about the violence and anger within it from that day on. I had always been struck by how much a play written four hundred years ago, exploring the behaviour of people four hundred years before that, showed so vividly how little in human nature has improved in nearly a thousand years, and on 11 September the phrase ''twas ever thus' had never seemed so depressingly apt. I'm glad, though, that the laughter did remain in the play that night – someone in fact remarked that it was stronger than ever. In Umberto Eco's *The Name of the Rose*, the powers-that-be in the story desperately try to keep hidden from those seeking it the secret of comedy. They don't like it up 'em, you know.

As for my King John – well, it's a strange but lovely part, neither flawed tragic hero nor out-and-out villain. More interesting than either, in a sense, he's a fascinating mix of traits and foibles: a catastrophically inadequate judge of people and of the way the world wags, he's foolish, vicious, frightened, and paranoid – it was said that he was so paranoid that he engendered paranoia in all around him. It seems abundantly clear to me from the script, and from all those snippets we know about the real man, that he was certainly all of these things, and that can, of course, be very amusing to the onlooker. I do hope, though, that in my performance people saw a glimpse of his pain too – the pain of a man in a job that he feels, with all his heart (and most of his mind), should be his, his by right, God-given, but with the creeping knowledge that he isn't good at it, a man in the wrong job, the job he wanted desperately:

> Is this Ascension Day? Did not the prophet
> Say that before Ascension Day at noon
> My crown I should give off? Even so I have!
> I did suppose it should be on constraint,
> But, heaven be thanked, it is but voluntary.
>
> (v.i.25–9)

He is not, as A.A. Milne said, 'a good man', nor is he, in my view, an evil one – although the makers of a TV Channel 5 documentary, that I saw whilst writing this essay and that nominated King John as one of 'the most evil men in history', would doubtless think of my attitude (and, I think, Shakespeare's) towards this beleaguered king as rather too forgiving. But then Shakespeare doesn't judge: he illuminates, and lets us think and feel what we will.

I find the fact that this misguided, worried man trusts the Bastard from the moment he sees him immensely touching. One of Shakespeare's great historical (or unhistorical) inventions, the Bastard in the play is the illegitimate son of John's brother Richard I, so he is literally John's nephew; but to John he is 'family', not for that reason, but because, from the moment the Bastard walks into the room, John loves him. He trusts him and for once in his life repays that trust with a loyalty of his own; he waits to see him before he dies and then does so (or so he did in our production) in his arms:

> O cousin, thou art come to set mine eye!
> The tackle of my heart is cracked and burnt,
> And all the shrouds wherewith my life should sail
> Are turnèd to one thread, one little hair;
> My heart hath one poor string to stay it by,
> Which holds but till thy news be utterèd,
> And then all this thou seest is but a clod
> And module of confounded royalty.
>
> (v.vii.51–8)

It seems that finding, keeping, giving love wasn't easy for King John; I'm glad that Shakespeare gave him the Bastard.

One of the great benefits of playing Shakespeare at Stratford is that you get to meet the audience – in the Dirty Duck pub or at question-and-answer sessions organized by the Shakespeare Centre and the Shakespeare Institute. At one such, a woman who obviously knew a lot about the real King John told me two things about him that I kept with me when playing him. One was that when he was dying he retreated to Worcester and took a great solace in his library – not an image one would naturally have had of him. The other thing I learned was that he was a very good father; apparently even his illegitimate daughter Joanna adored him. I changed the way I played part of his final scene on hearing that. I had always done the lines

2 Guy Henry as King John with Jo Stone-Fewings as the Bastard, *King John*,
Act v, Scene vii: 'O cousin, thou art come to set mine eye.'

> Within me is a hell, and there the poison
> Is as a fiend confined to tyrannize
> On unreprievable, condemnèd blood
> (v.vii.46–8)

as a general expression of John's torment (and Catholic guilt), but
now they became a direct explanation to his son Henry. I still pushed
Henry away afterwards, but far more gently, more kindly, than I had
done before.

If I were to play King John again I think I'd probably simplify the
performance, make it less flamboyant, perhaps explore the darker, more
sinister elements of him more. But on the whole I'll leave that up to
someone else, to the next actor to play him at Stratford, or wherever.
For me, I enjoyed playing him so much, probably more than any other
character I've ever played; and as I've never been more proud to be part
of a company than I was with that particular *King John* group, I think
I'll leave him be.

As for the play, which we as a company once knew so little about –
well, you couldn't accuse it of being perfect: there's a curate's-egg

quality to it, but we did get to love it, and although there will be those who didn't appreciate what we did with it, people *did* ask, all the time, why it's not done more often. As all we really do in the theatre is sit in the dark and tell stories, I'm really pleased that we found that Shakespeare's story of King John is one worth telling. I think, and hope, we'll see it again soon. I'll be jealous, mind.

Constance in *King John*

KELLY HUNTER

KELLY HUNTER played Constance in Gregory Doran's production of *King John* at the Swan Theatre in Stratford in the RSC's summer season of 2001, and afterwards at the Pit Theatre at the Barbican. Her other role that season was Mrs Garrick in *Jubilee*. Earlier work for the RSC had included Mariana in *Measure for Measure*, Lola in *Blue Angel*, and Isabel in *Talk of the City*. For the National Theatre she has played Linda in *A Chorus of Disapproval*, Constance in *She Stoops to Conquer*, and the title role in *Jean Seberg*. Roles elsewhere include Rosalind for English Touring Theatre (for which she won the TMA Best Actress Award), Nora in *A Doll's House*, Lady Teazle in *The School for Scandal*, and Sally Bowles in *Caberet*. She has worked widely in radio and as a narrator in orchestral concerts, and her televison credits include *Bad Blood*, *Family Tree*, *Life Force*, and *Silent Witness*.

There were two memorable events during the Stratford season of 2001: the first was bewildering and seemingly small; the second was the terrorist attack of 11 September. And, yes, this has everything to do with performing Shakespeare, and the part of Constance, and the play *King John*.

The earlier event was the announcement that the ensemble company system, which the RSC had been using to produce the plays of Shakespeare for the preceding forty years, a tradition dating back to the Lord Chamberlain's Men at the end of the sixteenth century, was to be dismantled in favour of a more 'modern', 'global', and 'flexible' system. Every time I've listened to the reasons behind this decision, and to the alleged need to knock down existing theatres and build bigger, brighter, better ones, the need to 'join the twenty-first century', my unease has increased because I've never heard them talk of the need to address the moral and aesthetic direction of a company whose prime purpose is to produce the plays of Shakespeare. In fact I've never heard them talk about Shakespeare at all.

So what's the connexion between these two events? Does it seem in terrible taste and an act of appalling presumption even to make one? It probably does, and please forgive it. The connexion is wholly subjective and entirely humble. On 11 September we happened to be performing *King John* twice, matinée and evening, so by nightfall we all, cast and audience, were in that strange limbo-land of shock that everyone experienced in their own way. But there was a need for the play – as simple as that. I am the last person to 'wax lyrical' about theatre, but it is not even theatre that I'm talking about: it's Shakespeare. My growing unease while performing in this season and watching these changes unfold for myself, derived from the sense that Shakespeare is the least important voice to be heard. Does it actually have to be spelt out, what genuine works of art are for: to relieve us from ourselves, to prompt us, to change and teach us? If the plays of Shakespeare are treated as anything less important, then we are all diminished. So I've spoken out, like Constance in *King John*. She sees the truth and speaks it, in a world of lies and liars. Where does it get Constance? Nowhere. But perhaps it 'gets' to the audience, who hear her say these lines to the fraudulent Austria:

> Thou little valiant, great in villainy!
> Thou ever strong upon the stronger side!
> Thou fortune's champion, that dost never fight
> But when her humorous ladyship is by
> To teach thee safety! Thou art perjured too,
> And soothest up greatness.
>
> (III.i.116–21)

To me, Constance is one of the few voices of reason in a play peopled with irrational, unreasonable voices – Hubert and Arthur being the obvious two others. She has moments of emotional instability, but they are the consequence of other people's immoral, illegal, and selfish behaviour. Of course we are talking about kings and queens, and this particular lot were famously cavalier and cut-throat. I read that when Henry II heard that his father was about to die he rode as fast as he could from France to England to ensure his title as king, even though it was rightfully his. But since Shakespeare's historical plays are not always historically accurate, it is the particular mindset of these characters, who bear little resemblance to their originals, and the specific familial constraints that they place on one another, that sparks one's imagination. In terms of research, therefore, there is very little reason to read anything other than Shakespeare's play – apart from the rest of Shakespeare's plays, which will always give you a clearer idea of the scale of play that you are in.

I may seem to be a complete pain, but I only work, learn, and rehearse from the Folio text. I'm perfectly happy to be teased about it, but no amount of teasing will make me learn a Shakespeare part from anything other than the closest document to the original that exists. The difference between learning from modern editions and learning from the Folio is chalk to cheese – but I think that's another essay.

It's funny that the reputation of Constance as a Shakespearian character seems to owe more to some early lines of Queen Eleanor than to an intimate knowledge of what Constance says and feels in the course of the play:

> Have I not ever said
> How that ambitious Constance would not cease
> Till she had kindled France and all the world
> Upon the right and party of her son?
>
> (I.i.31–4)

The one thing that was said to me about her – in that helpful way that people have when you've just got a part in a play – was that she is a crashing bore who just goes 'on and on and on'. Actually most people hadn't read, seen, or even thought about *King John* for decades, so that cheered me up: no milestone performances to be endlessly and fruitlessly compared to. Start with nothing.

The first thing I thought about was why does she have all those very long speeches. In fact about ninety per cent of what she says is laid out in very long speeches. Why does she not let others talk? Familial constraints for a start. And is she saying the same thing over and over? No: on the contrary, her thoughts change on almost every line and she is, more often than not, in an unconscious state of working out *how* she feels. She is a perfect example of Coleridge's description of how, in Shakespeare, a thought only exists as a direct result of the thought before it, 'like a serpent twisting and untwisting in its own strength'.

Reading the play I realized that every decision and feeling she has is experienced through her total obsession with being female: her marital status, her value as a child-bearing woman, and her success as a mother, specifically as the mother to the young and rightful heir to the throne.

She is always defining herself – as woman, widow, mother. With her very first line it is not enough for her to say that she is Arthur's mother; she finds it necessary to add that she is also a widow: 'O, take his mother's thanks, a widow's thanks' (II.i.32). Is she using her widowhood as a political means of eliciting the help of 'strong men' to fight her cause? Is she neurotically defining herself in the way that lonely and isolated people do? The answer is that she is doing both, and it is clear that she is perfectly able to inhabit her conscious and unconscious life within one line. In the most deeply unconscious of all her speeches she describes herself, to Salisbury, as a sick and fearful woman:

> For I am sick and capable of fears,
> Oppressed with wrongs, and therefore full of fears,
> A widow, husbandless, subject to fears,
> A woman, naturally born to fears . . .
>
> (III.i.12–15)

It is in this scene with Salisbury and Arthur that she begins to comprehend the full power of the opposing forces in her dilemma: 'belief' and 'life', 'nature' and 'fortune'. On hearing that the King of France has effectively betrayed her, leaving her a virtual outcast, she invites chaos to consume her:

> O, if thou teach me to believe this sorrow,
> Teach thou this sorrow how to make me die!
> And let belief and life encounter so
> As doth the fury of two desperate men.
>
> (III.i.29–32)

Stressed correctly, the words 'if' and 'let' are vital: they show a woman allowing herself to be changed by the unfolding events around her. 'Belief' stands for hope, 'life' stands for reality; and if this is my reality then I must absorb it and die.

This new defeatism takes her to a state of disgust at the world and to new words in her vocabulary: 'harmful', 'heinous', 'ugly' begin to define her state of mind. Salisbury, whom she was using as her confidant only minutes before, she now calls an 'ugly' man, a 'harmful' man (III.i.37,41). She then turns on her son who, with only one line to express himself in the scene, asking his mother to be 'content' (III.i.42), is treated to an outpouring of disgust at the potential deformities that he, Arthur, might have embodied, a sort of mother's nightmare vision:

> If thou that biddest me be content wert grim,
> Ugly and slanderous to thy mother's womb,
> Full of unpleasing blots and sightless stains,
> Lame, foolish, crookèd, swart, prodigious,
> Patched with foul moles and eye-offending marks,
> I would not care, I then would be content,
> For then I should not love thee.
>
> (III.i.43–9)

In her fury at being made an outcast, she has lashed out at the one person left in the world that she loves. And she is at once full of regret, and tells him, immediately, in the next lines of the speech, using the most gentle language that she speaks in the whole play, that nature has 'gifted' him with lilies and roses, that he is, indeed, 'fair' (III.i.51–4). This domesticity, the unjustified raging of a mother to her son, and the instant regret and attempted reconciliation, is the key to the relationship between Constance and Arthur. It shows that she loves him deeply, that she is involved with him psychologically. And it crushes Eleanor's argument that Constance is merely a politically motivated character who heartlessly uses her son as a pawn in her own struggle for power.

Crucially, Arthur is kidnapped a couple of scenes later and Constance never sees him again. In fact when he predicts to King John so accurately that his kidnapping 'will make my mother die with grief' (III.iii.5), it suggests that the little boy, too, is connected to his mother's state of mind, that he knows that she loves him.

In telling Arthur that he is fair, she falls upon the memory of his birth, an image that comes back to haunt her in her final scene:

> But thou art fair, and at thy birth, dear boy,
> Nature and fortune joined to make thee great.
>
> (III.i.51–2)

'Nature' and 'fortune': whereas the pairing of 'belief' and 'life' sent her into a dark and depressive state of mind, the pairing of 'nature' and 'fortune' could be seen to spur her back from depression into a state of revenge and anger. At first the anger is directed at fortune herself, whom she sees as a female rival adulterating with John, a rival who has forced her ally, Philip of France, to abandon her and become fortune's bawd. Of all the insults that she could use, she specifically chooses two that

3 Kelly Hunter as Constance (with Benjamin Darlington just discernible as Arthur), *King John*, Act III, Scene i: 'But thou art fair, and at thy birth, dear boy, / Nature and fortune joined to make thee great.'

denounce them sexually, 'bawd' for Philip and 'strumpet' for fortune (III.i.60, 61). This seemed to me to tie in with her female obsession; in fact, the more I read the part the more it seemed to me that her imagination never strayed far away from these female targets.

Her last speech in this scene takes on an entirely different tone as her anger at being outcast from the royal family rises and she turns her imaginative bile to the instruction from Salisbury:

> Pardon me, madam,
> I may not go without you to the Kings.
> (III.i.65–6)

In response Constance invents a new irony, a voice that we haven't heard before, and almost before our eyes she discovers the way to defy the status quo successfully by using language. And she uses it immediately to satirize both her own predicament and the world in which her predicament exists. She takes words that define royalty – 'state', 'greatness', 'throne', 'supporters', 'instruction', 'assembly' – and deflates their stature with her own heartfelt 'sorrow' and 'grief'. It is immensely

42

powerful, not only because her emotions are at a pitch of great intensity, but also because she is discovering a new way of using language and is garnering power as she does so:

> I will instruct my sorrows to be proud,
> For grief is proud and makes his owner stoop.
> To me and to the state of my great grief
> Let kings assemble; for my grief's so great
> That no supporter but the huge firm earth
> Can hold it up. Here I and sorrows sit;
> Here is my throne. Bid kings come bow to it.
>
> (III.i.68–74)

This new-found irony, wit, and power, which she uses to great effect to silence the wedding party later in the scene, contrasts entirely with her total lack of ability to hold her own when faced, in the first scene at Angiers, with her formidable mother-in-law, Eleanor of Aquitaine. In Act One Eleanor declares herself a 'woman of war' when she says 'I am a soldier and now bound for France' (I.i.150), contrasting with Constance's first lines of peaceful motherhood. The battle of the two women is already set up, before they meet, simply by their own definitions of themselves.

Although Constance has political strength at Angiers, championed at this point by France, she pitches in when silence would have been preferable and misjudges all her arguments. Her keyword seems to be 'grandam', as if she cannot get beyond her loathing for Eleanor, and is immediately obsessed, and thereby oppressed, by Eleanor's presence. As John and Eleanor try to tempt Arthur away, Constance becomes petty and bitter:

> Do, child, go to it grandam, child.
> Give grandam kingdom, and it grandam will
> Give it a plum, a cherry, and a fig.
> There's a good grandam.
>
> (II.i.160–3)

This is her first attempt at irony and it fails because it is too cruel. It completely backfires on her and the result is that Arthur bursts into tears, which Eleanor capitalizes on.

So I found a journey in Constance's use of language. In the 'public' scenes she is quite crude and hapless to start off with and only when she is abandoned by France, and has to fall back on her own wits, does she develop, very quickly, a powerful articulacy. Yet, privately, right from the beginning, she is articulate and able to talk, at length, about her changing state of mind.

It was the definition of these different states of mind that she inhabits, although she may appear to be repeating herself either in meaning or with phrases and words, that I concentrated on in rehearsal. The greatest example of this is the word 'grief'. With Salisbury she has called her grief proud and great – and meant it with all the growing, bitter irony that she invents for herself – but by the time she has lost her son she has had a true awakening to the real experience of grief and says, profoundly:

> Grief fills the room up of my absent child,
> Lies in his bed, walks up and down with me,
> Puts on his pretty looks, repeats his words,
> Remembers me of all his gracious parts,
> Stuffs out his vacant garments with his form;
> Then have I reason to be fond of grief?
>
> (III.iv.93–8)

Grief is no longer great, nor proud.

As we started to rehearse the play, I already knew that these internal journeys of language were very sustainable, and would keep my brain in the active state necessary for performing. I started to become obsessed with Constance's obsession with her own 'femaleness' as I saw how deeply entrenched it is in her psyche. When, after she has been betrayed by France, she disrupts the Dauphin's wedding, she asks the heavens to 'Set armèd discord 'twixt these perjured kings' (III.i.111), but she does so by 'marrying' herself to the heavens: 'A widow cries; be husband to me, heavens' (III.i.108). It seems she must be wife to someone. This 'marriage' is a real turning point for her, for it empowers her with a new perspective, immediately releasing her language into a speech of relentless rage and contempt aimed at Austria. Having allied herself to the holy and immortal force, she sees man, for the first time, in comparison to God:

> What a fool art thou,
> A ramping fool, to brag and stamp and swear
> Upon my party!
>
> (III.i.121–3)

44

And in the same scene she uses a more obvious female ploy as she sets herself up as a rival to the virginal young bride, Blanche, warning the Dauphin

> The devil tempts thee here
> In likeness of a new, untrimmèd bride
> (III.i.208–9)

– as opposed to me, a fully mature woman. Both women fall to their knees, pleading with the Dauphin, Blanche for peace and Constance that he take up arms against England. I wanted to express this rivalry physically, and developed a way of taking his hand, playing with his fingers right under the nose of his new bride, that was sexual and threatening. It seems to me that Constance will do anything at this point to gain ground; and all she has on her side – her 'armoury', as it were – is herself as a woman.

And following this 'female' trail, in her last scene, having lost Arthur, she asks 'How may I be delivered of these woes?' (III.iv.55), seeing herself as a mere vessel for childbirth, through which everything is born of her, even her woes. This scene has a very specific shape and rhythm that for ages I found almost impossible to decipher. I knew there had to be some inner life, some sort of change that occurs, and I couldn't see it very obviously in the language. There is a change, a subtle change of heart, that occurs half way through the scene. Remarkably, it hinges on her relationship to Pandulph; once I'd grasped that, a lot of things fell into place immediately. The change of heart is very simple: she says to Philip 'To England, if you will' (III.iv.68), implying that they should try to rescue the imprisoned Arthur, known to be in England. She seems to pull herself out of her despair and starts to bind up her loose hair as a symbol of solidarity with her imprisoned son. But then she turns to Pandulph, who earlier in the scene had challenged her state of mind with the totally unsympathetic line 'Lady, you utter madness, and not sorrow' (III.iv.43).

You have to look at Pandulph's first entry in the wedding scene to understand the impact he has on her. Just before he appears, Constance has married herself to God, asking God to wage war between England and France. Pandulph's immediate entrance into the play, with his call to France to take arms against England, gives her the belief that heaven has answered her prayers and that God is on her side – more specifically in the human form of Cardinal Pandulph. When pleading with the Dauphin she even uses the God-on-her-side argument when she says 'alter not the doom / Forethought by heaven' (III.i.311–12). But Pandulph gives her nothing. He doesn't even answer her pleas for the right to curse John in the name of God. He ignores her.

And when he calls her mad in Act Three, Scene Four, the first of only two lines that he addresses to her in the whole play, he, as 'God's messenger', shows her that God is indeed not on her side at all. This is when the change of heart occurs. The dawning realization that even God has forsaken her tips her into a maternal abyss of fanciful despair as she imagines meeting the rotten corpse of Arthur in the court of heaven and not being able to recognise him; and all notions of going to England, all notions of hope, are finally forgotten.

When we started performing the play I felt that I was left high and dry by not coming back in the second half. I felt cheated, in a way, of the 'pay-off' you can experience in the playing of Shakespeare's fourth and fifth acts, when the audience, and the play, are truly settled into the narrative. But I soon understood that Constance has her own 'pay-off' with her last scene and does in fact have a tangible dramatic arc all of her own, of beginning, middle, and end, which she plays out at its own steady, inexorable speed, thereby highlighting her isolation. I use the word 'steady' with reason. Constance repeats particular words twice over, giving the feeling of a heartbeat. She does this four times, never in the same speeches, but when you put them together it's as if you receive a coded message, a poetic account of the action: 'Forsworn – Forsworn', 'Arm – Arm', 'War – War', 'Death – Death'.

I have already written about the deepening of her understanding of grief. The other theme that comes back with a vengeance to haunt her is that of marrying herself to the metaphysical and of her 'armoury' of sexual powers, which she uses as a means of bargaining. But whereas earlier in the play she married herself to the heavens, now we see her, bereft of hope, marrying herself to death. It feels as though, in poetic and abstract terms, she is the embodiment of widowhood, a rampant loneliness, roaming through the play, ever more desperate to attach herself. This speech also has echoes of the raging she unleashed on Arthur; she is capable of going very deep down into a state of self-loathing and disgust at the human form itself:

> Death! Death, O amiable, lovely death!
> Thou odoriferous stench! Sound rottenness!

Arise forth from the couch of lasting night,
Thou hate and terror to posterity,
And I will kiss thy detestable bones,
And put my eyeballs in thy vaulty brows,
And ring these fingers with thy household worms,
And stop this gap of breath with fulsome dust,
And be a carrion monster like thyself.
Come, grin on me, and I will think thou smilest
And buss thee as thy wife. Misery's love,
O, come to me!

(III.iv. 25–36)

She has become almost a parody of her former self, or at least appears to be so, and this appearance of 'madness' rings a bell of psychological accuracy, in that if we observe a person in an extreme state of mind, that person can appear to us to be over the top, 'crazy', 'mad'. This is crucial in the playing of her last scene: the three men, King Philip, Lewis the Dauphin, and Pandulph, are all watching a mother grieve, and because they themselves are not grieving, all they seem able to do is watch her. Pandulph then labels her mad. But there is *nothing* in the text to imply that Constance is mad; in fact she is able to talk at length, with great lucidity, of the difference between madness and grief:

For, being not mad, but sensible of grief,
My reasonable part produces reason
How I may be delivered of these woes.

(III.iv.53–5)

The madness is in the eye of the beholder. The only man who comes close to feeling her pain is her old ally, Philip of France, and his empathy is, I think, heartbreaking. For what he observes is his own inability to comfort her. As the four of them stand, isolated from each other, ravaged by war, he notes the love in her unbound hair, and the way in which her tears have glued her hairs together

in sociable grief,
Like true, inseparable, faithful loves,
Sticking together in calamity.

(III.iv.65–7)

If only *people* were capable of that. The other echo of the earlier scene with Arthur is the memory of his birth, which triggers her nightmare

47

4 Kelly Hunter as Constance with Geoffrey Freshwater as King Philip of France, *King John*, Act III, Scene iv: 'Where but by chance a silver drop hath fallen, / Even to that drop ten thousand wiry friends / Do glue themselves in sociable grief.'

vision of death; and whereas in the earlier scene this memory was a source of comfort to them both, it now plunges her into despair and she uses a character from the Bible to make her point – as if still trying to connect with Pandulph on his level:

> For since the birth of Cain, the first male child,
> To him that did but yesterday suspire,
> There was not such a gracious creature born.
> (III.iv.79–81)

The other thing that really struck me about this scene is that she wants death to consume her; she does not want to take her own life. I had a very strong image of a woman roaming the freezing, deserted battle-fields, with little clothing, literally walking and freezing herself into the 'frenzy' of death that is reported of her later in the play (IV.ii.122). So the black undergarment that I wore for that scene was my idea, and the 'frenzy' was, I hope, implied visually in this, rather than through 'frenzied' acting.

I think I have laid out the scaffolding, but in performance you have to throw the scaffolding away – completely. The purpose of rehearsing is to imprint these details of thought deeply into your memory bank, so that your brain will be completely active when you come to perform the play. I cannot comment on Constance and call her names such as 'ambitious', 'unhappy', 'lonely', and so on, for if I did I would be doing no more than Lewis, and Philip, and Pandulph do, just watching and labelling. I realize that, in writing this, I have used the word 'immediately' a lot: I think that's important in playing this part. She dwells on nothing for very long and is often changed by events around her, or has an unconscious change of desire, sometimes in the space of one line. Her immediacy is vital to her; she needs it to survive in the midst of enemies. Those enemies are all around her in a world where she is cast as the political underdog. But I think her real enemy is the depressive state of mind that plagues her unconsciousness, her thoroughly Shakespearian disgust at the bleakness of the human condition.

The Bastard in *King John*

JO STONE-FEWINGS

JO STONE-FEWINGS played the Bastard in Gregory Doran's production of *King John* at the Swan Theatre in Stratford in the summer season of 2001, and later in London at the Pit Theatre at the Barbican. His other role that season was Orsino in *Twelfth Night*. Earlier work for the RSC had included Fenton, Guiderius, Richmond, Lucentio, and Surrey in *Henry VIII*. At the National Theatre he has appeared in *Ghetto*, *War and Peace*, and *Shadow of a Boy*, and among his theatre roles elsewhere are Jack in *The Importance of Being Earnest* and Julian in *The Misanthrope*. His films include *Wondrous Oblivion* and *All the King's Men* and among his television appearances have been *Young Arthur*, *Best of Both Worlds*, *Soldier Soldier*, and *The Prince*.

I was given lots of advice on how to play the Bastard in *King John*. 'He's a dark, comic chorus', I was told. 'No, no, he's the conscience of the play!' 'Well, Jo, it's a good part, in a little-done play, with at least one bastard of a soliloquy...' I decided early on not to research previous performances, but to treat it, as Greg Doran our director put it, 'like a new play'; and it had been so rarely done in the twentieth century that it felt to all intents and purposes as if that is what it was. It also felt, as we agreed on our first day of rehearsals, like an opportune time to be staging a production of it.

It was January 2001 and the papers were already trying to second-guess the coming general election, while the television seemed to be wall-to-wall politician. Meanwhile, at the RSC rehearsal rooms in Clapham, we were discovering that our four-hundred-year-old play contained scenes that wouldn't seem out of place on the ten o'clock news. The ya-booing kings' scene before the gates of Angiers was like a particularly heated debate in the House of Commons:

> KING JOHN From whom hast thou this great commission, France,
> To draw my answer from thy articles?

KING PHILIP From that supernal judge that stirs good thoughts
    In any breast of strong authority...
KING JOHN Alack, thou dost usurp authority.
KING PHILIP Excuse it is to beat usurping down.
QUEEN ELEANOR Who is it thou dost call usurper, France?
CONSTANCE Let me make answer: thy usurping son.

(II.i.110–21)

Cardinal Pandulph's scene with the Dauphin at the end of Act Three
(III.iv.107–83) could easily be an imagined tête à tête in a Millbank
spin-doctor's surgery. In fact, the more we dug into the play the more
we realized that here was a satire ripe for staging.

During early rehearsals Greg encouraged us to bring in pictures and
images to be used in company discussions about the play. The photograph, now infamous, of a Palestinian boy and his father caught in
West Bank cross-fire was an image of innocence caught in the wake of
larger events that seemed to echo Prince Arthur's journey in the second
half of the play. It is then that the emphasis shifts from cynical satire to
something darker and more heartfelt: an urgent, shorter-scened play,
spiralling out of control, that ends abruptly with the French army in
the quicksands, the English in a bog, and King John dead. In the final
scene there is a new political climate and a sense of uncertainty about
the next step.

Rehearsals for the play worked on three levels. We spent a lot of
time together as a company working through and understanding the
text, sharing impressions and exploring a collective perception of the
whole play. Then the individual scenes were worked several times with
those involved. Finally, there were the 'solus' sessions when Greg and I
concentrated on and discussed the character of the Bastard. Inevitably,
however, I found myself consumed by the role and much of the work
on the Bastard occurred at home, or on the train, or sitting staring at
cold cups of coffee.

The Bastard in *King John* differed, I decided, from Shakespeare's
other bastards. I looked at Edmund in *King Lear* and Don John in *Much
Ado about Nothing* in an attempt to define the genre. It seemed to me
that their journeys were far more formulaic and predestined, that they
were Machiavellian figures in the classic sense; like the Vice figures in
the early morality plays, they were set on their self-destructive courses.
I found my bastard less easy to define. Although Philip Faulconbridge (the name with which he begins the play) has drive, wit, and

self-awareness similar to Edmund's, his great need to get on is tempered by an innate wisdom:

> Which, though I will not practise to deceive,
> Yet to avoid deceit I mean to learn;
> For it shall strew the footsteps of my rising.
>
> (I.i.214–16)

Planning to rise without deceit is definitely not from the Machiavellian handbook. This ethic of integrity could be attributed to his being the bastard son of Richard the Lionheart. Richard is an absent presence that hangs over the whole play, a revered dead king, a national hero, and an uncomfortable comparison for the troubled King John. Perhaps, then, the Bastard's wisdom and nobility are inherent, in his genes. While this concept, in itself, is interesting, it is not so useful when trying to play the character. Such 'facts' cannot be played: one has to exist in the world of the play, and I had to find the man within that world. To understand him I had to rely on the text and follow the character's journey, gauging his reaction to events. Instead of looking for any character absolutes, Greg spoke of 'threading the necklace with different coloured beads' – that is, we are not sure what colour the next stage of the journey will be, but when we view it overall it makes some sort of pattern.

Looking at the play's events, I noticed immediately that the Bastard's meteoric rise is matched only by his ability to process what's happening to him. His 'quicksilver, mercurial mind' was a phrase constantly used by Greg – usually when I felt anything but mercurial. He learns extraordinarily quickly, like a newborn child. His mind moves rapidly from one idea to the next. His name also shifts, from Philip Faulconbridge to Sir Richard (though he is mostly referred to simply as 'the Bastard'). He also moves constantly from within to outside the action, stepping out to share his knowledge directly with the audience. Being an outsider makes him a slightly 'illegitimate' presence and this combines with a sharp observation and humour.

To understand him better I divided the Bastard's experience of the play into four segments:

1. The first part of the play is concerned with the exact nature of his parentage. His younger brother Robert comes to King John to suggest

that Philip is illegitimate and that he should therefore be denied his inheritance. When it is suggested that he may be Richard the Lionheart's son, he is surprisingly knighted by the king and given a new name (Sir Richard) and a new destiny. He then forces his mother to confirm his true parentage before he follows his new 'family' off to Angiers to fight the French. This quarter I decided to call his 'identity quarter'.

2. The second quarter occurs entirely in France, on the military campaign. When a stalemate is reached between the English and French, the Bastard convinces the kings to unite in destroying Angiers before continuing the war, only to be amazed when they decide to kiss and make up at the eleventh hour by uniting through a hastily arranged dynastic marriage. From this he learns the lesson of expediency or 'commodity'. When this new peace is just as quickly broken, the Bastard takes great relish in avenging his father's death by cutting off the head of the man who killed his father, the Duke of Austria. He is then sent to merry old England by King John to raise war funds by ransacking the church. This was, I felt, his Thatcherite Essex-man phase, or period of understanding 'self-interest'.

3. The Bastard then takes a break from the action of the play before arriving back at court full of news of dissent in the kingdom and of impending war because of a French invasion. He is sent by the king to try to win back the vacillating lords. Suddenly, out of the blue, his world is turned upside down when Arthur's body is discovered and it is suggested that the king had a hand in the murder. This section marks a period of 'self-awareness'.

4. The last quarter of the play is a period of redemption for the Bastard. He is convinced of Hubert's innocence and of John's guilt. This leaves him lost among 'the thorns and dangers of this world' (IV.iii.141). Confronted with the weakness of the king, however, he takes on the 'ordering' of the war (v.i.77). He leads the country into battle and emerges with a hard-fought-for philosophy. He argues for England's need to be 'well-sinewèd' to her defence (v.vii.88). He learns in this last quarter a 'collective responsibility'.

'What men are you?', asks King John (I.i.49) on meeting Philip Faulconbridge and his brother in the opening scene of the play. Philip jumps in and answers first:

> Your faithful subject I, a gentleman,
> Born in Northamptonshire, and eldest son,
> As I suppose, to Robert Faulconbridge,
> A soldier, by the honour-giving hand
> Of Coeur-de-lion knighted in the field.
>
> (I.i.50–4)

It's a bit of a mouthful, the Bastard's first speech. This chunk of information left me wondering initially which bit was more important. Should I weight one word or phrase more than another? The fact that he came from Northamptonshire intrigued me. Was this useful? What was a Northamptonshire accent like? Why was it there and why is it never mentioned again? (Perhaps this was a clue in itself and would have saved me weeks of red herrings – but it was an avenue I had to explore.) I idly mentioned this to the RSC's superb voice department and they promptly sent me a tape. 'The Northamptonshire accent', a rather plummy Radio Four voice intoned, '... unfortunately there isn't one'. It turned out that Northamptonshire has as many variations in its accent as it has in its borders. Although all this seemed a bit of a dead end, it did make me realize a few important things early on: (1) I'm speaking poetry and the accent must support this; (2) Who is to say what the Northamptonshire accent in our play's world should be? (3) Maybe this should be less about layering a character and rather more about stripping down to one. In essence I realized that any accent, any colloquialism, should come from me, and not from some helpful (or unhelpful) bloke with a tape-recorder. Perhaps Northamptonshire was representative of the 'country' as opposed to the 'court' or the 'city': the Bastard later remarks to Queen Eleanor that 'Our country manners give our betters way' (I.i.156). This seemed to be a more useful direction to go in. Another clue was his friendly interchange with a character called James Gurney, who accompanies his mother to court and leaves almost as soon as he arrives:

> BASTARD James Gurney, wilt thou give us leave awhile?
> GURNEY Good leave, good Philip.
> BASTARD   Philip? – Sparrow! James,
> There's news abroad. Anon I'll tell thee more.
>
> (I.i.230–2)

A country 'gent' so affable with his mother's servant points perhaps to someone more familiar with the kitchens than with the drawing room.

Looking for an accent I decided to go back to my own roots to find something appropriate. I grew up on the Welsh borders in Herefordshire. Like Northamptonshire, Herefordshire is rather a piggy-in-the-middle, with Wales to the west, Evesham and Worcester to the east, and Birmingham to the north; the accent takes influence from all three, with a Welsh lilt, a country burr, and a harsher nasal sound. I decided to select useful sounds. I have found in the past that the Welsh accent has a muscularity that works well with Shakespearian verse. There is also a south Walean 'erk' sound that toughens certain words. Some of the traditional 'country' sounds didn't work quite so well, however, and after Eddie-Grundying my way through a few rehearsals I decided to tone down the country burr. It was important, however, to find a distinction between the way the Bastard spoke and the voice of the court. Fortunately Guy Henry's King John was using his own cultured public-school tones, and I was able to find a rougher non-specific accent.

This roughness is reflected, too, in the energy the Bastard has in this first scene. Mirroring King John's dubious entitlement to the throne, the Bastard's legitimacy is also in question. At this point I don't think he has any game plan. He's not there to present an argument, just to pick one. Despite declaring that he is a 'faithful subject' (1.i.50), he behaves irreverently in front of the king. He interrupts his brother's story repeatedly, and undercuts and ridicules him. He suggests that he knows exactly where he comes from but that it has never been publicly acknowledged:

> Most certain of one mother, mighty king –
> That is well known; and, as I think, one father.
> But for the certain knowledge of that truth
> I put you o'er to heaven, and to my mother;
> Of that I doubt, as all men's children may.
>
> (1.i.59–63)

This rather disrespectful joke at his mother's expense prompts Queen Eleanor to call him a 'rude man' (1.i.64), but he charms her with a quick-witted response and wins recognition from the king as a 'good blunt fellow' (1.i.71). In fact his use of language and quick verbal trickery are major weapons in his armoury. He has a freedom and an honesty in this formal environment that prompts the king to call him a 'madcap' (1.i.84).

5 Jo Stone-Fewings as the Bastard with Alison Fiske as Queen Eleanor, *King John*, Act I, Scene i: 'I like thee well. Wilt though forsake thy fortune, / Bequeath thy land to him, and follow me?'

There is, however, a barely repressed anger through much of what he has to say. Where does this acid energy come from? And how should I play this 'madcap'? It struck me that he hates his brother, a hate born of years of insinuation that he is illegitimate, a family intrigue buried in deep embarrassment. I imagined a tough childhood.

> Zounds! I was never so bethumped with words
> Since I first called my brother's father dad!
>
> (II.i.466–7)

he announces later. Having been used to words as weapons, it follows that his main form of defence should be attack and that his wit should be so honed and savage. His use of language in this scene contrasts wildly with that of his brother, which is formal, carefully planned, and rather obsequious. I felt that I had two choices: I could use his anger in a cynical, knowing way, snide and cruel; or I could keep him more upbeat, open and entertaining, more devil-may-care. The latter seemed more appropriate. His energy felt very active, very front-foot, an energy, I was later to discover, that carries him through the play. Playing him 'knowing' also made him too calculated: learning moment by moment he was more open to the audience.

In performance, therefore, we emphasized both the different verbal approaches of the brothers and also their physical differences. The Bastard lampoons his brother's appearance:

> And if my legs were two such riding-rods,
> My arms such eel-skins stuffed, my face so thin
> That in mine ear I durst not stick a rose
> Lest men should say 'Look where three farthings goes!'
> And, to his shape, were heir to all this land –
> Would I might never stir from off this place,
> I would give it every foot to have this face;
> I would not be Sir Nob in any case!
>
> (I.i.140–7)

Joe England, who played Robert, is taller and slighter than I am. He played his character with a stiff alertness, whereas I found it helpful to reflect the Bastard's energy by being more free, by roaming about the stage. This culminated in delivering a blow to Robert's groin as a final two-fingers to his brother, once the Bastard had received his knighthood and been welcomed into the royal family.

I was starting to get the feel of this character. At this early stage I'd identified the Bastard as a number of things: an outsider, a fighter, a loud-mouth, a joker; but astute. So how was he going to look? Our designer, Stephen Brimson Lewis, liked, I was told, 'to work with the actors'. This sounded hopeful; the costume designs would come from rehearsals and the actors' ideas. True to his word, Stephen organized a character 'show-and-tell' session. We were to bring in any photographs or images of costume elements that we thought might come in useful. Stephen would also be on hand during rehearsals to discuss any new ideas. I found it difficult to think in terms of costume (perhaps that's the reason we have designers!) and rather than selecting ideas from a C&A catalogue I was keen to find an individual who displayed the Bastard's qualities, and see what they wore. I came up with Mohammed Ali, a fighter with a mouth, but unfortunately mostly dressed in silk shorts – not so helpful! My second attempt produced a bad photograph of James Dean, an archetypal outsider, but too moody and clean-cut; besides, I couldn't see myself working with a quiff for the rest of the year. I needed someone more contemporary and eventually dug out an old record cover of Ian Dury and his rhythm stick, dressed in a thick leather jacket and with a big grin on his face. I liked the idea of Dury, a lead singer in a band born of the punk-rock era. Here was a punk poet, an outsider with a wit forged from adversity. The leather jacket obviously scored some points, for I found myself fitted for one a few weeks later. The rest of the costume reflected the whole look of the production, which was a modern/medieval mix with the emphasis on practical clothes rather than costumes. Capitalizing on the Bastard's sense of movement, his shifting and upwardly mobile energy, I had flexible, unrestrictive clothing: no tight, formal coats, but a hooded top, short jackets, and a comfortable pair of military-style boots.

By the end of the first scene, this punky, slightly unkempt, country outsider has become 'Sir Richard', and part of the establishment. Although this extraordinary outcome should exceed his wildest dreams, the Bastard is already on to the next move:

> A foot of honour better than I was,
> But many a many foot of land the worse!
> Well, now can I make any Joan a lady.
>
> (1.i.182–4)

I was left alone on a bare stage with nothing but the throne of England for company. It's his first soliloquy, and a chance to get acquainted with the audience. It's a good opportunity to talk directly to them. I don't think there's any point in not acknowledging them, although some audiences are more willing than others. It's not really something one can rehearse. The first time I did it for the company there was a stony silence – I think it was close to lunchtime. It wasn't until the first previews in the Swan, surrounded by expectant faces on all levels, that the speech came alive.

Rehearsing this speech, I found that it divided into two halves, with a major gear-change half way through. The first half demonstrates the Bastard's pleasure in undercutting the establishment that he has just joined. He is rather like a kid in a playground, imitating the pretentiousness of the court. It is peopled with a gallery of characters that he relishes satirizing. I found that this was direct, crowd-pleasing stuff, finding funny voices and comic gestures to fit the 'pickèd man of countries' and 'dialogue of compliment' (1.i.193, 201) that he so clearly abhors.

And so to the gear-change. The second half of the speech begins with 'But this is worshipful society' (1.i.205). Initially I found this complicated, because it was not consistent with the jibes of the first half; it is more considered. The Bastard seems to be saying 'I can play this game, be part of this élite club, be in step with this new fashion'. He can play the outward show and flatter those around him at the same time:

> And not alone in habit and device,
> Exterior form, outward accoutrement,
> But from the inward motion – to deliver
> Sweet, sweet, sweet poison for the age's tooth.
>
> (I.i.210–13)

Whilst knowing, however, that this behaviour will ease his way to the top, he tempers it:

> Which, though I will not practise to deceive,
> Yet to avoid deceit I mean to learn;
> For it shall strew the footsteps of my rising.
>
> (I.i.214–16)

He smartly reminds us that, whatever he plays at court, he is still aware of his ultimate illegitimacy and thence his permanent state of presumption. Perhaps he would like to forget this fact, but it is an eternal thorn in his side. I decided to use this, and in performance it gave a reason for the gear-change and the sudden seriousness. His essential insecurity, and the fundamentals that he cannot change, mean that he must always be aware, that he must learn and play carefully.

The conversation that follows is short but fundamental. It establishes firmly 'Sir Richard's' true origins. He taunts his unknowing mother with mention of that other 'Sir', his stepfather Sir Robert, until she finally relents and quite simply tells him that 'King Richard Coeur-de-lion was thy father' (I.i.253). The directness of her admission seems genuinely to floor the Bastard – for the first time. When he finally speaks, he picks his words carefully:

> Now by this light, were I to get again,
> Madam, I would not wish a better father.
>
> (I.i.259–60)

During the following speech there is, I think, a choice to be made. Does he forgive his mother? The whole speech could be played with a growing sarcasm. After all, she has kept his true identity from him for far too long and it's unlikely that he's going to run into her arms:

59

in which case, perhaps he doesn't forgive her. The problem with this interpretation is that it makes it difficult to deliver the line 'With all my heart I thank thee for my father' (I.i.270). If, however, one plays him so thrown by the news that his response is forgiving and heartfelt, it makes no sense of the central section in which he satirizes the irresistibility of the Lionheart and the idea that no woman could refuse him. In the end I took elements of both. I began with the Bastard building in anger and sarcasm, literally keeping his mother at arm's length and not addressing her face to face, then finally exploding accusatorily on the lines

> He that perforce robs lions of their hearts
> May easily win a woman's.
>
> (I.i.268–9)

At that point, however, I had the Bastard look at his mother, let his guard down, and forgive her without reservation. After all, he now knows who he is, where he came from, and where he's going. To show that he has learnt from his former crippling life was the most interesting way of playing this speech.

By the time the Bastard arrives in France he's cock-sure of his new identity. Although a knight of the realm he has no courtly affectation. He cannot suppress his excitement at the prospect of battle. He interrupts the formal discourse of the kings, poking fun at his father's killer the Duke of Austria. He slightly oversteps the mark at one point, earning a reproof from King John: 'We like not this; thou dost forget thyself' (III.i.134). In performance I kept his energy up, being free in the space, roaming around the stage and the auditorium. To reflect this energy both Stephen Brimson Lewis and I decided that he should take his medieval grunge look into battle. The military-style boots would remain, chain mail and a padded jacket would go over his hooded top, and there would be copious amounts of smoke-coloured face make-up and fuller's earth. If anything he would be even dirtier than in the preceding act.

The Bastard's adventure in self-interest really begins with a slow realization that the rules of war are not quite what he expected. I discovered during rehearsals that as an outsider he has a unique perspective on this particular 'theatre of war'. As a new participant in the game his incredulity at the behaviour of the kings makes complete sense. War is about killing your opponent and should be total and absolute:

Cry havoc, kings! Back to the stainèd field,
You equal potents, fiery-kindled spirits!
Then let confusion of one part confirm
The other's peace. Till then, blows, blood, and death!
(II.i.357–60)

Although unattractive, perhaps, the Bastard's stance is an honest one. When the deadlock between the French and the English descends into farcical negotiations, however, and the marriage compromise is agreed, the Bastard is sidelined once more. It is from this familiar position that he once again bends the audience's ear with the 'Mad world, mad kings' soliloquy (II.i.561).

In performance I found that this soliloquy differed from his first in the sense that it is entirely in isolation and outside the action; and no-one interrupts it. I had been warned that this was a 'bastard' of a speech and it certainly seemed extremely dense on first reading. During it the Bastard observes that the world is 'mad' and that it is all driven by the accommodation of self-interest or 'commodity'. There is a lot of imagery, some of which is now fairly antiquated and difficult to convey to a modern audience: whilst it is lovely to describe the world as a bowling ball, and commodity as the weight inside it causing it to curve from its true path, an intimate knowledge of Elizabethan bowling is not usually high on the list of interests of, say, a sixteen-year-old from Solihull. I feared blank, uncomprehending stares. The word 'commodity' itself also presented a challenge. 'Tickling commodity' (II.i.573) is at the heart of the speech, repeated many times, and it's a word whose meaning has shifted. In order that the audience should appreciate its sixteenth-century meaning, Greg decided that it would need qualifying in the speech and suggested cutting 'vile-drawing bias' (II.i.577) and inserting instead the more twenty-first-century-friendly 'expediency'. It would help during the bowling imagery to provide a 'safety hook' for the audience. I don't have a problem with nips and tucks in the right places, and although it was a pity to lose 'vile-drawing bias' as it helped to inform the bowling image, the change did strengthen the argument for the audience.

Throughout the production's runs in Stratford and in London it was this speech that concerned me most. I felt that I had two basic interpretations, and I played with both. First, I felt that I could play it with a sense of angry frustration, railing at the impossible stupidity of the kings for brokering their compromise. The speech would end in a defiant resolution, the thought that 'if this is how the world is, I'll play them at their own game'. The second was less of a rant and more of a discovery. It had a feeling of staggered amazement at the world: 'I can't believe they did that, can you?' These two interpretations came from performing the speech on rainy Thursday afternoons and packed Saturday nights, and I instinctively felt my way towards whichever seemed more appropriate – though by the time we arrived at the Pit in London, which is a much smaller space, the speech necessarily became more conversational and intimate and I found that the second interpretation sat better.

The 'mad world' speech is an epiphany for the Bastard. He pieces together the strange events and realizes that he is a pawn in the game –

> Not that I have the power to clutch my hand
> When his fair angels would salute my palm
>
> (II.i.589–90)

– and then resolves with this new knowledge to take control and become a 'player':

> Since kings break faith upon commodity,
> Gain, be my lord – for I will worship thee!
>
> (II.i.598–9)

This new self-determination is acted on very quickly. The Bastard seizes on the resumption of the conflict to claim a prize for himself: he kills the man who killed his real father, arriving on stage with the Duke of Austria's head in his hands. I always took the opportunity in performance to have the Bastard's face and hands smeared with blood: he has taken relish in this action. He is further empowered by King John in the next scene when he is sent to 'shake the bags / Of hoarding abbots' (III.iii.7–8) – in effect to be a rogue tax collector with direct power from the king. He answers with

> Bell, book, and candle shall not drive me back
> When gold and silver becks me to come on.
>
> (III.iii.12–13)

He is excited at the mission and in a way he has found his niche, a course of action worthy of his talents.

The character then takes a long break and by the time he arrives back at John's court a lot of plot has occurred far from his beady eye and the play has taken a much darker turn. The French under the Dauphin have invaded England, the country is beset with discontent, John has rather desperately had himself recrowned, and there is rumour rife that he has had Arthur murdered. Re-entering the action I had to gauge the Bastard's energy rather carefully. I felt that during his adventures in tax-collecting he had matured and gained confidence. When we brought the production to London I had him wear a longer, more military-style coat at this point, a reflexion of his growing status. This short scene raised a tricky question, however: he has met the 'distempered lords' (IV.iii.21), heard the rumours about Arthur, even dragged a discontented prophet of doom with him to court, so why does he not question the king, or immediately worry about the French? The answer lay in his absence: he doesn't realize how bad things have become. He retains his humour, satirizing the prophet and his 'rude harsh-sounding rhymes' (IV.ii.150), providing some relief to the spiralling events. I always played him surprised, though, by the swiftness of John's death-sentence on Peter of Pomfret. The Bastard cannot, however, be suspicious of the king. I discovered in playing this scene that it was important to take this view, to maintain his innocence and not build in an enquiring look or an arched eyebrow. In other words, just play the text – and this pays dividends in his next scene, the scene around Arthur's corpse.

The stage is set for a show-down in Act Four, Scene Three. The lords are convinced of John's guilt, the Bastard is convinced of the king's right, and they then discover a dead child in the corner of the stage. In performance we found that cranking up the differences in opinion at the start of the scene led to a more dramatically interesting outcome at the discovery. It is the Bastard, however, who is first on the back foot. His moment of realization that the child is dead, that Hubert probably killed him, and that the king could be implicated in some way, marks his least vocal contribution to the play. Initially he cannot quite believe it (though in expressing this he intuitively perceives the truth of which only the audience is aware):

> It is a damnèd and a bloody work,
> The graceless action of a heavy hand –
> If that it be the work of any hand.
>
> (IV.iii.57–9)

He has to think quickly on his feet and it is not until after the lords' departure that he has time to try to make sense of what has happened. I wanted to convey his dilemma as he is left alone with Hubert. His anger at Hubert is tempered by disbelief, and in performance I made him unable even to look Hubert in the eye whilst he tests his innocence. In order to do so he paints a full picture of the dire consequences if Hubert is guilty, using his imagination and command of words to deliver some of the most vivid and beautiful imagery in the play:

> And if thou wantest a cord, the smallest thread
> That ever spider twisted from her womb
> Will serve to strangle thee; a rush will be a beam
> To hang thee on.
>
> (IV.iii.127–30)

Finally, and only when he looks Hubert in the eye, and hears his categorical denial, is he sure of Hubert's innocence and convinced of John's guilt and its terrible implications. His world is blown apart, his order gone, and he is once again left to his own devices:

> I am amazed, methinks, and lose my way
> Among the thorns and dangers of this world.
>
> (IV.iii.140–1)

It is at this point of revelation that the Bastard begins to formulate that zealous, forward-looking philosophy that carries him through to the end of the play. Perhaps this is another form of defence: there is no going back; he has to keep moving forward, to defend ultimately the only sacred thing left to him, the very idea of his country. This point marked for me his moment of 'self-awareness', moving towards his development of a social conscience.

The beginning of the fifth act and the final quarter of the Bastard's journey finds him having to face his own demons in confronting the king with the news of Arthur's death. During rehearsals Greg was keen to emphasize the intimate nature of this scene. At times it became more of a marital row than an argument over national security, an onstage struggle, messy and fraught, reflecting the conflicting emotions that the Bastard is trying to reconcile. It was, from the start, and so it remained, an exasperating scene to play. The Bastard has to keep changing tack in order to cajole, bully, and persuade John, while keeping in check his own panic and disillusionment with a man he had trusted. By the end of the scene, however, he is given 'the ordering of this present time' (v.i.77) – that is, the weight of responsibility for the entire country.

The fifth act of *King John* is witness to some large speeches from the Bastard, both in length and scale. During rehearsals we had a day with Max Atchinson, a speech-writer for politicians and someone with a passionate interest in the power of words. He took us through a session on the mechanics of public speaking, or, as he put it, 'how to make an audience listen'. He showed us a tape of various politicians, from Thatcher to Clinton, and the tricks they employed to sway an audience. It was interesting to discover these 'new' tricks in our four-hundred-year-old play. The use of metaphor to demonstrate a point, the rhetorical question followed by the rhetorical answer, the flashy 'rule of three' – as in 'The life, the right and truth of all this realm' (IV.iii.144) – all these devices were built into our play and only needed gentle coaxing out.

The end of Act Five, Scene Two became known to us as the 'outscolding' scene: the Bastard and the Dauphin in a demonstration of 'how to make people listen'. It is here that the Bastard gives a display of verbal fireworks, with all the rhetorical devices (including the 'rule of three') contained within his speech:

> This apish and unmannerly approach,
> This harnessed masque and unadvisèd revel,
> This unhaired sauciness and boyish troops,
> The king doth smile at.
>
> (V.ii.131–4)

The use of metaphor and simile is also much in evidence:

> To dive like buckets in concealèd wells,
> To crouch in litter of your stable planks,
> To lie like pawns locked up in chests and trunks,
> To hug with swine...
>
> (V.ii.139–42)

Even the rhetorical question and answer is used to defy the French:

> Shall that victorious hand be feebled here
> That in your chambers gave you chastisement?
> No! Know the gallant monarch is in arms...
>
> (V.ii.146–8)

The Dauphin is forced to admit 'we grant thou canst outscold us' (V.ii.160). The torrent of words is so effusive, however, that it almost extinguishes itself. The Bastard goes one metaphor too far, and has to

6 Jo Stone-Fewings as the Bastard with Guy Henry as King John, *King John*, Act V, Scene vii: 'And then all this thou seest is but a clod / And module of confounded royalty.'

catch himself. In performance I would use the explosion at the English lords to show that he had crossed the line: he has become too personal, losing his objectivity and the argument. The Dauphin pounces on this:

> We hold our time too precious to be spent
> With such a brabbler.
>
> (v.ii.161–2)

This fires the Bastard's indignation and he recovers to let forth a defiant salvo of image upon image of 'warlike John' and the 'bare-ribbed death' to come (v.ii.176, 177), images all the more vehement because of his awareness of how altogether unwarlike John had appeared at their last meeting. The Dauphin commands 'Strike up our drums to find this danger out' and we hear a flash of the old Bastard, truly back on form, as he swiftly rhymes 'And thou shalt find it, Dauphin, do not doubt' (v.ii.179–80).

The final scene was initially difficult to understand. Why does the Bastard return to John, a man he believes to be a child-killer? Again it is

because there are more pressing matters to occupy the Bastard's attention and he must suppress his feelings towards John. Whether he forgives
John, whom we had die in the Bastard's arms, remains ambiguous. It's
almost not significant: the importance of national unity in defence of
the realm transcends the death of a king. This is the lesson the Bastard's journey through the play has taught him. With the treacherous
lords returned to the court, the sudden death of King John turns all
eyes to Prince Henry. The Bastard immediately pledges loyalty and a
scramble for the attention of the new king begins. The messy struggle
between the Bastard and the lords always remained fairly fluid in our
production, with all of us rushing to kneel at Henry's feet. This probably had a lot to do with the now dead body of King John sprawled in the
middle of the stage: attempting to circumnavigate the old king and grab
the attention of the new one became an undignified brawl, pathetic and
comic. And yet out of this mess the Bastard calls for national unity and
collective responsibility, reminding characters and audience alike that

> Naught shall make us rue
> If England to itself do rest but true!
> (v.ii.117–18)

It is always interesting to know what an audience makes of a play, and
of our interpretation. It was particularly so with *King John*, since it was
so little known. Many people felt that we had discovered something
very exciting. During conversations and post-show talks it was often
suggested that the Bastard was the hero of the play. In playing him for
over a year, what had I discovered? Much within myself as an actor, and
much within the role. Every night we re-asked the question 'What men
are you' (I.i.49) and the answer was always slightly different. I would
disagree with any attempt to pigeon-hole the character as anything. He
is certainly capable of 'heroic' acts, yet able also to fall, albeit defiantly,
on his backside. What made him such a good character to play were his
inconsistencies, his failings, his humanity.

King Edward III

DAVID RINTOUL

DAVID RINTOUL played the title role in Anthony Clark's production of *Edward III* at the Swan Theatre in Stratford in the summer season of 2002. The production was later presented at the Gielgud Theatre in London. His other part that season was Ruy Dias in Fletcher's *The Island Princess*. His only earlier role for the RSC had been Prince Hal in the two parts of *Henry IV*. Other Shakespearian roles include Orlando at Birmingham Repertory Theatre, Demetrius at the National Theatre, the two dukes in *As You Like It* at the Globe, and Bolingbroke, Edward IV, and Richmond at the Phoenix (with Marlowe's *Edward II* at Edinburgh University adding one more to his remarkable tally of English monarchs). As a member of APTLS (formerly ACTER) he has also played Hamlet, Macbeth, Malvolio, Oberon, and Edgar on tour in the United States, Egypt, and the Far East. A wide range of other theatre work includes *A Mad World My Masters* at Chichester and at the Globe, *The White Devil* and *The Beaux' Stratagem* at the Lyric Hammersmith, and *The Rivals* and *Remembrance of Things Past* at the National. His many roles for television include Mr Darcy in *Pride and Prejudice* and four series of *Dr Finlay*.

1600, Friday 1 March 2002. At home. The phone rings. It's Roger, my agent.

'David. *Edward III* – Royal Shakespeare Company. Know anything about it?'

Nothing about the play, but I had heard that it was part of an interesting sounding season of rarely performed Elizabethan and Jacobean plays that the RSC was mounting at the Swan and that it was going to be directed by Ed Hall – with whom I'd worked a few months earlier on a Sondheim musical revue at Chichester – but that there had been problems and that he'd pulled out: 'A bit.'

68

'Well . . .' – Roger is a pretty unflappable cove, but was sounding a touch flapped – '. . . how does the idea of playing the king in *Edward III* and Ruy Dias in Fletcher's *The Island Princess* strike you?'

Heart ups the tempo a notch: 'Tell me more.'

'They're biking the scripts over to you now and it would be a good idea to read them as soon as they arrive because rehearsals begin on Monday morning and we've got to do a deal by eight o' clock this evening.'

Ah, right. 'Is it an offer?'

'Not exactly. They'd like you to meet the director, Anthony Clark. He lives in Birmingham.'

'Does Anthony Clark have a helicopter at his disposal?'

'Perhaps not. Look, read the plays and we'll work something out.'

'You know I'm flying to Glasgow early tomorrow morning to run a workshop for the Scottish Youth Theatre and that I'm speaking at Ian Bannen's BAFTA tribute on Sunday and recording a radio play in Edinburgh on Monday and Tuesday? If I can cancel the four-day audio book I'm reading in ten days' time, I could be with them first thing on Wednesday morning.'

'Yes . . . well, just read the plays and let me know what you think.'

The biker with the scripts is late – Friday rush hour. I sit down and read *Edward III* – quickly. My partner, Vivien Heilbron, reads *The Island Princess*. *Edward III* comes over as a stately, rather verbose verse drama with some fine writing; the part of the king is very long and obviously very challenging.

'How's *The Island Princess*?'

'Interesting.'

'What about Ruy Dias?'

'Can't quite make him out.'

'Is there another part in it that I should be playing?'

'No.'

I call Tony Clark in Birmingham. We've never met, but we've both served time at the Orange Tree Theatre in Richmond and Tony has talked to the director, our mutual friend Sam Walters, who has presumably confirmed that I don't have two heads. I like him and we have an 'if I offered it would you do it? . . . if I wanted to do it would you offer it?' sort of conversation. Next I call Greg Doran who is to direct *The Island Princess* and is in overall charge of the Swan season.

'What do you make of the parts?'

'Hard to say.'

'Would you like to play them?'

'Are you offering?'

'Yes.'

'Then it would seem churlish to refuse.'

Chivers Press kindly agreed to find someone else to read the audio book and a deal was indeed done by eight o' clock that evening.

So it was that I arrived for the first read-through at a church hall in Clapham on the following Wednesday morning. I hadn't worked for the RSC for twenty years (when I had played Prince Hal in the two parts of *Henry IV* on tour) and it was to be my first season at Stratford. I was completely unprepared – *tabula rasa*. *Edward III* was to open the season with *Eastward Ho*; they were about seventy per cent double cast and had been given a shared seven-week rehearsal period (short by RSC standards), each show having rehearsal-call priority over the other on alternate days. Because of the time lost by Ed Hall's departure and Tony Clark's appointment, we were already well behind and had four-and-a-bit weeks of shared rehearsal time until first preview. We were working under pressure. It was therefore a relief to look round the table that Wednesday morning: many of the company were old fiends and colleagues and as a group we gave off the hard-edged, experienced, amused confidence that the job needed. We were lucky to have Tony as director. He and designer Patrick Connellan were having to come to major production decisions on the spur of the moment, yet he managed to create a calm, pleasant atmosphere in which I felt able to look at this difficult and complex play in much greater depth than the time and circumstances would seem to have allowed.

Learning the lines, however, was a pain in the arse. With a bit of notice, line-learning can be a fairly gentle process, but not in this case. I couldn't trust that they would easily insinuate themselves into my head over the four weeks; I had to cram them in there double-quick. I'm not a particularly slow, or fast, study – just average – and I have a method. Whenever I go to Greece (which is as often as I can) I buy a small bundle of blue plastic-coated school exercise books. Into one of these I write out my lines in black ink and one-line cues in red. With 'day-glo' highlighters I mark alliteration in yellow, repetition in green, rhyme in pink, and bits that I consistently forget in blue. I put down the script and rehearse from this book as soon as I can. I read it before every performance. It becomes dog-eared, sellotaped, scribbled on, and it acquires enormous totemic value. I once left one on a plane and was utterly bereft. (It was found and I got it back.) During rehearsals for *Edward III* I would bury myself in this exercise book during the two bus rides that took me from Fulham to Clapham. I would wake at two in the morning, get it out of the bag, and study it for hours until the birds began to sing. I would gaze at it while eating horrible pies for lunch. The words did go in, but during the first performances it felt that I was dragging them out of my head. I didn't really feel at ease with them until well after press-night.

The Swan season consisted of twenty-eight actors and eleven musicians performing five plays in repertoire – the three that I wasn't in being *Eastward Ho*, *The Roman Actor*, and *The Malcontent*. Each show had to be capable of being struck, or set, in half an hour to allow a one-hour changeover between matinée and evening performance. (Fight and music calls were on stage at 6.30 p.m.) This meant that set-design was minimal: in our case, a tree, two umpire's chairs, and a gauze curtain with a medieval castle painted on it. Tony and Patrick didn't want us in full fourteenth-century fig, so the costumes were anachronistic, as they probably would have been in an Elizabethan production: modern mess-dress uniforms over which we wore armour or, for the English, red cloaks with the Garter emblem, twentieth-century civilian dress for the French refugees, felt-tip pens and notebook for Lodowick.

Mr Frederick R. Koch, who generously paid for the building of the Swan Theatre, did a very good thing indeed. It's a remarkable theatre: intimate, but with a public and, if you like, spiritual dimension way beyond its size. Playing Edward was rather like being in a new play: you don't really know what you've got on your hands until you've put it in front of an audience; with and through them you find out what sort of play you've got. To go through that process with a very good company in the Swan was a privilege.

What was it like? I'll go through the king's part scene by scene (using the scene numbers of our RSC text edited by Roger Warren).

Scene One Well, of course the king knows his own ancestry, but he wants his title to the French throne stated in court by a Frenchman. Acting decision: has he decided to declare war on France before the scene begins, or does the provocative invitation from Valois, delivered by Lorraine, tip him over the edge? Usually, I would say that if you can make a decision on stage, in the theatrical moment, then do. Here, however, because of the canny, controlling nature of the man, I go for premeditation. It makes sense that he would ask Artois to validate his claim on that particular occasion. Immediately after declaring war on France, however, he has to delay the campaign and go north to sort the Scots out. This is unwelcome and unforeseen. Note his decisiveness and speed in allotting tasks to his commanders. He can think on his feet: an impressive warrior-king. Note also his son's behaviour: unbidden he lays into Lorraine; unbidden he urges these seasoned campaigners 'cheerfully forward' (line 168) in the last couplet of the scene. When Edward tells him to

> forget thy study and thy books
> And ure thy shoulders to an armour's weight
>
> (158–9)

I don't think he anticipates any serious difficulty in getting Ned's backside out of the library and onto a horse: a chip off the old block.

Scene Two Edward starts the scene spoiling for a fight, only to find the 'stealing foxes fled and gone' (line 90). His dander's up, but he's frustrated to find no Scots to conquer: they've run away. On walks the delectable Countess of Salisbury – and wouldn't you like to conquer her? Transfer the energy from the Scots to the lady: a thumper of men, and a humper of women. Here, crudely, is the plot of the play: 'Fail to thump Scots . . . Fail to hump Countess of Salisbury . . . Thump French.'

He has enough self-knowledge to resist for a while. We talked a lot about

> What strange enchantment lurked in those her eyes
> When they excelled this excellence they have,
> That now her dim decline hath power to draw
> My subject eyes from piercing majesty,
> To gaze on her with doting admiration?
>
> (102–6)

Is this a pretty, public compliment or is he in private conference with the audience? It could be either, but I argued for the latter because of the word 'doting' (line 106). It seems too self-revealing an adjective for public consumption. Interesting, too, are the lines

> Lest yielding here I pine in shameful love,
> Come, we'll pursue the Scots. – Artois away.
>
> (117–18)

Again, I think the adjective 'shameful' (line 117) is too powerful to share with anyone but the audience, whereas the second line is clearly addressed to his fellow warriors – so he changes theatrical mode (soliloquy to open statement) in mid-sentence.

Acting decision: does the Countess of Salisbury find the king and his later advances repulsive throughout, or does she have an inward struggle to resist him? We thought the latter richer to act, and I think the script points in that direction. The sexual implication behind 'Being at the wall, enter our homely gate' (line 124), and in the countess's house and earth imagery, what about

> More happy do not make our outward wall
> Than thou wilt grace our inner house withal
>
> (143–4)

or the implied opposite to

> The ground, undecked with nature's tapestry,
> Seems barren, sere, unfertile, fruitless, dry
>
> (150–1)

– that is, fecund, young, fertile, fruitful, wet?

Scene Three
As an Aberdonian I enjoyed playing

> 'Even thus', quoth she, 'he spake', and then spoke broad,
> With epithets and accents of the Scot,
> But somewhat better than the Scot could speak
>
> (29–31)

and picking out the consonants in the last line with all the skill my RADA-trained organs of utterance could muster. This opening soliloquy, and the exchange between the king and Lodowick that follows, is one of the oddest sections of an odd play. Edward wants Lodowick, a fellow 'well read in poetry' and in possession of 'a lusty and persuasive spirit' (lines 53–4), to write a love poem on his behalf to the countess, along the lines of – and he then proceeds to burden the poor man with enough material to fill a not-so-slim volume of the stuff without giving him the time or space to jot down a single line. It's comic, of course, and the scene got plenty of laughs, but how consistent is it with the pretty formidable Edward we have seen in the opening court scene, or, indeed, with the ruthless thumper of the French we are to see later on? To what extent did consistency of character bother an Elizabethan playwright? All right, he's a bit of a thug – but Radovan Karodic is a poet, and Hitler liked to paint. Anyway, people *aren't* consistent: just play the moment full out and trust that the playwright(s) know(s) his/their job(s) and that the whole character will emerge from the sum of the parts. But I'm a twenty-first-century actor and I like to scratch about and make some sort of sense of my character and his actions. So he's the son of Edward II, a man well in touch with his feminine side, who was deposed, humiliated, murdered. He's not going down that road. His masculine side is so well to the fore that when his repressed, poetic nature is triggered, it erupts with a volcanic, ludicrous ferocity. Trite, perhaps – but actable. Lodowick is a puzzle, open to different interpretations. Wayne Cater's Lodowick veered towards being the king's licensed fool, and I was grateful to share this tricky scene with someone of his comic energy and talent, but I could equally see him played as a dry, baffled, John-le-Mesurier-type courtier.

And so, after a hundred and forty lines of high-energy outpouring (and I would defy any actor to play the scene at less than high energy) the countess enters. And does she get the benefit of the king's poetic invention? She does not. Instead she gets the old (yes, I suspect he's used it before) swearing trick: 'Swear to make me happy.' 'Of course.' 'Fine, you can make me happy by coming to bed with me.' The countess wriggles out of this with consummate skill and mental energy. 'As wise as fair', the king had said of her in the second scene (line 162). You bet. Oaths and swearing, the giving or breaking of one's word, recur throughout the play and emerge as its major theme.

Having tried the swearing trick on the countess, he tries the allegiance trick on her father, Warwick. He reminds Warwick of his oath of allegiance and Warwick confirms that to break it would be to break his 'faith with God and man' and thus to be 'excommunicate' from them both (lines 332–3). Having established this, the king continues:

> And therefore, Warwick, if thou art thyself,
> The lord and master of thy word and oath,
> Go to thy daughter and in my behalf
> Command her, woo her, win her any ways,
> To be my mistress and my secret love.
>
> (340–4)

7 David Rintoul as King Edward III with Caroline Faber as the Countess of Salisbury, *Edward III*, Scene iii: 'I wish no more of thee than thou mayst give.'

Note the phrase: 'if thou art thyself' (340). Your very identity depends on doing what you promise to do.

The scene raises questions: all subjects promise loyalty to the king. Can the king therefore do whatever he wants? Is this a one-way deal for him? The countess argues that marriage vows are more inviolable – but isn't inviolability an absolute? – than an oath of allegiance. The king argues the opposite to Warwick. Can there be a qualitative difference between oaths? Is this like a poker game: does a royal flush beat four aces? Surely an oath's an oath: if you swear to do something, you do it – full stop. But if you swear allegiance to a king *and* swear to remain faithful to your spouse and the king demands that you sleep with him, which oath takes precedence and why? The play is daring to ask the question 'Is the king above the law, or is the law above the king?', that dangerous question that dominated late sixteenth-century constitutional thought and lies at the heart of Shakespeare's *Richard II*. It is a question that would go on being asked, with increasing urgency, for the next half century, until it was answered, with terrible finality, when Charles I stepped onto the scaffold in Whitehall on that January morning in 1649.

In terms of common sense, though, we know that the king is pulling a fast one. He has moral responsibilities, he is a Christian king, he has given his own oath of allegiance to God, and to call in a subject's oath of allegiance in a way that conflicts with his responsibility as a king – in particular to try to force a father to pimp for his married daughter – casts him into a moral wilderness.

Scene Four Allowing his obsession to overrule his moral sensibility has driven Edward into a sort of madness (strong echoes of Macbeth here). Derby and Audley report that all is ready for war with France. Mired in his obsession, the king will have none of it:

> The quarrel that I have requires no arms
> But these of mine, and these shall meet my foe
> In a deep march of penetrable groans.
>
> (60–2)

Sexual and military conquest: hump and thump. What about conquering the obsession? Enter the Prince, and Edward sees in him

> His mother's visage, those his eyes are hers,
> Who looking wistly on me, make me blush.
>
> (86–7)

This elicits the crucial question:

> Shall the large limit of fair Brittany
> By me be overthrown, and shall I not
> Master this little mansion of myself?
>
> (92–4)

Answer – no. The countess is on her way. The mansion is undergoing an earthquake and everything's falling off the shelves. Self-examination gives way to self-justification:

> The sin is more to hack and hew poor men,
> Than to embrace in an unlawful bed
> The register of all rarieties
> Since leathern Adam till this youngest hour.
>
> (111–14)

I may be in the sack with a loyal subject's wife, but at least it keeps me off the battlefield. And what about 'The sin is more to hack and hew poor men' (line 111) from the mouth of a warrior-king? This is surely questioning, even subversive: certainly well beyond crowd-pleasing, patriotic chronicle. When we transferred to the Gielgud Theatre in London during the build-up to the American and British invasion of Iraq, the line took on a particular resonance.

The countess enters and opens with a dangerous gambit: the only way we can come together is by the death of my husband and your queen. So kill them: reduce the situation to its absurd conclusion, and thereby bring Edward to his senses – except that he agrees. Yes, I'll kill them; I'll swim 'through a Hellespont of blood' (line 152 – another Macbeth echo). The only way to jolt him out of his obsession is to threaten suicide by wedding-knife unless he swears (more oaths) to leave her alone. Finally, this works. Acting decision: is this a pre-meditated fall-back? Does she have the wedding-knives up her sleeve (or, in the case of our production, her dress), or is it a desperate decision, made on the spur of the moment (in which case, I suppose, she always has her wedding-knives about her)? Even if the countess is appalled by the king's advances, this is to me the most powerful passage in the play. Add the dimension of *mutual* attraction and it becomes particularly dense, rich, high-voltage. Acting decision for the king: when he says

> I am awakèd from this idle dream.
> Warwick, my son, Derby, Artois, and Audley,
> Where are you all this while?
>
> (196–8)

what happens between 'dream' and 'Warwick' (lines 196–7)? There's not much time to act the moment – the verse marches on. Is it a clear dawn after a dark night of the soul, or is the vacuum immediately filled by the obsession that has been waiting in the wings, the French campaign? The latter, for me – no hump, so thump.

Scene Seven The early part of the scene contains some of the clumsiest writing in the play. For example:

> KING I know not how we should have met our son,
> Whom now in heart I wish I might behold.
> *Enter Artois*
> ARTOIS Good news, my lord, the prince is hard at hand.
> And with him comes Lord Audley and the rest,
> Whom since our landing we could never meet.

> *Enter Prince Edward, Lord Audley, and soldiers*
> KING Welcome, fair prince, how hast thou sped, my son,
> Since thy arrival on the coast of France?
>
> (11–17)

The ritual exchange of unpleasantries between the kings is very actable, though. During it Edward says

> Imagine, Valois, whether I intend
> To skirmish not for pillage but for the crown
> Which thou dost wear and that I vow to have.
>
> (93–5)

One night the 'sk-' of 'skirmish' came out but the brain jumped ahead to the '-illage' of 'pillage' (line 94), so that what I said was ' . . . whether I intend / To *squillage*', which I had no choice but to follow with 'not for *pillage*'.

The scene sees the Black Prince rise to eminence. His campaign in northern France has gone well, he insults King John of France unbidden and with gusto, he is formally given arms, and he is awarded the dangerous honour of leading the 'vaward' or vanguard of the battle (line 220).

Staging decision: what happens to the English during King John's speech to his troops? Do they go off and re-enter for Edward's address? Do they 'disengage'? (We retreated upstage, out of the light, and turned our backs to the action.) Do they stay on and listen to John? (We might have experimented with this if we had had more rehearsal time.) We took the interval at the end of this scene.

Scene Eight Michael Thomas (playing King John) and I sat atop a pair of umpire's green chairs surveying the battle. I was uneasy about this because it seemed to make Edward an observer of the fight rather than a participant in it. To counter this I daubed a blob of fake blood onto my pate – which someone kindly pointed out gave me the look of Gorbachev and his strawberry mark. Edward is severely tested by the news that his son the Black Prince is surrounded and likely to be killed unless he, Edward, intervenes. His response

> Tut, let him fight, we gave him arms today,
> And he is labouring for a knighthood, man
>
> (30–1)

8 David Rintoul as King Edward III with Jamie Glover as Edward the Black Prince, *Edward III*, Scene viii; 'Arise, Prince Edward, trusty knight at arms.'

and, particularly,

> We have more sons
> Than one to comfort our declining age
> (36–7)

seem remarkably callous, and Audley's 'O cruel father' (line 67) quite justified. Well, historically he did have a stockpile of surviving children, but I take Edward's reasons for non-intervention at face value. Ned is in the vanguard of a battle, fighting for his knighthood. Of course he is in mortal danger, but to intervene would be to dishonour him. (Imagine a senior Battle of Britain RAF officer whose son flies Spitfires: does the boy get special treatment?) It doesn't mean that Edward is indifferent. I suppose you could play it that way, but it's richer to act the pain of making such a decision. There is an echo of *Henry V* when Ned reports the disproportionate French and English battle losses.

The RSC edition of *Edward III* was sold to the audience at a reduced price, and sure as eggs is eggs the person whose nose would be buried in it throughout the play would be sitting in the front row. One night I was delivering

And ever after dread their force no more
Than if they were but babes or captive slaves

(65–6)

when my mind went completely blank after 'babes'. I had to make some rubbish up and what I came out with was 'Than if they were but babes . . . , or . . . small babies'. The man in the front row didn't raise his nose from the book, but echoed, rather loudly, '*small babies?*'

Scene Ten Does Edward change during the post-countess scenes of the play? Does he learn anything about himself? Does he temper his behaviour in the light of his experience? There's not much evidence that he does. The one spontaneous act of mercy he comes up with is directed to the sick and indigent who have been expelled from the besieged Calais:

Go, Derby, go and see they be relieved,
Command that victuals be appointed them,
And give to every one five crowns apiece.

(30–2)

I enjoyed playing the next moment as if this kindness had taken me by surprise and that I had to justify it to Artois, who might see it as a weakness. 'The lion scorns to touch the yielding prey' (line 33). Not much mercy is shown to the powers that be in Calais, who offer a conditional surrender. In order to save the town from 'fire and sword', six of the wealthiest merchants are to present themselves to be 'afflicted, hanged, or what I please' (lines 72, 78). The focus of the play now turns, however, to the Black Prince and his pursuit of King John of France, rather than dwell on Edward's siege of Calais. A wise choice, I think, although Samuel Beckett may have disagreed. At any rate it gave me a very generous twenty-five minutes in the dressing-room.

Scene Sixteen In the event, only four burgesses of Calais turned up to take the rap. We had six actors and we had six costumes, but, try as they might, two of them couldn't make it. Ben Hicks had just played Audley's saviour, the (single) poor squire, and Tony Byrne was about to come on as King David of Scotland. Some quick changes are beyond the art of even the Stratford wardrobe department. We thought of amending the lines to

> Except within these two days *four* of them
> That are the wealthiest merchants in the town...
>
> (Scene 10, 73–4)

but if Monsieur Rodin could manage six – then on your imaginary forces work, and see two of them squatting patiently in Row C.

At the top of the scene we meet Queen Philippa who, redoubtable woman, has been a-thumping the Scots – 'That big with child was every day in arms' (Scene 10, line 45). Sian Howard's Philippa was, indeed, heavily pregnant and, to illustrate her bellicose nature, initially sported a breast-plate with a fine pair of Madonna (Ciccione)-like breasts – conical, brass, and dangerous-looking. I suggested that each breast might be hinged so that she could give suck in the heat of battle, but I wasn't taken seriously and this spectacular artefact now languishes in some RSC store.

The burgesses of Calais have to remind Edward of his promise not to destroy their town and slaughter its citizens and it is only Queen Philippa's intervention that stops him having them put to a cruel death. Note how dismissively King David of Scotland is dealt with: a captured king, and he's not given a single line. Little wonder that the play seemed to disappear when James VI came south.

Salisbury enters. Does the audience realize that this is the countess's husband? Does Philippa know of the attempted seduction? It's richest to play it that she does, which gives

> We thank thee for thy service, valiant earl.
> Challenge one favour, for we owe it thee
>
> (102–3)

an added frisson. 'I am in debt to you not just for the service you have done the state, but for the dishonourable way I behaved to you and to your wife, and I am delivering this apology in the presence of my own wife, who knows what I'm talking about.' It's a lot to load onto 'for we owe it thee' (line 103), but I think the audience got it.

What, however, are they to make of Salisbury's news? We last saw the Black Prince preparing to march triumphantly to Calais with the captured French king in tow. Now we hear that he's almost certainly been killed in battle. (Note the reverse echo of the second part of *Henry IV*, where another father, Northumberland, gets the false news that his son has triumphed in battle.) Some members of the audience I spoke to thought that they must have missed something and that the prince had indeed been killed, but most realized that he was alive: a long speech, therefore, and the parents' grief-stricken reaction – and all in response to what most of the audience realize is untrue. A bold piece of writing? Some would say incompetent. Odd, whatever. Edward's grief at Ned's supposed death rings true, albeit expressed as a bloodthirsty cry for revenge, as does his joy at the prince's return. When Ned suggests turning a warlike eye on

> Spain, Turkey, and what countries else
> That justly would provoke fair England's ire
>
> (233–4)

Edward's 'Here, English lords, we do proclaim a rest' (line 236), delivered as 'Steady on, son', usually got a laugh – legitimate, I think. The play ends

> God willing then for England we'll be shipped,
> Where in a happy hour I trust we shall
> Arrive three kings, two princes, and a queen.
>
> (241–3)

It's a splendidly daft line: 'and here we are on stage in front of you, so you can't say we haven't given you your money's worth'.

What of the authorship question? Shakespeare? A collaboration that may or may not have included Shakespeare? Someone else? First, a disclaimer: I'm not a scholar and I'm only too aware of the weight of scholarship that has been directed at this question. Of it I have read only Roger Warren's short introduction to the RSC edition and Giorgio Melchiori's full and impressive one to the New Cambridge. I'm out of my depth. Some observations, though: the play is certainly actable; it holds an audience; it has humour; but it's not what I as an actor would call buoyant. It needs skilful playing and it needs to be driven hard; a Ferrari it isn't. I wouldn't like to see an amateur production. It benefits from cutting. Early in rehearsal I brought in about sixty of Edward's lines that I offered to Tony as possible cuts. Unusually, I, the actor, was saying 'I think it would flow better if we cut this' and Tony, the director, was saying 'Let's see if we can keep it in and make it work'. In the end we lost about forty of Edward's lines and I was very grateful to see them go. The dialogue is often 'chunky': you speak, I listen; you stop, I speak; you listen – not much cut and thrust. There is a great deal of classical allusion: the mariner's, and Salisbury's, long speeches seem to come directly from the Greek theatrical tradition. It seems, and here I begin to speculate wildly, to be the work of a young man, well educated, with great linguistic and theatrical flair, but with little practical theatrical experience. It doesn't feel to me to have been written initially for performance in a large public theatre. It was published in 1596, about the time that Shakespeare was writing *A Midsummer Night's Dream*. I find it hard to imagine a writer who had acquired that level of experience, skill, and sophistication being sole, or even part, author of *Edward III*. Professor Melchiori suggests 1592–3 as the date of its composition. Even so...

This notion occurred to me during rehearsals – a hunch, no more. What if, in the years between Stratford and London, say in the mid-1580s, Shakespeare wrote a play called *Edward III* for an amateur performance, as a calling card, or what have you? What if, later, when he began to write for the voracious public playhouses, he revised this early work, either by himself or in collaboration? The problem with this supposition is that it makes the original writing pre-Armada (1588) and pre-second-edition-of-Holinshed (1587). Obviously the gung-ho patriotism (if taken at face value – the play is not without irony) would appeal to a post-Armada popular audience, but, more importantly, as Professor Melchiori points out, the mariner's description of the Battle of Sluys contains details of the defeat of the Armada described by Ubaldino in 1590. Also, could this imagined first version of the play have been written with reference to two of its sources, Froissart and Painter, but without reference to the 1587 Holinshed? Probably not, but note that I have cunningly allowed in my theory for a later revision.

Single author or collaboration? Collaboration was more common than single authorship in the Elizabethan and Jacobean theatre. I can't see the joins, but then I've been in two-author plays such as *The Changeling* and haven't seen the joins there either. There is a weight of opinion that says that Shakespeare wrote the Countess of Salisbury scenes and a person or persons unknown the rest. I'm not entirely convinced by this. Certainly the Countess of Salisbury scenes describe the most powerful dramatic action in the play, but does that necessarily imply that they were written by a more capable writer than the rest of the play? The opening of the following scene is pretty feeble, but does that falling-off necessarily imply a different hand?

If I were a betting man I'd be tempted to ascribe the initial authorship to a young Shakespeare. Here's an image: a summer pudding in a glass bowl. It's lined with bread and filled with blackberries, raspberries, and other summer fruit. A weight is put on top and the juice seeps through the bread. I don't quite get the fruit, but the juice is very vivid indeed.

King Richard II

Samuel West

SAMUEL WEST played the title role in Steven Pimlott's production of *Richard II* at The Other Place in Stratford in the summer season of 2000 and later at the Pit Theatre at the Barbican. It was his only role that season, his first with the RSC. Earlier Shakespearian roles had included Prince Hal in English Touring Theatre's production of the two parts of *Henry IV*, and Octavius Caesar in *Antony and Cleopatra* at the National Theatre. He returned to Stratford in 2001 to play Hamlet in the Royal Shakespeare Theatre. A wide range of other theatre work includes *Arcadia* and *The Sea* at the National, and leading roles at Birmingham Repertory Theatre, the Manchester Royal Exchange, and Chichester. Among his films are *Notting Hill*, *Howard's End*, *Jane Eyre*, and *Persuasion*. He has also worked as a reciter with a number of major orchestras and extensively in television and radio, where his roles have included Bassanio, Lysander, Bertram, Benedick, and Richard II.

I wasn't doing *Richard II* the night John Gielgud died – good thing too. The job of playing a large classical part (even a lesser-known one like Richard) feels like taking the crown, staggering along under it for a bit, and passing it on with gratitude to the next person lucky enough to have the chance. But though Gielgud had last played Richard many years before, he was still inseparable from it, and it wasn't until weeks after his death that I got it back, as it were.

I'd played Richard in a BBC Radio production six months before, and blush now to think that in seven days of rehearsal and recording I thought that I'd solved most of the part's puzzles. Even in my smuggest moment, though, I felt it would be fun and interesting to do it again on stage. The RSC almost immediately announced their millennium project 'This England: The Histories': all eight plays from *Richard II* to *Richard III* over a year, to be staged, finally, in order over a week for the first time in the company's history. This seemed like a noble and proper thing to attempt, and I wanted to be part of it. I met Steven Pimlott, he cast me, and I got to say the first line.

Richard II was the only one of the histories to be played in the Other Place, the RSC's smallest auditorium, for which David Fielding designed what came to be known as the 'White Box', a featureless, white-walled room. As well as directing *Richard II*, Steven was Artistic Director of the whole building and his vision of the White Box had much to do with the way the play and the performance turned out.

Because The Other Place doesn't have the design deadlines of the Royal Shakespeare Theatre, the 'main house', it's possible to work much more freely there. One of the remarkable things about these rehearsals was how unplanned they were (or how unplanned Steven gave us the impression they were: if he had all the answers at the read-through, he certainly wasn't saying so). On the first day he had the extraordinary confidence to say 'I don't know how we're going to do this – where it will be set, when it will be set, whether there will be a set – but we have enough time to decide for ourselves'. This set the tone for rehearsals. We called it 'white boxing', and we were proud of it. It was good to be at a read-through and not hear 'This is what you're wearing, this is the set, and don't stand upstage right because that's where the hydraulic platform goes'. We had carte blanche, and pièce blanche, and the answers to my usual questions at the very beginning of a job (why are we doing this, and what's the story we're trying to tell?) could be postponed. We knew we had about four of the eight weeks to decide.

It was clear at once that this was, even by the standards of the RSC, a very intelligent and well-spoken company. Steven's opera experience has given him a terrific ear, and he had cast a group who spoke the verse naturally, easily and very fast. All the same, at first, a lot of what had been written about *Richard II* did poison our thinking. The extreme formality of the language (it's virtually the only Shakespeare play completely written in verse; everyone – gardener, groom, king – speaks a five-beat line) frightened us off for a while, and we started thinking it was a play of masks, with no-one ever saying what they meant and hiding behind pageantry and formal vocal devices. Of course, sometimes they do, but as we got more confident (and with a company who could sound like they meant what they said, and weren't just using funny words), we began to notice that every character's vocal register is subtly differentiated, and that though the verse is for the most part extremely regular (and very often rhyming couplets), we were playing people who simply chose to talk that way – rhyming when they wanted to, sometimes interrupting to finish off someone else's couplet, and preferring pentameter as the best way to express themselves. This was a small breakthrough and from then on we became the masters and mistresses of the words and not the slaves of them.

Now we were free to try to define what the play meant to us then and there. Almost immediately we began seeing it as fable as well as chronicle – as a story that affected us all, and from which we could learn. Richard's problem seemed less about holding on to power and more about understanding his own mortality. This, of course, is something that everyone thinks about in the depths of some night or other: having been born, all I know is that I am going to die. And it is a solitary journey: we are born alone, we die alone, and any companionship along the way is an illusion. It was about this time that the word 'existential' first got used in rehearsals, and once we had all stopped calling each other wankers for using it, we found it very useful, and used it a lot. The play seemed to us to articulate a peculiar sort of existential angst that wasn't specific to Richard – those around him were as vulnerable as he would be if he lost power, and those succeeding him would come to know in time the poison of the 'hollow crown'. All human structures and hierarchy were artificial and would ultimately fail, and the only search worth the effort was the search to become nothing. This sounds very nihilistic, but in fact, as we worked through it, the play spoke to us with straightforward honesty. Our fin-de-siècle cynicism didn't need to take refuge in a production that looked backward to pageant and spectacle for its effect. Instead, we could start the new millennium with an unsentimental version and a fiercely analytical eye, and with the laboratory (or the operating theatre) of the White Box, anatomize the play and find out what it was about it that made so many of us uneasy.

Quite quickly it was decided to try to do the play with as little set and as few props as possible. Anything that went into the box was thrown into huge relief by the white walls – someone said that everything had inverted commas around it – so a few well-chosen things would do better than many random ones. And they were well-chosen, I think. We ended up doing the play with a chair, a coffin, and a pile of earth. Even the coffin looked more like an ammo box – its true nature wasn't revealed until the end of the play. When we were looking for a coffin for rehearsals, the RSC stores supplied this box with rope handles. It served so well that we ended up using it completely unaltered and as I write (during performance 100) it has held up very well. The earth was Steven's idea – he wanted a grave on stage at the beginning of the play to represent the murdered Gloucester, and we gradually realized that a hole in the ground wasn't as useful as a pile of earth (the word 'earth' occurs twenty-nine times, and 'ground' another twelve, and they both have prominent parts in some pretty famous speeches). The ground was England's ground, from which Bolingbroke takes his leave (and from which David Troughton, playing Bolingbroke, took a handful) when exiled, but it also stood for the dust of the grave, to the taint of which Richard believes himself immune. As the play went on, my relationship to this dust of England became less proprietorial, and I began to realize that I would return to it – we all would. The chair was a dining-room chair, wooden and utterly normal. It was painted gold and designated 'throne', but even in rehearsal most people couldn't bring themselves to call it anything but 'the chair'. Around the white walls sat another fourteen chairs, also painted white. This was, I think, one of Steven's most brilliant ideas. Up to the first day of technical rehearsal we had benches around the walls. By replacing them with chairs, Steven made the point that the 'throne', while painted gold, was just a chair after all. We invest the throne with significance, and we choose to call the person on it 'king' and encourage them to think that they have a separate, semi-divine existence by virtue of the seat they're in, but in the end (as Richard comes to realize) the throne is just a chair, and the king is just a man. So by the end of the third week the set was finalized, and the prop budget came to almost nothing.

We discussed lighting, and Simon Kemp came up with a design that, for the first time in my experience, was the same colour as the play in my head – a bright white political reality (lit with fluorescent lightboxes, mostly from above) and a darker world of shadow and plaint. Blue and purple sidelights threw long shadows, especially accompanying the women in the play, and the sense of existential doom that their being outside the political loop seemed to give them. Very strong, and very simple – the colour of a nightmare. Sue Wilmington's costumes were another matter – rich and varied, haute couture, not prêt à porter, hypermodern but in a palette that recalled the dark shadow world of the lighting.

By this time we had pretty much decided that we wanted the play set now, in the year 2000–1. The fate of the monarchy had never been more topical, and the question of who owned England seemed important. (I liked to say that we were doing a play about the Poll Tax riots, the Irish question, and who should succeed to the throne, set in 1398. Meeting Prince Charles after the performance, all I could think of to say was 'I hope we haven't put you off'.) Starting rehearsal two weeks into a new millennium made it a time for intense scrutiny. I make no secret of the fact that television's current direction sometimes depresses me, and I felt proud (and paradoxically modern) to be with a group who chose to spend a year with the RSC talking four-hundred-year-old language rather than waiting for an episode or two of telly that would pay them the same amount of money in a month. In the modern style of talking it is fashionable not to care – the casual aside, the back-foot shrug. Verse is impossible not to care about. The muscularity of the words in your mouth alone makes what you say matter to you. We were the true rebels, I thought – bucking the apathetic trend and staging our version of a four-hundred-year-old question that we still didn't have a good answer for. I was much more interested in asking the question properly than faking an unbelievable answer.

I'm going into so much detail about the rehearsal process because it defined, to a great extent, an approach to the style of the part that I hadn't thought of before. On the radio I gave a conventionally weepy, self-pitying, whiny sort of reading. It was probably fine, but it wouldn't suit what we were doing in the White Box. For a while – several months into the run, I suspect – I went too far the other way, and found the environment made me very cynical and waspish, always ready to deflect dangerous emotion with a self-mocking laugh. This was very useful for a while, and I found the part was much funnier than I remembered, but I think I ran the risk of this ironic detachment taking over (as it does sometimes in my own life) and showing a Richard who never quite lets the mask slip. And that's no good.

The existential fear we thought we'd found was a universal problem, and a timeless one. Our modern production needed a 'moral' to make it both modern and timeless. We decided on a prologue, cannibalized from Richard's great prison soliloquy in Act Five. In an intense purple light and to the sound of bells, the cast entered and turned to me, sitting in the audience, where I had been reading (or 'studying') a copy of the play. I was being called on to give up my position as spectator and take the throne. I put down my copy, stood up, walked to the doors and bolted them. If I was going to go through with this I had to make sure that everyone else was trapped inside the box with me, and wouldn't get out until we'd solved the problem. In fact, as I hoped we would prove, the thing about life is that no-one gets out of it alive anyway. I sat on the coffin and said to the audience (from V.v.1–5)

> I have been studying how I may compare
> This prison where I live unto the world;
> And for because the world is populous,
> And here is not a creature but myself,
> I cannot do it. Yet I'll hammer it out.

This was to be an exploration of the prison that we are all born into, and from which we are only released at the hour of death. I went on (from V.v.32–8):

> Sometimes am I king;
> Then treasons make me wish myself a beggar,
> Then am I kinged again; and by and by
> Think that I am unkinged and straight am nothing.

('This is what's going to happen to me; this is the argument of the play' – delivered quite flat and matter-of-factly.) Then I explained (using lines from V.v.31–41) that this wasn't just my story, it was everyone's. And that, with the benefit of hindsight, my journey as exemplum would be away from my state as king, and towards acceptance of my transitory nothingness:

> Thus play I in one person many people,
> And none contented. But whate'er I be,
> Nor I, nor any man that but man is,
> With nothing shall be pleased till he be eased
> With being nothing.

I put on my crown, jacket, and signet ring, and began the first scene with John of Gaunt. At the end of that, and by transposing the lines 'Then call them to our presence' (I.i.15) – it sounds like we moved a lot of lines (and why not?), but they were mostly at the beginning and end of the play – only then did I decide, hesitatingly, to step into the coffin box, on which was placed the 'throne', and take my seat. I always imagined that I could decide not to do the play if I wanted, that Gaunt was setting me up, that his son was a stirrer, and at the dress rehearsal I actually said 'no, I'm sorry, I don't believe you', and walked off. But, of course, Richard does go through with it – a scapegoat, but in the end a willing one. As I stood on the coffin and sat on the throne the lights shot up into blinding light and Richard's roller-coaster descent to death began. All sense of special knowledge or hindsight evaporated under the lights.

The fact that both audience and actors were trapped in the box, and Simon's lighting was designed to illuminate both constantly, went a long way to dissolving boundaries that sometimes let the jam-making classes sit back and let the gilt and splendour wash over them. We simply assumed that the audience was part of every scene they watched – the court in Act One, Scene One, the invited audience in Act One, Scene Three, my soldiers in Act Three, Scene Two, Bolingbroke's in Act Three, Scene Three, the Commons in Act Four, Scene One, my thoughts in Act Five, Scene Five, and so on. It kept people on their toes (literally at one point, when Bolingbroke made them stand to pray for the dead Mowbray), and meant that we could talk and stare at them and, for the most part, get hard stares back. Very few people fell asleep in this production . . .

THE PLAY

At the beginning Richard has a problem. Bolingbroke and Mowbray have been accusing each other of treason, and I think he's called them before him to make the accusation specific, in the hope that going 'on the record' will moderate the fierceness of their attack. Benson famously played with his dogs here, and Gielgud suggests cultivating a lazy silliness. I couldn't square this with Richard's obvious intelligence, and the wit with which he tries to diffuse the quarrel. He is a judge the jurisdiction of whose court has been called into question, and he knows exactly what's going on. He decides to go ahead, assured by Gaunt that his son Bolingbroke's complaint is newly provoked and not old news. I imagined a memo (in fact, I wrote one) from Bushy, Bagot, and Green to me saying 'To the best of our knowledge, Bolingbroke is not about to mention the Gloucester Unpleasantness'. Well, bad briefing: he does, and Mowbray stands accused. (We decided he was telling the truth when he says (I.i.134) he 'neglected' to kill Gloucester, and that Aumerle was the murderer.) Mowbray's my man in Calais, and I can't show him sympathy, at least in public. So I do what I can: I promise him equal treatment before the throne, and give him the floor, and he immediately becomes a liability. His insistence on going to trial by combat is a disaster: if Mowbray wins, John of Gaunt, the most powerful man in the kingdom, will never forgive me for letting his son die, and die a traitor, implicitly, since he lost. And if Bolingbroke wins (which is far more likely, since he's the better athlete), his power will be consolidated and I will stand covertly accused by the plot against Gloucester. So we retreat, regroup, decide to call off the duel at the last moment, and banish both appellants. There's a choice here: the cancellation can be a spur-of-the-moment decision, but I felt premeditated action was in keeping with the thoughtful Richard of the first scene. It's quite difficult to make this clear on stage – it must *look* for all the world as if we're going through with the duel. (We had fun with this: Mowbray and Bolingbroke were given huge fire-axes, and at one point we thought of spreading plastic sheeting over the front row.) In the end it's to do with the speed you stand up to call a halt, I think.

Richard's subsequent speech is well argued, and sounds reasonable. Even though banishment is severe, it's not tyrannical, and could even be considered a merciful and prudent way of dealing with a troublemaker and an insider with an embarrassing story to tell. It seemed important to base Richard's decisions in reason as far as possible, and always to play the part from his point of view, without 'comment'. Looked at this way, he becomes a man who is doing very well, thank you, running the country in the face of fierce opposition from old-fashioned and out-of-touch Tory squires who think of nothing but their dogs and wouldn't know a sonnet if it bit them. My court included Gower and Chaucer as well as dancers and actors; French fashion and tastes prevailed, and this was how I preferred it. Through a clever marriage I'd concluded peace with France (where I was born – unlike Bolingbroke, the 'true-born Englishman' (1.iii.309)); I'd been in my minority for *ages*, and I wanted a go at the wheel myself. During rehearsals I made notes for myself and left them around my flat. One was 'NB to Uncles: governing England is my job – fuck off.' As for trial by combat, that was simply medieval. The subtext was 'fine for grandpa, but we don't do things like that any more.' When Richard hears the word gun, he reaches for his culture.

The little scene with Richard's hangers-on (1.iv) has always been important. We shied away from the bath-house and turned it into a mock-interrogation, where Aumerle magnificently defended himself against charges of fraternization with the enemy, and I tried to keep a straight face. Bushy, Bagot and Green weren't so sure of his innocence – the closeness that Richard and Aumerle share is one of royal blood, and others aren't members of that particular club. At one point when I couldn't keep up the pretence I kissed Aumerle, which seems to have been taken as an explicit indicator of homosexuality. While I've no doubt that Richard and Aumerle slept together at Eton, all I was expressing was closeness and love to one of my class. It was very useful in delineating the growing rift between Aumerle and the three spin-doctors (Manchester Grammar boys all), and went some way to rescue them from accusations of foolhardiness: if they weren't sure about Richard going to Ireland or confiscating Gaunt's estate, they daren't say so, since he and Aumerle clearly saw the whole thing as a huge joke.

It's a long part, and the more reasonable Richard seems to start with, the greater his stupidity in deciding to take Gaunt's stuff after his death. I saw that as his first really unforgivable act, and justified it (zooming around in Gaunt's still-warm wheelchair) by thinking that Richard has reigned in the shadow of uncles all his life. 'When', he thinks, 'does my life belong to me?' I have been told that I ought to be declaring war on France (this in front of my French wife!) and when York started going on about being Edward's last surviving son, I put my fingers in my ears and sang loudly. Richard was a spoiled brat in this scene (and a violent one, who twice had to be kept from hitting Gaunt), but the more he is supported in his behaviour by his circle, who have long since decided whose side they're on, the more likely he is to return from the war in Ireland with that unassailable self-belief that sets up his fall. It is as if after twenty years of uncertain rule, Shakespeare pops in for the last two just as Richard thinks he's getting the hang of it, and shows him how wrong he is.

So Richard disappears off to Ireland for one sixth of the play. I never knew what to do in the gap, apart from get a haircut (I called it my antrim). If you're playing Hamlet, you need a break in Act Four to prepare for the fight, but as Richard you get most of Act Two off and you've hardly started. The only advantage is that you can come back from Ireland bursting with belief. Steven's note was 'while you were out, your daughter was raped', and he encouraged me to take the line of a militant mother witch, cursing Bolingbroke for harming her child.

The seesaw must be a big one: for Act Three, Scene Two to work, Richard's effort to drag himself out of despair must be genuine, and ultimately successful. The evangelism of Richard's tone and the way he takes the image of himself as the sun and runs effortlessly with it through an eighteen-line extended metaphor suggested to me that he had a mad certainty about his relationship with God. In the past, doubt over which of the king's two bodies he's in has nearly upset him; how much better to allow himself the absolute certainty that he was God's anointed representative on earth, and should behave that way? I went to see the Wilton Diptych in the National Gallery – Richard had it painted in the late 1390s as a travelling votive panel. The angels behind the Christ child are wearing white harts and broom pods (*planta genista*) – both Richard's badges. They're his team: they're on his side. I decided that the angels Richard thinks will fight for him are not imagined but real, and I pointed to where I could see them in the sky. This was where one of Cicely Berry's exercises became especially useful. In rehearsal one day, as I spoke about the invincible nature of kingship, Cis suggested building a throne out of all the stuff we had in the rehearsal room. At that time this included a hospital bed, a bench or two, the coffin, cushions and flowers. I ran around excitedly building up the throne, getting the others to help me (luckily I knew the lines quite well), and was helped to the top of the wobbly pile just at the triumphant moment when I saw the angel. Then in came Salisbury and took one of the cushions away. I didn't know he was going to do this. I got down, and he took the flowers from my hand and threw them into the sea. I stood on the shore as he, and later Bagot, came on with more and more bad news, and with each piece of bad news removed another piece of my wobbling throne. Occasionally I would try to shore it up, but there was always more bad news, and eventually I stood alone on an empty shore, all evidence of my power gone. The physical shock was considerable, and very useful as sense memory when familiarity had dulled the edges of the scene.

In the great speech beginning 'No matter where. Of comfort no man speak' (III.ii.144) Richard comes face to face with the reality that flattery has kept from him: that he may be a king, but far from kingship giving him special protection, it dooms him. Kings die, always. That's what they do. At 'Bores through his castle wall' (III.ii.170) I took off my hollow crown and poured a handful of dust through it. The crown became the waist of Death's hourglass. I liked this piece of business, not least because I thought of it, and it was used on the poster. And the speech, which is often a great wrenching aria, became in our production a complaint that Richard's court had lied to him; that he wasn't semi-divine, just one of the boys. In words of one syllable, as so often in moments of emotion in Shakespeare,

> I live with bread, like you; feel want,
> Taste grief, need friends. Subjected thus,
> How can you say to me I am a king?
> (III.ii.175–7)

'Subjected' is of course a pun, and a conscious one. Richard has a terrible capacity for mocking himself with puns at his lowest moments. I sometimes took to phrasing it 'How can you *say* to me I am a *king?*' It was more active: 'How dare you flatter me "all this while" when it is clear to all of us that what I am is a man, and a pretty poor one at that?' I think this is the fulcrum of the play, where Richard consciously realizes for the first time that title and hierarchy are meaningless, and nothing can stop his slide towards the grave.

The most difficult question every actor has to answer is why does Richard give in so easily. It can't remain a problem – you have to make sense of it. After another exercise when I was held down on the throne by Aumerle and Carlisle as I struggled to pull it out from under me, I suddenly decided I wanted to stop. It was as if Richard had said 'God, I hate this – I wish I could give it up', and for the first time it occurred to him that he could. What crystallized this movement and made it active was the realization that in giving in, like all good 'Sub-Dom' relationships, the submissive is taking charge. By saying 'you can't sack me, I resign', Richard regains the moral high ground, and willingly looks forward to handing over a crown which only he knows is poisoned. By abdicating responsibility, he gains his own freedom.

> Must he submit?
> The king shall do it. Must he be deposed?
> The king shall be contented
> (III.iii.143–5)

had (I hope) a new note of surprise in it. Richard uses the repetition of 'the king' as an attempt to shore up the power of his 'name' (III.iii.146) now his armies have gone, and finally fails with a mixture of emotions, one of which is relief.

9 Samuel West as King Richard II with David Troughton as Bolingbroke, *Richard II*, Act IV, Scene i: 'Here, cousin – / On this side, my hand; and on that side, thine.'

The parliament called in Act Four, Scene One to crown Bolingbroke and depose Richard is called in Richard's name, but has not his authority. There's a gap in the succession, and Richard determines to slip through the gap and cause havoc. Our Act Four was an odd reversal of most others: the gage scene, which almost always gets unintentional laughs, was kept tight and serious by a combination of testosterone and extremely fast playing, and the deposition, which can be the most monstrous wallow, became a romp. I came in wearing a crown of thorned red roses (Bolingbroke's flower), carrying a white rose as sceptre (my own flower-power, which I had to give up), wrapped in a George cross flag and whistling 'God Save the King'. Richard has never had a court fool; he is free now to be his own one. He's clever and angry enough to exploit the fact that no-one knows who is king. Why should he go quietly, when the hypocrisy of his subjects provides so much ammunition? At the end of the abdication speech (a routine, read from Bolingbroke's A4 folder), I took the crown of thorns and sceptre, dropped them on the grave, and draped England's flag over it all. Then I produced my own pen, signed the abdication, and pushed Bolingbroke into the throne, thrusting the crown down about his ears.

The still centre of the scene is, I think, 'I must nothing be' (IV.i.200) – Richard's ultimate goal, and one he has no way of knowing he will ever reach. I called for a mirror because I was no longer sure I *had* a reflexion. When I found out that I did, the breaking of the mirror, for which we used the coffin box stood on its end, became a conscious desire to cut the crap – lose the glister, and reduce the king's two bodies to one, the real one, the one not constructed of flattery and self-deception. (For a long time we thought Richard's face could appear on a TV screen, through which he would throw the crown.) To break the mirror I pushed the box over, and, falling horizontal, it became a coffin. The flattering glass removed, all that gaped beneath was a grave. Self-knowledge came in an almost euphoric rush, and Bolingbroke and I played the last exchange as a vaudeville stand-up duo, until banishment to the Tower, which is where I realized I needed to be, in order to work on becoming nothing.

At this point in the play (the beginning of Act Five) Richard is resolved to die. He has no parents, no children, no crown, no job, and he's on his way to prison to make his witness when the worst thing possible happens – he meets his wife in the street. Catherine Walker (who played Isabel) and I found that this scene repaid trying to avoid the playing of it. The last thing Richard wants is to be reminded of ties to this earth, but his wife gets the rise out of him and provokes him to prophesy. This is particularly satisfying when you know that the predictions you're making to Chris Saul, playing Northumberland, will be acted out by him in both parts of *Henry IV* the next day. Even then, it is a marvellously unsentimental scene, both lovers trying to cope, playing games, pretending not to care and yet unable to leave. Eventually we had to be ripped from each other's arms.

Richard's great final soliloquy began with me dragging in the box on my back like a cross, then standing in it and fixing my hands through the loops so that I couldn't move. The physical obstacle was useful, and forced the mind to roam. The first time I'd used our mantra 'I have been studying' line as prologue, I was speaking as an actor about to enter the play; now I had become my own willing gaoler. I was shot in the back by Exton and hushed into the coffin by the groom, who had been forced to take part in the murder. After my death, sitting on my coffin, Bolingbroke repeated 'I have been studying . . .' to end the play as his own unwilling gaoler. He finished with 'Yet I'll hammer it

10 Samuel West as King Richard II, *Richard II*, Act V, Scene v: 'I have been studying how I may compare / This prison where I live unto the world.'

out' (V.v.5), and went off to the Swan the next day to do exactly that as Henry IV. I was underneath him, lying in the box that had finally become my resting place, and the throne chair was set on top, just as at the beginning. The audience was left to imagine if Edward III had been in the box in the first scene.

My father once met Brecht's widow, who told him that the alienation effect was 'simply something Bertie invented to protect himself from over-indulgent actors'. If, as the Introduction in the Penguin edition of *Richard II* suggests, we sometimes think of Richard as 'a voice, and a voice with tears in it', then I believe our production represented a radical re-think. The motto might have been one we put in the programme, from *Waiting for Godot*: 'They give birth astride a grave, the light gleams an instant, then it's dark once more.' Beckett's phrase, not Shakespeare's, and our response, not (I imagine) Shakespeare's. But it felt like the right time for such an honest, unsentimental view of life, and I hope my performance was made to fit.

Bolingbroke in *Richard II*, and King Henry IV

DAVID TROUGHTON

DAVID TROUGHTON is an Associate Actor of the Royal Shakespeare Company. He played Bolingbroke in Steven Pimlott's production of *Richard II* at The Other Place, and the title-role in Michael Attenborough's production of the two parts of *Henry IV* at the Swan Theatre, both in the Stratford summer season of 2000. The productions were later staged in London at (respectively) the Pit Theatre at the Barbican and at the Barbican Theatre. David Troughton's wide range of earlier roles for the RSC had included Bottom, Cloten, Hector, Kent in *King Lear*, Holofernes, Caliban, the title role in *Richard III*, Lopakhin in *The Cherry Orchard*, Fitzdottrel in *The Devil is an Ass*, and Zanetto/Tonino in *The Venetian Twins*. He has also worked extensively for the National Theatre (where his roles include Captain Hook in *Peter Pan*) and in London and provincial theatre and his film and television credits include, among much else, *Dr Who*, *David Copperfield*, *Our Mutual Friend*, *The Winslow Boy*, *Cider with Rosie*, and *Madam Bovary*. His essay on his performance of the title role in the RSC's 1995 production of *Richard III* was published in *Players of Shakespeare, 4*.

By any standards the RSC's millennium project to produce all eight of Shakespeare's history plays from *Richard II* to *Richard III* was something special. It had never been done before and even productions of the better-known quartet of *Richard II* to *Henry V* had been rare. The fact that different directors, designers, and spaces were to be used for different sections of the octet made the project even more artistically unusual and exciting. For me there was the particular joy of being able to take Bolingbroke through three plays, a privilege shared by the actors of Northumberland and Hal; others (Hotspur, Falstaff and his followers, and so on) had two. It was important, though, as one anticipated the project, not to get overawed by the whole thing: one was still, one had to remind oneself, just an actor, creating a character.

Not that the character seemed in the least consistent or coherent through the plays when I came to re-read them after accepting the role. For a start, they are so very different in style: an all-verse play for *Richard II*, and what seems at first like an all-prose play for *Henry IV*. The king and the court do, of course, speak verse, but it's a very different kind of verse from *Richard II*. So my first questions to myself were about correlating the two even as far as speaking the lines was concerned, let alone creating a character. At the same time as these initial anxieties, I was doing a certain amount of reading on the historical background, though, as usual, this was soon displaced to the back of the mind as real work on the text and on the subtleties and textures of the language – the words and rhythms that your character uses, what other people say about him, what you say about other people and how you say it – began to dominate my preparation. I had never seen a production of these plays, which is really the way I like it. Some of my colleagues take a huge interest in the performance history of their roles; I'd much rather not know. I come to it, I hope, as a blank sheet, and if I happen to make the same decision on a particular passage as an actor thirty years ago, then perhaps that's in the writing.

We rehearsed *Richard II* and the first part of *Henry IV* at the same time – and those two rehearsal periods were as chalk and cheese. In *Richard II* we had an entirely new concept for The Other Place, a brilliant, clinical, white box. We also had a total production budget of ten thousand pounds – a tiny fraction of what is spent on designs for the main stage. Adrian Noble had withdrawn rather late from directing the production and Steven Pimlott was brought in at short notice. So we had a budget that precluded anything much in the way of designs and sets, and a director who hadn't had anything like the usual amount of time for research and preparation: brilliant – we, the actors, were free to do anything! *Henry IV*, for the Swan Theatre, was altogether different: a totally different space, obviously, and all marked out ready for rehearsal, and in Michael Attenborough a director who is a stickler for the verse and the passion and energy of the language – which is splendid – but who has such a strong idea from the outset of exactly what he wants theatrically, and is so enthusiastic about it, that the early stages can be a bit overwhelming. As a result I was much further ahead, all through the rehearsal period, on the first part of *Henry IV* than ever I was on *Richard II*, though when I got the job I had anticipated the pleasure of developing the character from the earlier play into the later.

It turned out, however, to be the other way round, with ideas developed for Henry being tried for Bolingbroke. It wasn't until *Richard II* was playing, and we had an audience (always the fourth dimension for that production), that the process began to work in the expected order.

Moving from the first to the second part of *Henry IV* was a much simpler process. We opened *Richard II* and immediately afterwards the first part of *Henry IV*, then went straight into rehearsal for Part Two. The actors knew each other and those whose characters carried on knew their characters and were beginning to see continuities. For example, I took the violence of the language in Henry's deathbed speech to his son about the chaos and humiliation that will descend on England when he is king (Part Two, IV.v.120–38) from the very similar tone of the deathbed speech of my father, John of Gaunt, to Richard II, about the shame he is bringing on England (*Richard II*, II.i.57–68); so the energy and anger and defiance that Alfie Burke had found in Gaunt's final speech resurfaced in my last scene as Henry IV. I simply couldn't see the man lying in bed dying quietly; when people die they often find in their last breaths an extraordinary energy – which, in turn, hastens their demise. But I shall return to this scene later.

The way we were playing *Richard II* meant that the mood of futility and fatigue, perhaps even pathos, that emerges clearly in Henry in Part Two was not entirely new. On the page Bolingbroke in *Richard II* can seem a rather one-dimensional character. His verse is very staid, and he speaks a lot of rhyming couplets; indeed, he speaks nothing but rhyming couplets in the final scene. Through rehearsals this scene developed into a kind of nightmare of recognition of what was going to happen to him, with people coming in like automatons to announce rebellions and executions, hammering out the rhymes so that it all took on a nightmarish quality, and concluding (at least in one of the several endings we used in the production) with me repeating Richard's words from the prison scene with which Sam West's Richard II had in fact opened the play:

> I have been studying how I may compare
> This prison where I live unto the world . . .
>
> (V.v.1–2)

The man has thus come through the play to the realization that being a king is nothing: we've watched him disintegrate, from the moment of getting the crown – that moment for which he's yearned – to this moment of realization that life is nothing, that death is nothing. The crown he's sought so longingly is like a cancer; as soon as you get it it starts to eat you away, to kill you. No sooner has he achieved it in *Richard II* than he starts, in the very next scene, to worry about his son: 'Can no man tell me of my unthrifty son?' (v.iii.1), a sequence that is exactly repeated at the end of Part Two of *Henry IV*, as anxieties about the whereabouts of the crown, and of his eldest son, oppress his mind. This worrying about the succession goes right through the plays and connects with his sense of the cyclical nature of events. 'What a funny thing life is' is the gist of his reflexions to Warwick, taking Northumberland's treachery as an example:

> 'Tis not ten years gone
> Since Richard and Northumberland, great friends,
> Did feast together, and in two years after
> Were they at wars. It is but eight years since
> This Percy was the man nearest my soul...
> (Part Two, iii.i.53–7)

With Richard, against Richard; with me, against me: and as these contemplations continue, he realizes, in his final scene, the truth of what Richard had said, right at the beginning, about the consequences of his usurpation:

> For all my reign hath been but as a scene
> Acting that argument.
> (Part Two, iv.v.197–8)

He sees himself here as a victim, his allotted role in life having been to take the crown, to defend it, to struggle for peace; but his real role is now, in death, when he can conclude what he was put on this earth to do, and give his crown, in peace, to his son:

> And now my death
> Changes the mood, for what in me was purchased
> Falls upon thee in a more fairer sort.
> (Part Two, iv.v.198–200)

And then, at last, he can be at ease with himself, at ease with 'being nothing', which is what Richard talked about (*Richard II*, v.v.41). The more we played them the more the three plays started to arc from one to another in ways such as this.

Bolingbroke believes, I think, in his Catholic way, that the rebellions that have persisted through his reign are his punishment for the sin of taking the crown, for usurping it from God's anointed. He took it, though, for the best of motives, for the sake of the nation. How he took it doesn't matter: in the unavoidable revolution there were unavoidable deaths. The nation, though, is inextricably connected in his mind with his own dynasty; and the future of both depends upon his errant son. Alongside all the national politics is an ordinary father and his ordinary sixteen-year old son and a relationship between them that has, all too familiarly, failed, so that Hal has chosen an alternative father-figure in Falstaff. Bolingbroke needs desperately to get Hal back on board, and there are two major scenes dealing with this, one in each part of *Henry IV*. The one in Part One is brilliantly written in its exploration of all the tactics that we use as parents: anger, loving kindness, emotional blackmail, they're all there. But the emotional blackmail with regard to Hotspur is his strongest weapon, as I shall explore later.

Hotspur, of course, is one of those deep, dark secrets, those guilt-trips, that are going on inside Henry, and at the beginning of Part One we learn that this has been eating away at him for a year. It has altered his language, too: from Bolingbroke's very regular verse in *Richard II*, with antithesis occasionally, in argument, the Henry we hear at the beginning of Part One is using a metaphorical, antithetical, poetic language, full of dark adjectives. The change of costume, from the modern dress of our *Richard II* to the more or less medieval costume we had in *Henry IV*, seemed to me exactly to reflect this change in Henry's linguistic register. He has had a year between the plays, apparently in penance and prayer, but it's finally time to stand up and start doing something about the country; but even as he does so he betrays this weird fixation on Hotspur, that 'son who is the theme of honour's tongue' (Part One, 1.i.80), who is so good to his father, such a great soldier. Hotspur and Henry meet only twice in *Richard II*, but we had tried to make those moments as powerful and striking as possible, to set up this obsession at the start of *Henry IV*. This is, I think, why Henry is so adamant about Hotspur's prisoners. Legally Hotspur is in the right, but Henry is desperate to get those prisoners from him, partly because he needs the ransom money to finance his crusade, but more importantly because of the feelings of envy and guilt that Hotspur provokes in his mind and that are in danger of making him vulnerable. Henry is a politician and a

tactician; he needs to be ruthless as both if he is to control the politicians
and tacticians around him.

With these general ideas in mind about the continuities and devel-
opments in the role through the plays, I want now to look in more
detail at our productions' treatment of the sequence of Bolingbroke's
scenes.

At the beginning of *Richard II* Bolingbroke and his supporters are
taking their first bite at Richard. They know that Mowbray is only the
agent, that the real guilt lies with Richard himself. The scene is very
much a public show, and because of the point at which Shakespeare
has chosen to pick up his chronicle sources, many of the audience will
have no idea who this murdered man they all keep talking about, this
Gloucester, is. What they see are two men desperate to fight each other,
and Richard desperate to avoid that, then having to allow it, and then
stopping it again by banishing them both. It's important to remember
that Bolingbroke is very high up, very close to the crown, a prince fighting an ordinary lord. Our production presented the first scene so clearly
as a put-up job that I even had a letter from someone who thought that it
was actually Bolingbroke who had killed Gloucester and was now trying
to frame Mowbray – well, at least he was responding to part of what we
were trying to suggest! The casting worked well here too, with an 'older
generation' – David Killick (York), Chris Saul (Northumberland), and
Alfie Burke (Gaunt) on my side – and Sam West (Richard) and a group
of much younger actors on the other. Audiences could see it as Old
Conservative versus New Labour if they wanted to, with my side grumbling at the new-fangled way that England is now being run: 'We want
our lands back; we want to run the country as we used to; we won't pay
taxes – the government should get its money as it always has, by raiding
France.'

Then Bolingbroke has his absence from the play – twenty minutes
in playing time, many months historically – and in his first scene back,
with Northumberland (Act Two, Scene Three), he's remarkably quiet.
He's got a lot to think about, of course: historically the fact that Richard
had prevented him from coming to his father's funeral and forbidden his
marriage; in the play the fact that Bushy, Bagot, and Green are selling
his lands for their own profit. In our production Northumberland and
I got our own back on Bushy and Green by shooting them in the head

in front of the audience – and that phrase 'in front of the audience' was all-important in this production. It wasn't like being watched in a normal theatre; the audience was in the white box with us, becoming our thoughts and desires, or sometimes actual characters in the play, lords and ladies, or jurors. Every word I spoke, every look I made, was directed at them. Bolingbroke is a politician, and in this production every single thing he did was politicized.

I don't think Bolingbroke intends a revolution when he returns. Everything seems to fall into place for him, to present itself to him on a plate; he doesn't have to do anything. In Wales he is prepared to fight Richard for his own Lancastrian inheritance, but Richard equivocates and says he can have everything: 'Your own is yours, and I am yours and all' (III.i.197). To Bolingbroke that means that Richard wants to give up; he is handing over the crown, without a bloody revolution. From that moment on Bolingbroke is certainly intent on gaining the crown, though that doesn't mean that he wasn't telling the truth earlier when he claimed that all he wanted was to get back his lands. He and Northumberland have to engineer things a bit in the parliament scene, which they think is going to be merely the symbolic formal enactment of a political process that is already decided – and the anarchy of the scene of the gages is an interesting prelude to what is to come. Things start going wrong the moment Bolingbroke gets the crown itself. Sam West, playing Richard, used to ram it onto my head, and make me look silly – in front of the audience, in front of the media. Bolingbroke starts off thinking he's in control of the scene, overriding Northumberland's protests about allowing Richard to speak; he thinks Richard is simply going to give up his crown quietly and everything will be all right. But the more Richard finds his voice, the more Bolingbroke loses his. Richard outdoes him, upstages him; Bolingbroke may be gaining the political power, but he's certainly losing the theatrical contest. I used to say 'Go some of you, convey him to the Tower' (IV.i.315) in a state of violent anger and exasperation; Richard's behaviour, his performance, had driven Bolingbroke to that.

Yet I began the scene in total control, actually forcing the audience to stand in respect for Mowbray when the Bishop of Carlisle gives the news of his death (IV.i.98) – though they were perfectly well aware that my apparent surprise at the news is feigned and that I knew of his death all along. It's a put-up job, part of the apparatus of power, which is seen at work again when the Bishop of Carlisle is arrested the moment

11 David Troughton as Bolingbroke with David Killick as the Duke of York and Paul Greenwood as the Bishop of Carlisle, *Richard II*, Act IV, Scene i: 'Go some of you, convey him to the Tower.'

he finishes his long speech against the abdication. You can't win, you see: one of Carlisle's speeches is the cue for the audience to stand; his next triggers his arrest. These are the times we now live in; this is Bolingbroke's 'new world', as one of the challengers calls it as the gages go down earlier in the scene (IV.i.78). But in my frantic struggle to adjust and remove the crown after Richard had rammed it on my head, the contest to keep control of the theatrical situation is lost. That crown doesn't fit him: physically, mentally, and metaphorically he cannot cope with it. He hates putting it on, it's so painful to wear, though he has to wear it for certain occasions; but he won't let go of it either, and certainly won't let anyone else have it. It is killing him, but he clutches it to his chest for the rest of the three plays.

The first task of Bolingbroke's kingship is to decide whether to execute my uncle's son, my cousin Aumerle. There are laugh-lines in the scene with the Duchess of York, obviously, but nothing very funny about the basic political situation. Half way through I turn to the audience and say

> Our scene is altered from a serious thing,
> And now changed to 'The Beggar and the King'.
> (v.iii.78–9)

It is Bolingbroke's first reference to an idea that he is still talking about on his deathbed, to all his reign having been 'a scene / Acting that argument' (Part Two. IV.v.197–8), the argument created by his usurpation. During the scene with the Yorks I used to keep turning to the audience as if asking them whether this could be real, a boy's mother pleading for mercy and his father for execution. Aumerle is undoubtedly a traitor, and Bolingbroke is now a king, and should kill him; but he can't, because he's 'family'. Before he achieved the crown he would unhesitatingly have shot him in the head, but now he has the crown his sense of guilt is softening him: 'I pardon him', he says to the Duchess, and adds (turning, in my performance, to the audience), 'as God shall pardon me' (v.iii.130). But when you are in power you cannot think like that. You must root out the political opposition, and kill it; and there can be no more drawing the line at family:

> But for our trusty brother-in-law and the Abbott
> Destruction straight shall dog them at the heels.
> (v.iii.136–7)

The English ruling classes at this time were a family, all related. That is what the Wars of the Roses were all about.

And having spared one father's brother's son, in his next scene the corpse of another father's brother's son is laid at Bolingbroke's feet. Did Bolingbroke really ask for that? Exton says that he did, but no-one ever hears him say it. The audience have to make up their own minds – something that we were always trying to force them to do in our production, with all the play's rhetoric projected out to them, very politically. I used to speak the words 'though I did wish him dead' (v.vi.39) aside to Exton, though moments before the lines

> A deed of slander with thy fatal hand
> Upon my head and all this famous land
> (v.vi.35–6)

had been pushed deliberately out to the audience, to the media. Of course Bolingbroke loves the fact that Richard has been murdered, though in public the politician has to say the opposite and pretend to mourn.

At this point in our production, everyone was walking out on Bolingbroke, the final person to go being York, who put the golden chair on the coffin and left me alone – except for the ever-watching media-audience – alone in my little white box, just as Sam West's Richard had been alone at the beginning. I tried seven or eight different endings through the run, but the one that probably worked best was the repetition of the lines with which Sam had started the play –

> I have been studying how I may compare
> This prison where I live unto the world
>
> (V.v.1–2)

– though when it was announced a while before the production closed that Sam would be playing Hamlet in the following season, it was only with difficulty that I resisted starting 'To be or not to be', to see what reaction I might get from him lying there in his coffin.

Our production of *Richard II*, then, remained very fluid throughout its run. *Henry IV* – presented in the much larger space of the Swan, of course (and when it moved to the Barbican, indeed, it was in the main house) – inevitably lacked some of this fluidity, and in terms of costume and staging was rather more conventional. Its brilliance, it seemed to me, was in the speaking, for that is Michael Attenborough's real strength and joy. I tended, I think, especially in Part One, to be a little extravagant vocally, but though the Swan may give the impression of an intimate theatre it doesn't seem to me to work well unless you are reasonably 'large' in it. Henry's verse in Part One, moreover, fits that approach, for once he gets up (off his knees, literally, at the beginning of our production) he is very successful, crushing the rebels at Shrewsbury and following this with an energetic plan for the next campaigns in the north and, with 'son Harry' (Part One, v.v.39), in Wales. Everything seems to be rosy – and then, when we first meet him in Part Two, he's wandering around his palace grumbling that he can't get to sleep. There is an obvious parallel here with Falstaff, whom we first meet grumbling about his diseases. Falstaff is dying of the pox; Henry is dying of the crown, and the guilt of taking it, which is eating him away like a cancer. It is exhausting being king, for you can only be reactive; in *Richard II*, as Bolingbroke, he could be proactive, a mover and shaker. But in *Henry IV* he is the one being shaken: 'So shaken as we are, so wan with care' (Part One, I.i.I.).

Henry begins Part One expressing his yearning to go on crusade. This seems to me to be an absolutely genuine desire, not an attempt by Bolingbroke the politician to 'busy giddy minds / With foreign quarrels' (Part Two, IV.v.213–4). Thus to risk his life fighting, as he would see it, for God, is a way of trying to expiate the sin of his usurpation. Just as Bolingbroke's verse changes between *Richard II* and *Henry IV*, so does the man who speaks it. Once he gets the crown, things start to go wrong politically and personally. The guilt has started to eat away at him; it's as though the year that elapses between the plays has hugely changed him. The fulfilment of that one aim of getting the crown was one thing; keeping it is quite another, for once you've got it, the only thing to do with it is to stop anyone else getting it. A crusade would help only him; it wouldn't help the country, it wouldn't busy any giddy minds – bashing the French is the only version of that that his nobles recognize.

I have no doubt that Henry has Hal watched. Though in our production my King Henry and Falstaff were symbolically present on stage together for a few moments between the first and second scenes of Part One, Henry never speaks of Falstaff – 'passages of life', 'rude society', 'vile participation' (Part One, III.ii.8, 14, 87) are the sorts of phrases he uses to avoid doing so, and even when he specifically asks where Hal is, no-one will mention Falstaff's name: 'With Poins, and other his continual followers' (Part Two, IV.iv.53) is as close as they get. And yet, in the parley with Worcester and Vernon before Shrewsbury, Falstaff (as a commander of troops, presumably) is present with Henry and the rest of his officers, and Falstaff's one utterance in the scene is remarkably astute: 'Rebellion lay in his way, and he found it', he says (Part One, v.i.28), ostensibly of Worcester, though it's uncannily appropriate to Bolingbroke's own career in the preceding play. We created a brief moment in our production – after I had rejected (for fear of losing my heir) Hal's offer to take on Hotspur in single combat (Part One, v.i.102–3) and as we were all girding up for battle – when I looked at him and Falstaff together and thought 'O, God, I don't want them meeting any more'. Henry's inability to speak of Falstaff is part of his failure as a father; he is popular with the people, that is part of his success as a politician, but with his own son he has no idea how to behave at all. Hal's search for an alternative father is a cry for help, because his own father wants him for only one thing: to be his successor.

Had Worcester and Vernon taken Henry's offer of love and redress of grievances and surrendered their army, I have no doubt that Henry would have had them all executed, just as John of Lancaster has the rebel leaders at Gaultree Forest executed in Part Two: like father, like son. John of Lancaster is an interesting character. In our production Dickon Tyrrell played him very religious, always trying to please his father; and Henry just ignored him, for he has time for only one son. All the others, the Gloucesters, and the Clarences, as well as the Lancasters, can go hang. I decided to get angry with the solicitousness of Clarence on 'Nothing but well to thee, Thomas of Clarence' (Part Two, IV.iv.19), for all Henry wants to know at that point is where his son is. 'But, daddy', you can almost hear Clarence thinking, 'I am your son', and Henry's unspoken reply is, 'Yes, I know, but I mean *the* son.'

Hal is late for their big meeting in Part One. This may be part of a little power-game, but it's probably accidentally – in much the same way as the chair on my right hand in all the council scenes is always empty. Henry goes through many different tactics in his long harangue to his son. First there's the terrible emotional blackmail of 'let me wonder, Harry, / At thy affections' (Part One, III.ii.29 ff.), with its undertow of 'you can't possibly love me if you do all this'. Then he moves into the political arguments, the ways in which it is necessary to behave in order to 'pluck' – an interesting choice of verb – to 'pluck allegiance from men's hearts' (Part One, III.ii.52). This is the role he himself has played as media-man, and his pride in the skill with which he has performed it is very clear in all he says here. Then come the threats, with the stories of Richard's self-demeaning behaviour (with the constant implication that Hal should remember where all this ended) and the warning that 'For all the world / As thou art now was Richard then' (Part One, III.ii.93–4). And finally, at the mention of Ravenspurgh, I used to think to myself 'I'll just try the Hotspur card', and say 'even as I was then is Percy now' (Part One, III.ii.96). This, at last, gets a reaction out of Hal, for earlier, in the pub, he'd been revealing his own concern about Hotspur by mocking him for killing Scots before breakfast (Part One, II.iv.100–107). Hal, it there emerges, is needled by this young man Hotspur, partly because he knows that his father so admires him. So when I pick on Hotspur and ask Hal if he knows what this 'Mars in swaddling clothes', this 'infant warrior' (Part One, III.ii.112–13) – those are the words I choose, and they offer wonderfully unlikely pairings – has done, my goading of Hal is absolutely calculated. I am now attacking his manhood: 'Are you aware what he's done? Are you? He's captured this huge

Scotsman – "renownèd Douglas" (III.ii.107) – you wimp!' And when I go on to accuse him of being more likely to take the enemy side, I really get to him:

> Why, Harry, do I tell thee of my foes,
> Which art my nearest and dearest enemy?
> Thou that art like enough, through vassal fear,
> Base inclination, and the start of spleen,
> To fight against me under Percy's pay,
> To dog his heels, and curtsy at his frowns,
> To show how much thou art degenerate.
>
> (Part One, III.ii.122–8)

At last I see the glint in his eye and know that I've unlocked the door and got to him. That's the way to get to this boy, through Hotspur, and in that way too I can expunge some of the guilt of my own feelings about the young Percy.

It is an extraordinary example of tactical argument on Henry's part; his skill as a political strategist is here supremely clear. It then takes just one speech from Hal to bring them together – metaphorically, anyway, for though I used to put out my arms to him here, he never noticed, and no embrace was achieved. Perhaps Hal doesn't want to notice, or perhaps he simply doesn't see; that ambiguity was important in our production, and I think right. It's like one of those moments when you go to kiss your father – and it turns confusedly into shaking hands. Hal has said that he's sorry; he has said that he will fight alongside his father; but there has been no expression of the love of son to father, which is what Henry misses. But whether Henry could achieve the embrace, even if Hal were looking, remains a question. He simply doesn't know how to touch his son properly. So I just used to give him a little push on his shoulder with my fist, and the awkward moment passed.

They are together, but for how long? Henry needs Hal in the battle – Hal's a good soldier and can lead troops – but he needs him more as a symbol of royal unity. He also needs to protect him: he won't let him fight Hotspur and when Hal is wounded Henry's anxiety is plain: 'withdraw thyself, thou bleedest too much' (Part One, v.iv.1–2). Henry is protecting him, the heir, all the time – and then, ironically, the heir protects Henry, and that is the final proof of Hal's loyalty:

Thou hast redeemed thy lost opinion,
And *showed* thou makest some tender of my life
In this fair rescue thou hast brought to me.
                    (Part One, v.iv.47–9, my italics)

And at this point in our production there was an embrace, an embrace
that the heat of battle made very brief and that their armour prevented
from being in the least intimate, but which was still freer, I think, than
would ever have been possible in a room. Henry is at last together with
his son and the mood at the end of Part One is triumphant. Of course
the problems are still not over. They have to divide their power (always
a risky thing to do) in order to deal with Glendower in Wales and the
Archbishop of York in the north, but the principal rebel army has been
defeated. At the end of Part One I had a big double-handed broad-
sword, and though my Henry was so exhausted that he could hardly lift
it, he still found the desire to slaughter Worcester and Vernon almost
irresistible. If he had had a gun, I believe he would have shot them, as he
shot Bushy and Green in *Richard II*. Henry can understand Worcester's
behaviour – Worcester is simply a bastard, and he knows about them –
but Vernon was the one he thought he was getting to in the pre-battle
parley, and Vernon failed to stop the fighting. So Henry's line 'Other
offenders we will pause upon' (Part One, v.v.15) always seemed to me
to signal a hasty pulling back, with a sudden change of subject – 'How
goes the field?' (Part One, v.v.16) – as he takes control of himself and
realizes how badly he is behaving in front of his son. It is left to that
son, with his gracious and elegant pardon of the Earl of Douglas, to do
what Henry should have been doing.

The second part of *Henry IV* presents actors with the difficulty of
keeping up the theatrical energy through what is, in effect, one long
'dying scene'. There's a sense of the characters being all covered in
cobwebs and disease, saying the same sorts of things as they said in
Part One, but now it's all falling on deaf ears. They are all older now,
the country is going down in wrack and ruin, and the king is going with
it. He has a scene in which he can't get to sleep; then a scene with an
adviser in which they are apparently going to write a letter about what
they're going to do but indulge instead in a reverie about life and fate,
and whether or not all the things that are happening are just inescapable
'necessities' (Part Two, iii.i.88); and finally for Henry comes the scene
in which he has a sudden relapse and asks for his crown to be placed

beside him on his pillow: 'Set me the crown upon my pillow here' (Part Two, IV.v.5). The line is immensely important, though it is hard to convey to a modern audience the symbolic idea of the crown on the pillow being temporarily in obeyance, waiting for the king to die before it is placed on his successor's head. To remove it is an act of sacrilege – almost as bad as stealing it from Richard II.

As an actor approaching Henry's death-scene, you are obviously anxious not to be boring: you don't want to be playing it on one last, frail breath all the way through. So you look for a cue in what he may be dying from. Historically, of course, no-one knows what Henry IV died of – leprosy was suggested, because his nose is supposed to have dropped off, though when they looked into his coffin a year later, before he turned to dust, he had a perfect face. So I decided that my Henry was dying of cancer, and because he says, just before he is carried out to die, that 'my lungs are wasted so / That strength of speech is utterly denied me' (Part Two, IV.v.216–17), I took lung cancer as the illness. There are a lot of half lines in Henry's speeches here, and having made this decision about the illness, it seemed to me appropriate to use the missing half lines to show the audience how ill he was. In this way you avoid acting illness on the line: you can use normal energy when you have verse to speak and then take a big heave of a breath in the missing half line, thus suggesting that you have urgent things to say, and that you can still speak perfectly well – but only briefly. Henry is an energetic man, and always has been, and that energy is still there, still a part of the character, even as he approaches death.

That is why I decided that he must get out of his bed for the final berating of his son. The anger inside him for what Hal has done – for what he has done *to me*, throughout his life – all comes together in this final speech. The language is extraordinarily fierce and passionate:

> Have you a ruffian that will swear, drink, dance . . .
> England shall double gild his treble guilt;
> England shall give him office, honour, might;
> For the fifth Harry from curbed licence plucks
> The muzzle of restraint, and the wild dog
> Shall flesh his tooth on every innocent.
> (Part Two, IV.v.125–33)

That really *has* to be done as an outburst, just as John of Gaunt spoke to Richard II; and just as Alfie Burke's John of Gaunt used to get out of

12 David Troughton as King Henry IV with William Houston as Prince Hal,
2 Henry IV, Act IV, Scene v: 'God knows, my son, / By what by-paths and
indirect crooked ways / I met this crown.'

his wheelchair and crawl across the floor after berating Richard, I used
to start crawling towards the exit as Hal began his speech of excuse and
explanation. That is part of the joy of doing the three plays together. If I
had only done the two parts of *Henry IV*, it would have been possible to
play Henry as a weak man, a man racked with guilt. But if you've seen
Bolingbroke's energy in *Richard II*, you've got to keep flashes of that
in *Henry IV*, especially in Part One. Having shown the development of
Henry's illness through Part Two, it is immensely rewarding, just as the
audience thinks he's about to die, to surprise them with the power of
the old Bolingbroke bursting forth again at the end. 'Now, neighbour
confines, purge you of your scum', he says (Part Two, IV.v.124), perhaps
referring to the prisons that were close to the theatres of Elizabethan
London, but to me, as I said this line, the 'confine' was always the
white box of The Other Place in which we had done *Richard II*, and I
used to push the line right out, remembering the way Bolingbroke had
always addressed the audience in the white box – addressed them as the
politician he is. So this became that politician's bitter farewell speech

to the crowd: 'I give you my son, Riot', is what he's saying; 'this is all I have been able to achieve.'

Then, of course, Hal has his long speech of self-justification, and Henry believes him – or is taken in by him. Whether Hal means it or not, I don't know; whether he has a tear-stick in the wings, I don't know; but whether it's genuine or not, Henry believes him. So the last thing I say to him is to 'busy giddy minds / With foreign quarrels' (Part Two, IV.v.213–14): 'Go and beat up the French, like we always used to, to take your subjects' minds off the problems at home; go to the Falklands and beat up the Argentinians and get re-elected; give them something to shout and cheer about; do it the old way, like we used to in Edward III's day.' And Hal takes my advice.

I think Henry dies believing that he couldn't have done anything different. He has fulfilled his role in life: 'all my reign hath been but as a scene / Acting that argument' (Part Two, IV.v.197–8). Fate laid out the carpet for him, and he had to tread it; you can't go against fate. He is quite calm at his death; none of what has happened, he believes, has been his fault. I used to look at all my sons and say 'My worldly business makes a period' (Part Two, IV.v.229), and feel quite contented about it. Henry is not a tragic figure in the grand sense, but there is something pathetically tragic about him. At the end I felt that I had achieved my goal in giving everything to my eldest son, who has learned enough to rule – and to rule in *my* way. He is going to invade France, and you don't have any problems about ruling over here if you give the lads a war in France.

> Doth any name particular belong
> Unto the lodging where I first did swoon?

Henry asks, and is told

> 'Tis called Jerusalem, my noble lord.
> (Part Two, IV.v.232–4)

The prophecy that he has clung to for so long seems, albeit ironically, about to be fulfilled, and he asks to be taken off to the Jerusalem Chamber to die. For my Henry, however, in spite of all the hopes and yearnings, there was never going to be an arrival in a Jerusalem of any kind: he died as they were carrying him off the stage.

Lady Percy in Parts 1 and 2 of *Henry IV*

NANCY CARROLL

NANCY CARROLL played Lady Percy in Michael Attenborough's production of the two parts of *Henry IV* at the Swan Theatre in the summer
season of 2000 and afterwards at the Barbican Theatre. Her other role
that season was Celia in *As You Like It*. Earlier work for the RSC had
been in *The Winter's Tale* and *The Lion, the Witch, and the Wardrobe*.
Other theatre work includes Ophelia at Bristol Old Vic and Cordelia at
the Almeida. She has also worked in television and radio and her films
include *A Lonely War*, *Richard Eyre*, and *An Ideal Husband*.

I received my instructions to attend an audition for the RSC summer
season of 2000 towards the end of a run of *Hamlet* at the Bristol Old Vic
in late November 1999. I knew I was reading for the part of Lady Percy
in the two parts of *Henry IV*, to be directed by Michael Attenborough.
Promptly I booked the 8 a.m. train for the following morning.

Although I had studied the plays at A-Level, my recollection seemed
to stretch little beyond Anthony Quayle's sozzled Falstaff waddling
along the streets of Eastcheap in the BBC video – not terribly useful for Lady Percy, even with the help of an avid imagination. So I
set about an absurdly irrational attempt at speed-reading the play in
between Ophelia's scenes during that evening's performance – one of
those hysterical moments when you question how you arrived at this
point in your life, but secretly love every crazy minute of it. Between
nunneries and Gadshill and reluctant kings and player kings I alter-
nated, darting up and down the stairs, quizzing colleagues in the wings
about sub-plots – complete madness, really. I can no longer remember
what I thought I knew. I do, however, vividly remember forgetting all
of it completely as soon as I walked though the doors of the Barbican
Theatre the following day.

I had been with the RSC the year before as a Narnian spear-carrier in
Adrian Noble's production of *The Lion, the Witch, and the Wardrobe* and
as a be-frocked looker-on in Gregory Doran's version of *The Winter's*

Tale, so to be offered a chance to come back, with speeches to enjoy and journeys to find, was mind-blowing. When Narnia had first landed in Stratford, Michael Attenborough's production of *A Month in the Country* had been on at the Swan, so we had silently shared corridors; but this was our first verbal exchange. Adrian Noble greeted me with all the smiles and support I could have wished for in my search for inner calm. A ridiculous choice of skirt, however, quickly re-established all my anxiety: my long peach satin, bias-cut, number slunk low and tastelessly for the better part of the audition, leaving bright purple tights and a tucked-in thermal vest to speak for themselves. My long-standing worry in auditions is how to sit in my chair: to this day I can never commit to sitting forward or back. If you sit back you feel relaxed, open, even marginally objective towards the proceedings; but are you in danger of appearing to be disinterested? If you sit forward that often helps to focus your nervous energy on the job in hand, but although engaged and physically involved in the meeting, do you then appear to be desperately over-interested? I find it very hard to disguise nerves with a calm posture; even if you manage to slide comfortably into your chair, your limbs feel like lost property awaiting collection. I find it helps to greet the chair with as much respect as you give the director; that way you both know where you stand – and hopefully the chair won't put up a fight.

There then followed a series of auditions with the directors of the other productions planned for the 2000 season. Generally a member of the company will appear in up to three plays in the repertoire. (The task of piecing together and scheduling the company's work must be overwhelmingly hard, requiring the skills of a prophet as well as those of a mathematician.) About a week after my final meeting I received 'the call': I had been offered the part of Celia in Gregory Doran's production of *As You Like It* and of Lady Percy in the two parts of *Henry IV*. I won't try to describe my hysteria in full, but it wasn't shy and it lasted through Christmas and the New Year, and up to the first day of rehearsals on 9 January.

We rehearsed Part One of *Henry IV* in Saint Peter's Church in Clapham, several months before rehearsing and opening Part Two. This oddly grand, badly lit, damp rehearsal room was home for about ten weeks. Two large spaces separated a kitchen and a lobby; the latter, despite arctic conditions, was quickly occupied by hardy smokers.

(The absurdity of the lengths they go to continues to bemuse and amuse me.) The kitchen had a large wooden table around which we laughed, moaned, feasted, chewed the fat, and grew into a company. Such kitchen times are as big a part of the production process as reading and rehearsing. Like a pack of wild animals we closely observe one another's food, fur and pheremones, sniffing out a common language and shorthand, in order that we may convincingly play members of the same family, lovers, wives, allies, and patriots. The first encounter of faces, the first words you exchange, begin the passage – 'Hello, I'm Adam; you're my wife' – and secure your seat on the roller-coaster.

The part of Kate Percy is that of Harry Hotspur's wife in Part One and his widow in Part Two; we see her primarily in relation to him. Her entire role consists of just three scenes, with two central speeches. But those speeches, Kate's words, hold a healthy, top-ranking spot in the young-female-performer auditioning canon. This was a fact previously unknown to me, but became an important part of my rehearsal experience – and instantly reduced my confidence in verse-speaking to that of a mountain-goat! There is, however, a reason why these speeches are often spoken in isolation: Kate's declarations, as wife and as widow, driven by her love and loyalty to Hotspur, are exquisitely structured monologues; stories that begin, peak, and then must end; arguments that contain a persuasive balance of emotion and of logic.

Kate's speeches must be to some extent self-contained, for it is only through these words that the audience can know her. She is not central to the plot, only to her husband. She is referred to on just two other occasions, once by Hotspur (I.iii.140) and once by Prince Hal, who mocks the Percies' relationship and way of life and contrasts them directly with his own:

I am not yet of Percy's mind, the Hotspur of the north, he that kills him some six or seven dozen of Scots at a breakfast, washes his hands, and says to his wife, 'Fie upon this quiet life, I want work.' 'O my sweet Harry,' says she, 'how many hast thou killed today?' 'Give my roan horse a drench,' says he, and answers, 'Some fourteen,' an hour after, 'a trifle, a trifle'. (Part One, II.iv.100–7)

The Percy scenes are dense with information. We see three married couples during the two parts of *Henry IV*: the Mortimers, the Northumberlands, and the Percies (although to make any of them sound like the 'couple' next door is hilariously inappropriate). Hotspur's relations with his wife, however, are given the air to breathe a life and to develop an importance that the others don't achieve and that warrants closer analysis.

As I read the first of the Percy scenes in Part One (Act Two, Scene Three) on my own before rehearsals had begun, the words felt immediately weighty and serious. Our first meeting with Kate is her last attempt to penetrate Harry's cloud of quarrel and concern. She knows less than the entire auditorium, and her words are driven by almost rhetorical questioning:

> O my good lord, why are you thus alone?
> For what offence have I this fortnight been
> A banished woman from my Harry's bed?
> Tell me, sweet lord, what is't that takes from thee
> Thy stomach, pleasure, and thy golden sleep? . . .
> Some heavy business hath my lord in hand,
> And I must know it, else he loves me not.
> (Part One, II.iii.39–66)

To say that it was a surprise to me to learn that this scene has traditionally been played lightly, with insults thrown at one another purely flirtatiously, would be a massive understatement. Even at the first read-through – when all that you can do is to hope that your tongue is in place, let alone your instinct – the scene appeared to have a natural emotional build to it, a build that is ultimately cut short by Hotspur:

> But hark you, Kate
> I must not have you henceforth question me
> Whither I go, nor reason whereabout.
> Whither I must, I must.
> (Part One, II.iii.105–8)

When Mike Attenborough started rehearsing this scene with Adam Levy (who played Hotspur) and me, he felt that it was such a full moment that it should be put on its feet straight away. This is scary at the best of times, but with such intimacy and intensity between the two characters, the task felt more than humbling. But holding our scripts tightly, we jumped full splash into the deep end. Yet to be on the book made it very hard to discover where rehearsals would take us – so Mike asked us to be off the book by the time we met again for the second rehearsal of the scene: Aahgh!

13 Nancy Carroll as Lady Percy with Adam Levy as Hotspur, *1 Henry IV*, Act II, Scene iii: 'And when I am a-horseback I will swear / I love thee infinitely.'

It seemed clear to us that Hotspur's physical drive is emphasized in the revelations this conversation provides about his relationship with his wife. Kate's dissatisfaction is set up clearly within her first lines: for two weeks at least their relationship has lacked communication and consummation. She opens the scene with a bold reference to this recent droop, to being 'a banished woman from my Harry's bed' (II.iii.41). Other such references follow, hard-hittingly, through her long opening speech:

> Why hast thou lost the fresh blood in thy cheeks,
> And given my treasures and my rights of thee
> To thick-eyed musing and curst melancholy?
>
> (Part One, II.iii.46–8)

And there Kate breaks the iambic meter for the first time with that feminine ending (in every sense of the word) to line 48. The use of words such as 'treasures' and 'rights', it might be said, hardly suggests a humble sexuality. One might go so far as to say that this recent lack of sexual intercourse is a driving intention for her through the whole scene, for it would not be inappropriate to imagine that Harry Hotspur is as fiery in the boudoir as he is on the battlefield. And Shakespeare's language rarely includes literary coincidences; the most far-fetched innuendo has been prudently placed. Even in Hotspur's name there are connotations of virility: 'spur' has a meaning beyond its equestrian and military sense. It is also clear, from Kate's opening speech, that her regret at the absence of Harry's usual qualities implies a very different situation under less extreme circumstances:

> Tell me, sweet lord, what is't that takes from thee
> Thy stomach, pleasure, and thy golden sleep?
>
> (Part One, II.iii.42–3)

Shakespeare has a story to tell. The climax of the first part of *Henry IV* will come in the final fight between Prince Hal and Harry Percy. The dramatic weight of this moment holds the audience's attention because they have witnessed and travelled the journeys made by these two men for the play's length. They have made an emotional investment in their stories, and the inevitable death of one or both therefore makes for gripping theatre. Their importance and impact as leaders of armies, and as makers of history, and of this story, stems from the audience's emotional connexion with them as people; and for Hotspur, an important part of that comes from his relationship with his wife. Shakespeare seems to remind us that the historical characters, and the legends, of England's past actually lived tangible lives: we are allowed to see that their strength lies in their vulnerability, their ideology derives from their reality, their very humanness comes from their interaction with, and their reactions to, the characters that Shakespeare puts with them.

In Kate Percy, then, Shakespeare has created a strong, intelligent woman of high social, and dramatic, status. He gives her, however, little or no opportunity to relate to the other two women with whom she comes into contact: in Part One, her Welsh-speaking sister-in-law, Lady Mortimer, with whom she cannot converse; and in Part Two, her mother-in-law, Lady Northumberland, with whom she does join forces to dissuade Northumberland from revenging his son's death, but, again, without addressing her directly. Her negotiations remain solely with men, providing the listener with that considerable rarity in these plays, a female argument. Kate openly rejects the notion of honour, and of justice, and their preservation, in the bleak face of mortality. In Part One this comes from fear; in Part Two from the harsh reality of Harry's death.

Kate's is the first female voice in the play, and its introduction provides a deliberate diversion in its journey. And this is not accidental – things rarely are in Shakespeare's plays. In a cycle of plays dominated by men, and by legends, moulding the course of England's history, the female voice, at Warkworth, at Bangor, and in Eastcheap, provides the audience with a different perspective, and this is of considerable consequence to the plays' development. Actions and reactions, effects and repercussions, lives changing lives, human greatness and human weakness, in peace but here, essentially, in war, are presented in all their intricate interdependence. Every word, every moment, is necessary to move the tale on, and the role of Kate Percy is an essential part of that complexity.

In our production the Northumberlands were given an additional moment, a silent encounter, at the end of the first scene of Part Two, Michael Attenborough having decided that this was necessary to complete the Percy story. Towards the end of that first scene, after Rumour has initially misconstrued the truth, Northumberland is informed of his son's death. There follows a traumatic, grief-stricken diatribe of volcanic proportions that his lords and messengers must watch and try to temper:

14 Nancy Carroll as Lady Percy with Adam Levy as Hotspur, *1 Henry IV*, Act III, Scene i: 'Come, Kate, thou art perfect in lying down.'

Now bind my brows with iron, and approach
The raggèd'st hour that time and spite dare bring
To frown upon th'enraged Northumberland.
(Part Two, I.i.150–2)

In our production, having superficially accepted the news, he turned to go, but discovered his wife and daughter-in-law in his path, silently standing, anxiously anticipating what he already knows. We felt that this provided a good moment for the audience, for with the knowledge of what they have just watched they can complete the scene for themselves. (If members of an audience are left to do this sort of thing for themselves, without being patronized, and without the risk of sentimentality, then their experience of the story is fully their own, and therefore the greater; such moments are always among my favourites.) Having failed, in Part One, to sway Harry from his war-making intentions, Kate now refuses to allow her father-in-law the same freedom: her strength here in Part Two stems directly from her fatal acceptance and surrender in Part One.

In Act Two, Scene Three of Part Two Northumberland is preparing to leave Warkworth and making plans to avenge his son's death and thereby appease his own guilt and remorse for having abandoned Hotspur in his hour of need. It is Rumour who describes Northumberland as having been 'crafty-sick' (Prologue, line 37), but Harry Percy himself had said much the same thing on the eve of the Battle of Shrewsbury:

Sick now? Droop now? This sickness doth infect
The very life-blood of our enterprise.
(Part One, IV.i.28–9)

It is here that we see a social and moral structure to Shakespeare's character relationships. He gives us, in this time of crisis, the idealists and the realists, those that are led, the innocents, and those that lead – the history-makers, who attack and defend, in the name of a greater good, the high morals of loyalty and honour. The two parts of *Henry IV* are essentially morality plays, but the romance, and the consequences, of an existence driven by such morals, and whether they survive in the cold, life-and-death reality of war, is brilliantly set up by Shakespeare through the slaughter of his most passionate moralist, Harry Percy. And Harry Percy's life, and his reputation after death, are defended most eloquently by his wife, who will suffer, and does suffer, most by his death:

> in speech, in gait,
> In diet, in affections of delight,
> In military rules, humours of blood,
> He was the mark and glass, copy and book,
> That fashioned others. And him – O wondrous him!
> O miracle of men! – him did you leave . . .
>   so came I a widow,
> And never shall have length of life enough
> To rain upon remembrance with mine eyes,
> That it may grow and sprout as high as heaven
> For recordation to my noble husband.
>
>   (Part Two, II.iii.28–61)

These are her final words in the play.

As a woman Kate Percy can stand, objective, to the reasons for, and the virtues of, war; as Hotspur's wife those virtues are rendered meaningless by his death. As Falstaff puts it, 'Honour hath no skill in surgery' (Part One, V.i.133). As the personifications of all that is anti-war, of the living of life, Shakespeare gives us not only Falstaff and his Eastcheap entourage, but also Kate Percy. Kate is a nubile (if I say so myself), fertile young wife, deeply loving to her husband and his equal intellectually – very modern assumptions, perhaps, but there, surely, in the play, and fabulous to perform. She unravels the riddle of virtue and rejects it as quickly as Falstaff: 'Give me life' (Part One, V.iii.59).

In the late autumn of 2000 the Stratford summer company moved its wares to Newcastle, and the two parts of *Henry IV* transferred from the Swan to the Playhouse, where we played for a month before moving to the Barbican in London. Es Devlin's design for the Swan had been inspired: a dark, brooding, earth-encrusted scoop that represented the land of England over which the plays' characters fight (literally and metaphorically). When Es had first shown the company her set-design back in January she relayed to us the advice of a designer colleague who had had experience of working in the Swan's unique space: 'Don't fight the Swan, because the Swan will always win'. An actor's experience is very similar. When on stage in this theatre you are seen and heard from literally every side, and the front rows are within inches of you. At the beginning this feels terribly exposing, but it quickly changes to a sensation of irresistible warmth: you feel and hear the audience's reactions as quickly as you say the words, particularly when the story you are telling has the emotional density and intensity of that of Kate and Harry Percy. The reactions of the audience, whether they are hot and restless or still and involved, thus become intrinsic to the experience of playing the play.

When we moved to the Playhouse in Newcastle the space at first felt restricted and less hospitable to our production. Falstaff was unable to make his entrance through a latex hole in the ground as he had done at Stratford, and the stage floor could not be lit from below to make it look like burning coals, making a blazing celtic symbol on the floor of the King's council-chamber. Newcastle, however, offered our company something equally brilliant: not only was this an exciting and welcoming city, but the home territory, the original location, of the Percies' story. The names of Northumberland allies – Hotspur, Douglas, Worcester, Percy – are all over the city and we were able to visit the great Percy castles and strongholds that defended the coastline of north-east England, the historical locations of some of the scenes I had been playing.

When I played Kate Percy my experience of working closely opposite another actor in two-handed scenes was less than limited. To play a lover, a spouse, a sibling, requires understanding and trust, a trust on which, for the length of each scene and its story, and for each moment in it, the two actors depend and rest upon each other's voices and movements. Like two members of a team, they bounce and pass the ball to one another to keep the game from drooping. And I could not have wished for a bouncier, stronger, curlier, more generous, more rocket-powered team-partner than Adam Levy. We performed Kate and Harry Percy together from the beginning of one spring to the end of the next, in three cities, for thousands of expectant ears, in every mood and in every weather, but on stage there was not one minute of one performance that did not make my heart race and my toes curl.

Falstaff in Parts 1 and 2 of *Henry IV*

DESMOND BARRIT

DESMOND BARRIT is an Associate Actor of the Royal Shakespeare Company. He played Falstaff in Michael Attenborough's production of the two parts of *Henry IV* at the Swan Theatre, Stratford-upon-Avon, in the summer season of 2000, and later at the Barbican Theatre in London. His extensive earlier work for the RSC had included Trinculo, Feste, Gloucester in *King Lear*, both Antipholuses (for which he won an Olivier award for best comedy performance), Malvolio, and Bottom. His many roles for the National Theatre include Charlie in *Three Men on a Horse*, Brazen in *The Recruiting Officer*, and Toad in *The Wind in the Willows*, while during seasons at Chichester, York, Lincoln, Cardiff and elsewhere he has played, among much else, Lady Bracknell, Sir Toby Belch, and Pozzo in *Waiting for Godot*. His films include *Oliver Twist*, *A Christmas Carol*, *Alice Through the Looking Glass*, and *A Midsummer Night's Dream* and he has also worked extensively on radio and television. In the summer of 2003 a further glimpse of his Falstaff was to be seen on screen at the Olivier Theatre as part of a 'flashback' scene during the National Theatre's production of *Henry V*.

I was in Chicago directing a university production of *The Comedy of Errors* when the RSC's invitation to play Falstaff reached me. I rushed off to the university library and looked again at the plays and realized that the role was a really exciting challenge; that is always what makes me say yes to a part, as it did in this instance. People had been telling me for some time that I'd be perfect for Falstaff – no doubt alluding to my girth. It was not, however, a role I had especially coveted, though I had greatly admired the late Sir Robert Stephens's superb performance of the part on the only occasion I had seen the play in the theatre. I remember being enthralled by Stephens's portrayal, though as I had no idea at the time that the part would ever come my way I omitted to take the notes that would have allowed me to steal all his good ideas.

I regard the two parts of *Henry IV* as just one long play, offering those actors whose characters continue through the two parts the rare luxury of six whole hours to develop a character rather than the usual three. Our rehearsal schedule meant, however, that we had to rehearse Part One and get that on stage before we started rehearsing Part Two, a procedure on balance probably easier to deal with than trying to keep both parts in rehearsal simultaneously and opening them back to back. When we came to re-open the production at the Barbican, however, we did re-rehearse the two parts together and open them on one day, and I am sure that that is the way to see them, actors and audience feeling that they have climbed Everest together and sharing a great sense of achievement.

The mood of Part Two is infinitely more melancholy than that of Part One. Part Two is all about disintegration, the disintegration of relationships (especially that of Hal and Falstaff) and the disintegration of life, from the sickness of the king to the senility of Shallow and Silence down in Gloucestershire. The mood of Part One, in spite of its war scenes and the deaths they bring with them, is much more one of affirmation, affirmation of youth (even if only pretended in Falstaff's case) and of living: 'Give me *life*', as he puts it in the middle of the battle (Part One, v.iii.59; my italics). But he begins Part Two facing up to his own physical decay, and that idea of decay, the decay of youth, of friendship, of life, follows through the play, ending with Hal's grim allusion to the width of Falstaff's grave in the final moments. The two parts together thus make a sort of life journey.

I did some reading about the reigns of Henry IV and Henry V as part of my preparation, but didn't find it terribly useful for Falstaff. He is distantly based on the historical character Sir John Oldcastle, of course, but reading about him really didn't inform very much. After all, it's reading the play that's the only really useful form of preparation. I always go through the text underlining and taking out all the references that are made to my character and try to decide whether or not they are true – and even if they seem not to be, it's always worth remembering the old adage that 'there's no smoke without fire'. But all the real work of preparing a performance happens in the rehearsal room, and it's no good arriving there with a fully worked-out character – or, in this particular case, with any fixed idea about how you are going to look. I had imagined Falstaff in a costume based on horizontal lines to draw attention to his girth, with a thick leather belt below the waist to emphasize the paunch, but the costume designs were more vertical than horizontal. Most of my own weight is around the middle, so I needed some padding around the shoulders, and plenty of layers, to fill the costumes out.

A lot of time was spent on my wig. I started off with something half way down my back, and this went through various phases of modification – the Moses-look, the Rastafarian, the 1940s film starlet – until I began slowly to look more like Falstaff. I hate wearing facial hair: it's painful, and you have to be very careful how you talk, for it does have a way of falling off, as I have witnessed on stage on many occasions, even at the Royal Shakespeare Theatre. So I decided to grow my own beard, and a splendid colour it turned out to be, a sort of reddish-grey. By the time we had been playing for a while and these initial surprises and experiments were over, I came to take my appearance for granted, and couldn't imagine Falstaff looking any other way: to look in the mirror was to see Falstaff gazing back at me.

The play has a tantalizing way of referring every now and again to Falstaff's past – as a page to the Duke of Norfolk, perhaps (Part Two, III.ii.25), or as a young man 'not an eagle's talon in the waist' (Part One, II.iv.323), but the amount of firm biographical information that you can glean from the text is very slight. We decided that he was probably from a fairly well-to-do, titled family and that he had had some sort of military career in the past but that its restrictions went against the grain. In breaking away from his family he has, of course, cut himself off from its wealth and for the last fifteen years or so he has been getting by, on credit and highway robbery, in the company of the likes of Bardolph and Pistol, fellow-regulars in the snug at the back of the Boar's Head. It is here, we decided, that he met Poins, and, through Poins, Prince Hal. We discussed the possible circumstances of their meeting quite a lot. Poins seems to come from the minor aristocracy, and is a bit of a lad, and we imagined him encouraging Hal one day (perhaps a year or so, maybe two years, before the play begins) to come down to the pub to meet a fat man with a great line in funny stories and limitless gags up his sleeve – and all this just for the cost of a few drinks. And since that meeting with the king's son, Falstaff's whole existence has changed – and highway robbery has inevitably become a somewhat less risky way of earning a living. People like Falstaff are charismatic; his wit covers a huge area and Hal finds him fascinating because of this. It would be absurd to call him an alcoholic: he enjoys his drink, obviously, but he enjoys food, and sex, and laughter just as much. It is life that Falstaff enjoys, life that he asserts.

As we first encounter the relationship between Hal and Falstaff their friendship seems to be at a peak. Before the end of their first scene, however, Hal is referring to the '*base* contagious clouds' in which he has surrounded himself and declaring that this friendship is only for 'awhile' (Part One, I.ii.193, 196, my italics). It is obviously important that the actor of Hal shouldn't play the end of Part Two at the beginning of Part One, but the speech nevertheless alerts the audience to the precarious, the temporary nature of the relationship – aspects of it to which I believe Falstaff himself must, however, be oblivious. For all Hal's refusal ever to answer any of his questions about what may happen 'when thou art king' (Part One, I.ii.16, 23, etc), Falstaff clearly imagines the future King Hal ruling perfectly efficiently, but taking Falstaff along with him, no doubt with his own wing of the royal palace for a residence. There is something of the overgrown schoolboy about Falstaff, and of schoolboyish pranks about the going-on on Gad's Hill, and with the youthful zest that people of Falstaff's age have usually long outgrown comes a blind faith that people and situations are never going to change. Falstaff lives for the moment, without too much thought about the future, and he clearly feels that he has handled his relationship with Hal perfectly satisfactorily in the past and can continue to do so in the future. Even at their sole meeting in Part Two, after Hal and Falstaff have been months without seeing each other, Falstaff still imagines that things are just the same between them and that nothing has changed or will change. But in life things always change: their next meeting will be at the new king's coronation.

For the actor of Falstaff to be anticipating all through the preceding ten acts that final confrontation at the end of Part Two would, however, be to destroy the play. I do not think that Falstaff pretends his feelings of affection for Hal; they are, I believe, quite genuine. Nor do I think that Hal fails to realize that Falstaff is aware of the material advantages that the friendship of the heir to the throne brings with it. But I think that the gains of the friendship are mutual gains, not to be measured in material terms. Of course Hal provides a form of shield to the consequences of their law-breaking, but to reduce to its surface meaning Falstaff's statement that Hal's 'love is worth a million' (Part One, III.iii.135) is to be literal-minded about a casual witticism that Falstaff coins just to get himself out of an awkward corner – as well as to forget the fact that in trying to find a way of expressing how much they love, people often resort to material comparisons.

For me, then, Falstaff's affection for Hal is real and profound; I don't think you can play it as anything but genuine, or the relationship becomes so shallow as to make the play altogether uninteresting. I do not find in it anything of that homosexual element that some commentators on the play have wanted to detect – indeed, if Hal fell for some of the Falstaffs one sees illustrated, the only conceivable explanation would have to be the prince's previously very sheltered life. Certain directors might wish to develop this approach, but for me that derives from too much speculation about Shakespeare's own sexuality. The relationship between Falstaff and Hal seems to me much more interestingly related to that of a father and son, and the love between them very much greater than could be explained by Falstaff's greed or ambition. There is enormous mutual understanding and awareness between them. They are clearly the two most intelligent people in the play, but which is the mental superior of the other it would be impossible to say: they are an excellent match for each other. Hal is always aware when Falstaff is lying and exaggerating, and Falstaff always realizes that awareness. Hal is no doubt more devious than Falstaff, whose exaggerations and pretences have a harmless, transparent quality to them: Hal allows Falstaff to go so far, Falstaff knows (fairly accurately) how far that is, there is no malice involved when he is caught out, and the whole thing is a sort of competitive game. Falstaff's use of language in these contexts is, of course, far more interesting and exciting than Hal's, far more intelligent perhaps; but ultimately it is Hal who has the power.

Shakespeare has, in Falstaff, famously created a physically large man, and it is a fact of life that large men can get away with things that would never be allowed in thin men: what in the latter would be regarded as sharp or acerbic will be seen in the former as merely cheeky, even jolly. Falstaff's charisma even stops audiences – and perhaps other characters in the play – from thinking too hard about what, for example, he has done to his army of ragamuffins: 'good enough to toss, food for powder, food for powder' (Part One, IV.ii.64–5). I was aware from the audience response to this that they regarded it as no more than rather roguish of him, and were as apt to blame the ragamuffins for being so easily led, as they were to blame Falstaff. Of course we don't get to meet any of these ragamuffins, or their bereaved wives or daughters, so the attitude to Falstaff as a sort of loveable scoundrel isn't really tested. In Part Two we do encounter some of the conscripts in person, but there we never find out what happens to Mouldy and Wart and Feeble and Shadow – and there turns out to be no battle at Gaultree Forest for them to fight in anyway. That balance between Falstaff's ability to inspire affection in most of the people with whom he comes into contact (on stage and in the theatre), and the frequent unscrupulousness of his self-interest, is an important one to find in performing the role.

Falstaff (in spite of the promise in the Epilogue to Part Two) doesn't make it into *Henry V*. In the two parts of *Henry IV* Shakespeare has interwoven the political and military scenes with the Eastcheap low-life scenes in a fantastic balance. Whether this could really have been continued into a third play I don't know – it might even have got monotonous. But *Henry V* is much more serious in its attention to war than its predecessors, and Falstaff's presence might have undermined Henry slightly. The low-life characters in *Henry V* are directly involved in the war; Falstaff in *Henry IV* stays on the periphery of the conflict, always running around the edge of the battlefield, never across the middle of it.

I have been dealing so far with some general aspects of the character of Falstaff, and of the world in which he moves. I want to turn now to some more specific scenes and episodes in our production and in my performance, starting with the remarkable first entrance that Michael Attenborough devised for me: 'Now, Hal, what time of day is it lad?' (Part One, I.ii.I). Up through the floor I pushed, by way of a sort of rubber flange that we came to know as the sphincter. The first question I asked, of course, was where I was coming from and the answer that it was from another room in Hal's apartment seemed to beg for the response that most people have doors rather than rubber flanges in their apartments in order to get from room to room. Even a trap-door might have made some sort of sense, as though Falstaff had spent the night in Hal's cellar, having collapsed there while in search of another bottle of sack. The idea of this curious entrance, of course, was symbolic: our production was part of the RSC's 'This England' project to present all eight of Shakespeare's history plays, and the subject of those plays was this island, this England, this earth that we live on, and the director wanted Falstaff, as a man of the earth, to be seen to be born from and of the earth. My suggestion then was that we needed to separate this symbolic birth from the more naturalistic scene that followed it and we achieved this by having David Troughton, playing Henry IV, remain on stage after the end of the first court scene while Falstaff struggled into life from below the stage. Hal's real father and his surrogate father were thus seen simultaneously on stage together in a moment of fairly obvious, but, we felt, pertinent theatrical symbolism.

When you start a play you need, I think, to do so with broad brush-strokes. I decided, therefore, that we needed to say a lot about Falstaff's relationship with Hal in their first scene, and that we needed to do that physically. So we made it morning and we suggested that Falstaff had stayed at Hal's place overnight, as no doubt he does quite often when he passes out somewhere in the prince's apartments. We start their play off, therefore, by demonstrating the great emotional closeness between them, making it as physically intimate as possible without it looking like a homoerotic scene. They have a great understanding these two, and like all great mates they can cope with waking up in the morning after a night of heavy drinking and face another day with a few jokes at which neither of them gets offended. The arrival of Poins is clearly unwelcome to Falstaff: we had decided, as I said earlier, that it was Poins who had brought Hal and Falstaff together, but I think that Poins, as so often happens, has become jealous of the relationship that has blossomed from the introduction he made, and Falstaff is aware of that, and of Poins's constant attempts to turn that little dagger in his back. Falstaff, though, can deal with Poins.

The great tavern scene (Act Two, Scene Four) shows the relationship between Hal and Falstaff at its most vivid. We considered the idea that Falstaff's exaggerations over the number of men in buckram are merely a performance to entertain Hal, but this seemed to me far too contrived an interpretation. Falstaff getting involved in his fantastic story is what I chose to play, becoming, indeed, absolutely carried away by it. I don't think he even hears the little interjections by Hal and Poins in his excitement, and Hal simply allows him to go too far and to get himself tied up in knots: he wants to see if Falstaff is clever enough to get himself out of it when he (Hal) chooses the moment to bring him down to earth with a bump. That's how their relationship works and this is no doubt just one representative example of something that happens all the time. And when he says 'By the Lord, I knew ye as well as he that made ye' (Part One, II.iv.261–2), I think that's exactly what occurs to him absolutely on the spur of the moment. This is a clever, witty man,

15 Desmond Barrit as Falstaff with William Houston as Prince Hal, *1 Henry IV*, Act I, Scene ii: 'What a devil hast thou to do with the time of the day?'

thinking on his feet; the excuse isn't something he's had up his sleeve from a few moments earlier in the conversation. Of course he knows that he's been found out, that no-one is in the least taken in, and that he can't go any further – which is why, of course, he changes the subject: 'Hostess, clap to the doors! Watch tonight, pray tomorrow!' (Part One, II.iv.270–1).

But if Falstaff isn't performing during the story of the men in buckram, I'm sure he is when he goes to answer the door and returns with the news from Sir John Bracy, the 'villainous news', of 'that same mad fellow of the north, Percy, and he of Wales . . . what a plague call you him? . . . Owen, Owen, the same . . . ' (Part One, II.iv.326–34). There, surely, he is putting on a performance, and there you hear his fantastic use of language almost as clearly as in the play-acting that follows.

In both halves of that episode (when he plays the king and when he plays Hal) Falstaff keeps harping on the question of his own banishment. His insistence is curious, a product, perhaps, of that way we sometimes have of trying to joke about the subjects that are of deepest concern to us, to lighten them by being humorous. There may also be an element of testing Hal, to see what the response is going to be. For a long time he doesn't get a response at all, and then it comes, with devastating directness: 'I do, I will' (Part One, II.iv.466). It's the one thing he didn't want to hear, and before he has the chance to say 'look, you didn't really mean that, did you?', things happen to deflect the scene in another direction. I'm sure he just pushes it to one side, unable to believe it might be true, for I do not think that at this time Falstaff even begins to think that banishment might be a possibility.

When the war begins and Falstaff watches his young friend busily despatching messengers hither and thither, his response is very telling:

> Rare words! Brave world! Hostess, my breakfast, come!
> O, I could wish this tavern were my drum.
>
> (III.iii.202–3)

I don't think Falstaff is a coward, although, like me, he would rather avoid conflict unless it's inevitable. When fighting begins he contrives, if he can, to be a couple of fields away, for he values life, and his own life, infinitely more than heroic death. He makes that wonderfully clear in the 'honour' soliloquy (Part One, v.i.127–40). His perhaps slightly surprising presence in the preceding parley between the two sides, with his single devastating contribution, concerning Worcester, that 'Rebellion lay in his way, and he found it' (Part One, v.i.28), gives him the opportunity to observe the posturing of the two sides and provides a springboard for that speech on honour. Just prior to this we have heard him admit, as he led his troops towards the battle, that 'if I be not ashamed of my soldiers, I am a soused gurnet' (Part One, IV.ii.11–12). His admission to Hal that they are 'food for powder, food for powder' (Part One, IV.ii.63–4) is clearly callous, part of that breadth and complexity of character that makes him so interesting to play. He has enlisted the riff-raff of society after allowing the more well-to-do to buy themselves out, but, as I said earlier, we never meet the soldiers he leads to Shrewsbury, so can hardly take their fates too personally. Falstaff is an opportunist and a rogue and this episode makes that clear.

I used to play the 'honour' soliloquy as a sort of dialogue with the audience, with them asking the questions: 'Can honour set to a leg?', and Falstaff replies 'No'; 'Or an arm?', and Falstaff replies 'No'; 'Or take away the grief of a wound?', and again he replies 'No' (Part One, v.i.131–2). Falstaff is here placing himself, I think, as an intermediary between the war and the audience, forcing them to wonder why men go to war at all, asking, and answering, the questions that are in their minds.

For all his deftness in evading conflict, Falstaff does find himself at one point in the battle having to face up to Douglas, a situation from which he escapes by pretending to be dead. I used sometimes to wish we could have a close-up on the following moment when Hal discovers the 'corpse', for the treatment of this in Orson Welles's film *The Chimes at Midnight* is very funny. Welles's Falstaff is lying there in full armour pretending to be dead, but from the slits in his enormous helmet Hal can see, on this cold day, the breath seeping out and therefore knows that Falstaff hears him when he mocks him with 'Embowelled will I see thee by and by' (Part One, v.iv.108). In the theatre, with close-up out of the question, I found that the best way to play it was for Falstaff to 'act dead' as convincingly as possible, taking Hal in, and as many of the audience as didn't know the play – which is what creates the best laugh when he suddenly gets up, indignantly repeating 'Embowelled?' (Part One, v.iv.110). That means, of course, that Falstaff hears Hal say that only a love of 'vanity' would make him have a 'heavy miss' of his friend (Part One, v.iv.104–5), but performing a reaction to that at the same time as pretending to be dead is not really an option, and when he gets up Falstaff is too busy with the corpse of Hotspur – and inflicting that wound to his thigh is as disturbing as Falstaff's opportunism gets – to comment on what the prince has just said. I was lucky that our Hotspur, Adam Levy, was light enough for me to carry off the stage at every performance, which not all Falstaffs are able to do. 'I look to be either earl or duke', he says (v.iv.140), as he leaves with his burden on his back, a symbolic exit, as someone remarked to me, of comedy and fiction bearing tragedy and history from the stage at the end of a history play.

Or, rather, at the mid-point of a history play, for as I said earlier, the two parts of *Henry IV* seem to me to be one long play, through which the character of Falstaff develops as a whole. A year has passed since the Battle of Shrewsbury, and though there's clearly been no dukedom for Falstaff, he does now have a page, so obviously Hal has allowed him to get away with his lies and has made sure that he's looked after. It is, however, a long time – six months, we thought – since Falstaff has seen Hal. The king, we soon learn, is very ill, so Hal has had to be preparing himself for kingship. Falstaff, too, is ill – very clearly so, in our production – the pox and the gout having manifested themselves on his body, so he has not been in a position to pursue Hal too much himself. But he still has his pretensions about being well dressed, and wants to know about 'the satin for my short cloak and my slops' (Part Two, I.ii.29), even if his body is crumbling. I suspect that for the last six months he's done little more than survive and try to maintain the small semblance of dignity that he has left.

An ongoing motif of Part Two is Falstaff's conflict with the Lord Chief Justice, that authority figure who represents the opposite of everything Falstaff stands for and whom he longs to dethrone. At the end of the play the Lord Chief Justice will lock Falstaff up in the Fleet, but in their two earlier scenes together, Falstaff does, I think, have the upper hand. It's a well-matched conflict, though, in which the Lord Chief Justice acquits himself well, particularly in his speech presenting the undeniable physical evidence of Falstaff's age and frailty, the very things he doesn't want to admit to:

Have you not a moist eye, a dry hand, a yellow cheek, a white beard, a decreasing leg, an increasing belly? Is not your voice broken, your wind short, your chin double, your wit single, and every part about you *blasted* with antiquity? (Part Two, I.ii.182–6, my italics)

Falstaff replies 'I was born about three of the clock in the afternoon, with a white head, and something of a round belly' (Part Two, I.ii.188–90) – 'I've always looked like this' – making light of it with another of his typically evasive replies. But the speech does get to him, I think, even though he bounces back – in the same way as we have seen him bounce back from Hal's jibes in Part One. Earlier, his method of evading the Lord Chief Justice's questions had been that string of obsessive enquiries and comments on the king's health, a piece of rudeness matched in their second encounter when Falstaff ignores him and starts asking Master Gower to dinner. None of this is ineptness on Falstaff's part, of course: it's a deliberate way of putting the justice in his place. But he gets his come-uppance in the final scene when Hal puts Falstaff's future directly into the hands of the Lord Chief Justice, who is now holding all the cards. But I shall come to that later.

Asking the Lord Chief Justice for a loan of 'a thousand pound to furnish me forth' at the end of their first encounter (Part Two, I.ii.225–6) is Falstaff's final insult to him in that scene. It is a sum of money that has haunted him ever since it slipped through his fingers at Gad's Hill: 'There be four of us have taken a thousand pound this day morning... Taken from us it is. A hundred upon poor four of us' (Part One, II.iv.153–7) – though there's no reason at all why Falstaff should have any idea how much the sum of money was that they snatched in the dark; it's just a fictitious amount that he invents. Then in the next Eastcheap scene we learn that he has accused Hal of owing him that same thousand pounds – he sidesteps the accusation with the response 'A thousand pound, Hal? A million, thy love is worth a million, thou owest me thy love' (Part One, III.iii.134–5). Falstaff, of course, lives constantly on credit; borrowing 'lingers out and out' his 'consumption of the purse' (Part Two, I.ii.238–9), and his greatest success in borrowing turns out to be with Justice Shallow, as we learn at the end of Part Two, when they are at the coronation: 'O, if I had had time to have made new liveries I would have bestowed the thousand pound I borrowed of you' (Part Two, V.v.11–13) – that same magic sum again. And though the idea of spending the whole thousand on new clothes must be an exaggeration, it is interesting – particularly in the condition that he's in – that it does cross Falstaff's mind that he might have spent a lot of money on his looks, so as to appear, perhaps, more fantastic and impressive even than the king.

His constant creditor is Mistress Quickly, who has been 'fubbed off, and fubbed off, and fubbed off, from this day to that day, that it is a shame to be thought on' (Part Two, II.i.32–4). She puts up with it because she is in love with him – and she's in love with him right through to the time when she so movingly reports his death in *Henry V*. Indeed, I think her marriage to Pistol is much more of a sham than a marriage to Falstaff would have been. She loves this man, this lovable rogue, and she continues to do so even though he behaves so sexually blatantly with Doll Tearsheet in front of her eyes. Love is blind, they say, and (as one sees in television shows all the time) partners are ready to forgive the most blatant infidelities, so that, for years, Falstaff has (as the Lord Chief Justice puts it in their second encounter) 'practised upon the easy-yielding spirit of this woman... both in purse and in person' (Part Two, II.i.113–15).

'I hope you'll come to supper?' says Mistress Quickly (Part Two, II.i.158) after Falstaff has, yet again, 'fubbed off' one of her attempts to get some of her money back, and thus the big tavern scene is set up. This is the first time, we thought, that Falstaff has seen Hal in six months, so that when Hal comes in, in spite of the fact that he is playing a trick on him, Falstaff is so overjoyed to see him that all he wants to do is to hug his boy. What happened in our production was that Hal hugged Mistress Quickly instead, depriving Falstaff of the position he wants to be in. And then Falstaff has to extricate himself from the accusations of insulting Hal which he does with another of his magnificent evasions: 'I dispraised him before the wicked that the wicked might not fall in love with him' (Part Two, II.iv.314–15) – a wonderful lie that nobody in their right mind would believe, reminding us once again of Hal's willingness to go along with Falstaff's lies if they 'may do thee grace' (Part One, v.iv.155). Then, with his exuberant justification of what he's said – that Bardolph's burning nose, and Doll Tearsheet's diseases, and Mistress Quickly's lending him money, are all evidence of their wickedness – Falstaff tries to win Hal back to him again, to recreate their earlier jovial, happy, witty relationship and the love that they shared. But Hal is whisked away from him by that message from the court and Falstaff is left saying 'Now comes in the sweetest morsel of the night, and we must hence and leave it unpicked' (Part Two, II.iv.362–3), referring ostensibly to Doll Tearsheet, but in fact to the one true love that he has, to Hal, who has already been taken away from him.

That may be why Falstaff turns up in Gloucestershire. Things aren't working for him at this time and he needs to find somewhere else where he might be important, and one of those places might be among these yokels who find even his most obvious witticisms terribly funny. 'If he had been a man's tailor he'd ha' pricked you', he says to Shallow (Part Two, III.ii.151–2), and when Shallow laughs I played 'Yes, you've got that one, well done!', and the same with Silence's reaction to 'Master Silence, it well befits you should be of the peace' (Part Two, III.ii.89–90): 'You're on to that one, are you? Well done. Ha, ha, ha!'. Falstaff realizes that their sense of humour is very basic, and just sends them up. He also realizes that there's money in the country, plenty to eat, and plenty to drink, that nobody's short of anything, that recruits who will buy themselves out are easy to find, and that, at last, there's the possibility of getting that thousand pounds that has eluded him for so long. And he gets it, too: 'As I return, I will fetch off these justices' (Part Two, III.ii.291). What's more, he suddenly finds himself with people much older than himself, or, with the recruits, with bumpkins and buffoons, so that here he can feel superior to (and younger than) those around him, looking down on them almost, as if they belonged on a much lower level than himself. It was an absolute joy performing the Gloucestershire scenes, particularly after all the fighting in Part One.

More generally, indeed, I found Part Two much easier to play than Part One. In Part One Falstaff seems to drive nearly all the scenes he's in; in Part Two others do the driving and Falstaff is more of an observer. His soliloquies seem to be reflexions on other people and what they've said, about their state, and condition, and background, compared with those in Part One, which are his own reflexions on honour, and life, and other such abstract matters. Thus after Prince John has ticked him off for being late arriving at the battle, he is provoked into musing that 'this same young sober-blooded boy doth not love me, nor a man cannot make him laugh' (Part Two, IV.iii.86–7) and from that observation of Prince John comes the sherris-sack soliloquy. I think Falstaff really believes what he says there, that wine in your body gives you a positiveness, a manliness, that those without wine lack – so, as always in acting, a funny speech is only funny for the audience if the actor doesn't try to be funny with it, but plays it for real. The same quality of wry observation of people is there in his soliloquy about the justices – 'I do see the bottom of Justice Shallow...' (Part Two, III.ii.291–321) – and in his analysis of the odd relationship between Shallow and his servants, Davy and the rest:

It is a wonderful thing to see the semblable coherence of his men's spirits and him. They, by observing him, do bear themselves like foolish justices; and he, by conversing with them, is turned into a justice-like servingman. (Part Two, v.i.58–62)

But though he clearly enjoys this Gloucestershire interlude, Falstaff's real priorities still reveal themselves: 'I will devise matter enough out of this Shallow to keep Prince Harry in continual laughter the wearing out of six fashions' (Part Two, v.i.71–3). His next meeting with that same Prince Harry will reveal the futility of these hopes.

I always work on the assumption that the audience doesn't know the play, and I certainly did that for the rejection scene. I was surprised, therefore, when it was suggested to me that members of the audience would be embarrassed for Falstaff when he so noisily and naïvely interrupts the solemn ceremonial. I think that reaction can only be felt by people who know what's going to happen; others will be cheerfully anticipating that now that Prince Hal is King Hal it's simply a question of his making everything right for Falstaff. I had a very grand hat for the occasion, and replacing it carefully on my head at the end was a way of restoring a little dignity to Falstaff before the final exit – just as,

16 Desmond Barrit as Falstaff with Benjamin Whitrow (left) as Justice
Shallow and Peter Copley (right) as Justice Silence, *2 Henry IV*, Act v,
Scene iii: 'Boot, boot, Master Shallow! I know the young king is sick
for me.'

a few years earlier, my Malvolio had pulled himself up and tidied his
hair before finally leaving the stage. Keeping dignity is, I think, always
far more touching on stage than bursting into tears: bravery in the face
of adversity, and all that.

Whether Falstaff has any deeply hidden, sub-conscious inkling of
what is going to happen to him it is hard to say, but in no way is he
consciously expecting it; he's the sort of person who always goes for the
optimistic option. I think he believes that now Henry IV is out of the
way he can at last become Hal's father. Though he and Hal haven't met
much in Part Two of the play, there has been no indication that there is
anything wrong with their relationship – though, of course, when you
don't meet up with friends for a long time it isn't always easy to rekindle
what was there before. Falstaff's silence is the really extraordinary thing
about this meeting. 'Reply not to me with a fool-born jest', Hal says
to him, cutting him off from what Hal clearly thinks is going to be a
joke in response to Hal's statement that 'the grave doth gape / For thee
thrice wider than for other men' (Part Two, v.v.56–8). But I don't think

Falstaff was going to reply with a joke at all, the sort of 'no, *six* times wider' response that Hal seems to be imagining. I think that, for once in his life, Falstaff was going to beg for forgiveness. 'I know thee not, old man. Fall to thy *prayers*', Hal had begun (Part Two, v.v.50, my italics), and Falstaff takes that in, I think, and in response to Hal's glibness and cruelty is going to appeal to him to remember their past, their great friendship, the good times they have had together. But he isn't given the chance to speak at all.

When Hal has gone Falstaff makes an unprecedented admission of debt: 'Master Shallow, I owe you a thousand pound' (Part Two, v.v.76). When something as devastating as this occurs, people always talk about anything but what has just happened, and so, to lighten the moment, Falstaff talks about something that is not of huge consequence – for, compared to what has just happened to him, even a debt of a thousand pounds is not of huge consequence – and tries to make light of it. And then what Hal has said starts to sink in, and he begins to realize that what has happened is a bit heftier than he's tried to pretend. He then starts trying to convince himself that he mustn't worry about it, that Hal is only behaving like this because he has to do so in public: 'I shall be sent for soon, at night' (Part Two, v.v.92–3). I used to say that, not to the other characters on stage, but to myself. He's trying to be firm with himself: 'Things *will* be all right'. But, of course, he knows that they won't be and that there will be no going back. Then the Lord Chief Justice comes for the third round of their contest, and takes him away to prison. And the crime for which he is being imprisoned is that of loving someone too much, the crime of being a good friend – well, and a bit of a rogue as well. Hal has to move on; there is no choice. And Falstaff, I'm sure, dies of a broken heart.

Falstaff is certainly the most complex part I've ever played, and probably the most rewarding. Theatre roles are traditionally divided into the 'comic' and the 'straight', but Falstaff is neither of these – and both. He's serious and comic, honourable and ruthless, user and used. 'Give me life', he says in Part One (v.iii.59), and that becomes even more important in Part Two, because for Falstaff life means Hal, and Hal's presence. As I've said, I don't find the homosexual reading of the relationship useful; Falstaff's love for Hal is a paternal love, that deep, elemental love of parent for child; and so the sense of 'give me life' in Part Two is 'give me Hal back – *please* give me Hal back'. The role excited me, and stretched me, and I hope put finally to rest that snide comment in a review of one of my earlier Stratford performances, that I was 'the RSC's answer to light entertainment'. Falstaff is such a complicated, extraordinary, profound human being that it is hardly surprising that the word 'Falstaffian' has had to be added to the English language to describe him.

King Henry V

ADRIAN LESTER

ADRIAN LESTER is an Associate Artist of the National Theatre and played the title role in Nicholas Hytner's production of *Henry the Fifth* in the Olivier Theatre in the summer of 2003. It was the National Theatre's first production of the play and Nicholas Hytner's inaugural production as incoming Artistic Director. Among Adrian Lester's earlier Shakespearian work had been the title role in Peter Brook's production of *Hamlet* (at the Théâtre des Bouffes du Nord and at the Young Vic), Rosalind in Declan Donnellan's all-male production of *As You Like It* for Cheek by Jowl (a performance for which he won the *Time Out* award for best actor), and roles in a National Theatre production of *A Midsummer Night's Dream*, in *The Winter's Tale* at the Royal Exchange, Manchester, and in *Love's Labour's Lost* in the film directed by Kenneth Branagh. A wide range of other theatre work has included an Olivier award for the role of Bobby in *Company* and a second *Time Out* award for his performance in *Six Degrees of Separation*. His films include *Day after Tomorrow*, *Dust*, *Final Curtain,* and *Born Romantic* and among his television appearances are *Girlfriends*, *Jason and the Argonauts*, *Ball and Chain*, and *Silent Witness*.

When Nicholas Hytner offered me the role of Henry the Fifth, I must say I was hesitant. I had just done Hamlet, for a year, and my business sense was telling me that it was time to do some film or television work rather than another Shakespeare. To be offered this fantastic job just as I was feeling that I wanted to do something other than theatre seemed like a serious case of mistiming. I didn't really know the play: I'd done some scenes from it at school, I'd seen the Olivier and Branagh film versions, and Prince Hal's first soliloquy from Part One of *Henry IV* had been my audition piece at RADA. It wasn't a part I'd coveted, but after I'd read the play it was much harder to step away: this wasn't, I decided, going to be just another production of a play; it was going to be an event, and it was impossible to think of not doing it. The fact that the production was to be in repertoire at the National for six months, so was going to be nothing like the usual year-long commitment to eight performances a week that some of my recent theatre work had been, was also relevant to the fact that I accepted gratefully.

This was the National Theatre's first ever production of *Henry V*, it was to be in the auditorium named after the star (and director) of a famous film of the play, and it was Nicholas Hytner's first (his 'flagship') production as Artistic Director of the National. Yes, in many ways it was going to be an event, but that simply added to the usual pressure of starting work on a big part. It's odd, but I found that the added pressure actually helped. The fact that the director and all we actors were aware that this was a slightly bigger deal than usual meant that the work, the time spent on research, all the areas of yourself that you have to reach into in order to bring the character onto the stage, would be worthwhile.

My preparation before rehearsals took two main forms, both connected with history: the history contemporary with the play's first production, and the history that was being made while ours was in rehearsal. I also spent some time looking again at Kenneth Branagh's film, not for my own role, but to try to get an angle on the soldiers, Llewellyn and Bates, Nym and Pistol. For the Elizabethan history I talked at length to my brother-in-law, Paul Hamilton, a professor of English at Queen Mary College in the University of London. He gave me a vivid sense of the condition of England during the closing years of Elizabeth's reign, which was when the play was written. The Protestant state of England, with something of a poor-relation mentality with regard to the great Catholic powers of Europe – Spain and France and so on – and with enemies not only on the continent, but in Ireland, Scotland, even Wales, was in fact quite cut off and small. Shakespeare's play actually created a 'Great Britain' on the stage, before there was any such thing, with Llewellyn, Macmorris, and Jamie all uniting behind an English king (even though he was born in Wales) who goes off, noble and resilient and godly, to fight the French – and who, as history guaranteed, and with the help of God, wins. The God that this Henry worships emerges as rather a Protestant God, to whom you can get down and pray anywhere and any time, without the need for formal set prayers or priests to intercede.

The great and successful king that Shakespeare presents, however, to Elizabeth and her court, and to audiences in the popular theatre, succeeds by making war – a heroic, just, and honourable war. Yet the play's presentation of war is altogether quite negative. There is a constant tension between the heroic and noble King Henry and the destructiveness of the war he wages. This tension or conflict provides a strong element of drama – and is, of course, responsible for the two opposing poles around which attitudes to the play (and productions of it) have always circled.

My other pre-rehearsal preparation was to watch a lot of news broadcasts – one of those rare occasions when sitting with your feet up watching television can genuinely be classed as 'work'. We knew, of course, that something was going to happen with Iraq when Nick first approached me to talk about the part, though at that point, and in spite of all the talk, I didn't really believe it would come to war. Although he already knew that he was going to open up the Olivier stage and use its great expanse to show groups of soldiers on the battlefield, Nick wasn't at all sure at that time whether he was going to do the play in a medieval setting (all swords and armour), or early twentieth-century (more accessible, perhaps, but still with a touch of chivalry), or fully modern. But as events continued, and war in Iraq drew closer, he knew that there was, under the circumstances, no way to do this play but in modern dress. So I spent a good deal of time comparing the presentation of the news of the approaching Iraq war on various television channels, British, American, and (via the internet) a few other countries as well, trying to see the way information is packaged to suit consumers, and those purveying it. It was basically the same story, but relayed in different ways depending on what reaction the media wanted to instill in their particular audiences – very much the way, I discovered, that Henry V deals with his own situation.

My sympathies always lie with the people that I play. Anything else isn't playing, it's judging. Although I might not, myself, choose to do what this person has done, I must completely understand why they chose to do it. So, with that in mind, I think that Henry is a great leader, always capable of revealing the appropriate facet of himself to deal with a situation – whether it be finding the right key in the final scene with Kate, or inspiring his men back to the attack on Harfleur. If you believe that a great leader is someone who thinks that the needs of the few, or the needs of people in other countries, are as important as the needs of the majority in his own country, then clearly Henry is not a great leader, but in playing the part I have to believe that he is, and

147

that his priorities are, for him, the right ones. So I learned a lot from watching the world's leaders placing themselves under public scrutiny during the weeks that led up to the war in Iraq.

I also got to know the *Henry IV* plays a little better, since it's a rare thing to have two whole plays' worth of evidence about your character's past. Henry's first soliloquy in Part One, 'I know you all' (I.ii.192), with its image of the clouds hiding the sun, which is himself, reveals the kind of ego necessary to fill the role of king to which he was born. That idea of being 'wondered at' (I.ii.199) comes through at the beginning of *Henry V*, with the bishops talking incredulously about his reformation that 'came ... in a flood' (I.i.33), and this allowed me, in my first scene, to use the fact that people aren't quite sure that they know him any more, the fact that they're a little uneasy, and at the same time relieved, that he's become something completely different. The death-bed scene with his father in Part Two of *Henry IV*, with its advice to 'busy giddy minds / With foreign quarrels' (IV.v.213–14), is also fascinating: settle discontentment and grumbling in your own country by having a war with someone else – precisely what Mrs Thatcher did in the Falklands. And here, as we rehearsed, Britain was in the middle of an invasion of Iraq and Tony Blair was appealing to history to be his judge, just as Henry V claims that 'our history shall ... speak freely of our acts' (I.ii.231–2): the parallels were uncanny.

It was decided fairly early on that we would make a video of part of the play-acting in the tavern scene of Part One of *Henry IV* (the section – II.iv.410 ff. – in which Falstaff pretends to be Hal's father). Nick had decided from the start that he wanted to use video at the beginning of the English-lesson scene between Alice and Kate: at the start of the scene and as a way of anchoring, or earthing, it, they would be watching part of Henry's address to Harfleur. This developed into the use of video for various sections of the play. A few speeches became 'addresses to the nation' because we were very aware of how much the media were fighting the Iraq war in the public mind, while troops were fighting it in Iraq itself. In the end, all our scene-changes came to be covered by such video clips, and for the scene in which Mistress Quickly announces the death of Falstaff (Act Two, Scene Three) we had them looking nostalgically at a video of that joyful evening in the pub. Des Barrit, who had recently played Falstaff at Stratford (see the preceding essay in this volume), repeated a bit of that performance. I wondered whether Henry might, like Mistress Quickly, have kept a secret copy of that video, but I think he has firmly left all of that behind him; it's all gone, and he is now totally absorbed, perhaps consumed, by the job he is doing.

I saw the text with the cuts that Nick was proposing before rehearsals began and had the opportunity to ask for anything back that I missed and thought should be restored. Unusually, apart from cutting just a couple more lines, that text remained constant right through rehearsals to performance. Within the basic decision to do the play in modern dress, the costume choices for battle dress were dictated by the military situation – apart, that is, from Peter Blythe's elegant Exeter, who took the option that some high-ranking officers do, of not wearing quite the standard uniform (he chose to have no helmet or flak-jacket, and to carry only a pistol). I decided that Henry in battle-dress should look exactly like any of his soldiers. His pack would be slightly larger, though, for as the commander I felt that he should carry spare stuff for his men – powder for their feet (it's part of a platoon sergeant's duty to check his men's feet), extra rations, or whatever. Looking after his men is paramount in Henry's conduct of the war: he marches with them, he leads them, he's always there. For the final scene of peace negotiations in France it was decided that I should be still in uniform, that second most formal of army uniforms, known as 'number twos'. A suit would suggest that I have come for political negotiation; the uniform would make it clear that I have come to accept a surrender, and the fact that it's not the full black-hat formality of number ones would also make a statement about Henry's attitude to his defeated enemy. But I shall come to that scene later. I want now to go through the play examining some of the issues that lay behind the decisions we made for each of Henry's scenes.

I felt that Henry had probably been king for a couple of years when the play opens. The historical Henry V had been fighting in his father's civil wars since his early teens as well as handling problem areas in his father's government, and my Henry was certainly not chairing his first cabinet meeting when the issue of war with France is discussed. I felt it was important that the decision should be seen to be made there, on stage, in front of the audience: in the world of politicking in which our production took place, it might be possible to imagine such a decision having been fixed in advance, behind closed doors, but that, I think, would have made what happens on stage less alive than it should be.

Henry knows that he has to get the cabinet with him; he also knows that the country is desperate for money after years of civil strife and that the two options for solving this problem are either to confiscate the lands 'which men devout / By testament have given to the Church' (I.i.9–10), or to invade France and take the wealth they need from there. Henry is indifferent at this point – but he *has* to get the money from somewhere and so he has already begun to investigate both options.

When Henry steps into the room and sits down, the audience already knows that the church people are going to argue for war with France – as a way of keeping their lands – and that they are ready to give a bigger sum of money to finance the war than the church has ever given to a monarch in history. Henry hasn't decided, though we learn (I.ii.247) that he has already sent an embassy to France with a version of his claim. The rest of the cabinet think that the issue of church lands is the main item on the meeting's agenda, along with a few other routine matters, but Henry immediately raises the question of France and asks the archbishop to speak on the matter. This, and the solemnity of his instruction to the archbishop not to lie, not to 'fashion, wrest, or bow' (I.ii.14) his reading, because people will die as a result of what he says, takes them all by surprise.

Canterbury goes through the five reasons why the Salic Law is absolute rubbish, and as he's speaking, and most of the others find it hard to follow, Henry is concentrating, sometimes listening hard, sometimes thinking. He realizes that the French are lying to him and making a fool of him, and this insult to England becomes a powerful driving force, something that will make him seem weak if he doesn't go to war. All the time he's watching Canterbury very closely, so that the archbishop really has to work hard to make sure that he follows Henry's wishes. This is one of those 'guided discussions' in cabinet to which Clair Short referred (after her resignation), and the guiding is all being done by Henry. The cabinet has to be convinced, and so does Henry: he demands that the archbishop make his argument good so that he can believe it and then be able to sell it to the public.

The Dauphin's 'merry message' (I.ii.299) hits Henry quite hard – like sending a reformed alcoholic, who's now leading the country, a bottle of Jack Daniels – and his anger is only just held in check. There seems to me to be a glimpse of the old Prince Hal here, of the capacity for anger of the young man who used to get drunk, the kind of anger you might see outside a pub as a fight starts. And the insult is delivered in front of Henry's cabinet, who are all aware of his history and watching him closely, so the mockery leaves him absolutely seething, holding himself in his chair to make sure that what he says remains within a political context. He narrowly succeeds in channelling this anger into a brilliant line by line insult to the Dauphin, managing also to blame the Dauphin for the war for which he has just asked the archbishop to take responsibility. (Henry, consummate politician that he is, always manages to shift responsibility for his actions onto other people.) Here his anger flares, he directs its rage, and then he puts it away again and calmly announces the end of the meeting, leaving the members of his cabinet even more uncertain about how well they know the powerful king who emerged so suddenly from the reprobate prince. Never before have I played a character where it is so essential to play every scene for all its worth, without trying to make connexions with other scenes; the audience will make the links themselves and (if they can) make up their minds about Henry. The discussion of what kind of person Henry is must be continued, not answered, through my performance: if I try to answer it, it's dead; if I don't answer it, it remains alive and keeps moving.

The anticipation of violence in some of Henry's language in this first phase of the play is remarkable:

> France being ours, we'll bend it to our awe
> Or break it all to pieces
>
> (I.ii.225–6)

he says after the decision for war has been made, and then sends his uncle Exeter to the French king with the message (delivered in our production as he sips tea from a china cup) that

> if you hide the crown
> Even in your hearts, there will he rake for it.
>
> (II.iv.97–8)

You can easily walk away with a romantic chivalric impression of this play, but there are some things about it that absolutely reveal the savagery of Elizabethan warfare, the chopping and hacking through armour that was necessary to kill people, the real sensation of blood on your hands. In such moments the fierce determination of the man is very clear, and it's a determination that doesn't have to be pushed; he *will* cut into their chests and rake around in there for the crown if that is where they hide it. 'This is what we'll do, so have a think, and get back to us' is the gist of Exeter's message. It's very simple: the most powerful things are always said simply. And once again in this embassy we see the politician's careful passing of responsibility: if you don't give in, the blood and tears and groans and cries will all be 'on your head' (II.iv.105).

Before Henry embarks for France he faces the conspiracy of Cambridge, Grey, and his friend Scroop. Having banished Falstaff at the end of the preceding play, it is perhaps a little surprising to discover that he has now allowed someone else to become his intimate. There is no scene in which to show this friendship, only Henry's lament that Scroop's treachery has destroyed it. I decided for rehearsal purposes that Scroop must have been the sort of person that the new king most admired: intelligent, balanced, wise, observant, 'not working with the eye without the ear' (II.ii.135) – a model member of the cabinet. One of the usual questions posed when you are working on a character is 'Who am I?'; it seems to me that 'Who do I want to be?' is much more interesting, and for Henry, I think, the answer was Scroop. This was the person with whom he shared his anxieties, who listened to his worries and gave advice, who knew 'the very bottom of his soul' (II.ii.97); and his betrayal really, really grates for Henry. His long speech reveals that he finds it almost impossible to believe that it has happened, so that all the questions, all the sarcasm, though seemingly directed at Scroop, are in a sense directed at himself and force him, for the future, to be distrustful of virtually everyone except Exeter:

> thy fall hath left a kind of blot
> To mark the full-fraught man and best endued
> With some suspicion.
>
> (II.ii.138–40)

The episode isolates him and from that moment on, whatever the difficulties or problems, he has no-one to talk to. If Scroop were still there I'm sure he wouldn't go wandering off on his own in the dark on the eve of Agincourt, talking to the men in disguise, soliloquizing, praying. The loneliness of the leader, the isolation of kingship, are brought into sharp focus by the destruction of this friendship.

Henry's political loneliness is to some extent reflected, of course, in the theatrical loneliness of the actor playing the role. Hamlet has Horatio to talk to, but there is no confidant for Henry. The responsibility for upholding the narrative line of the evening is always going to rest with the actors in the leading roles. You've got to get it right, and so your preparation in the wings before a scene, or your period of reflection after a scene, is inevitably that little bit more intense, that little bit more dogged, than for many others in the company. I felt this very much with Henry.

As Scroop and his fellows are dismissed to execution and Henry is facing away from the rest of the men, there is a moment when a chasm of loss begins to open up in front of him. But a statement about the beginning of the war is required, the television cameras are ready to roll, and he snaps out of his thoughts, re-arranges his expression, and turns to face the media with a polished address to the nation. The leader is required to put the needs of the few a long way behind the needs of the many, and he, after all, is only one of the few. What he feels is not important; whether he sleeps at night is not important: 'We doubt not of a fair and lucky war' (II.ii.184) – and off he goes to Harfleur.

I believe the soldiers simply *have* to be retreating when Henry begins 'Once more unto the breach' (III.i.1). That is the way Kenneth Branagh presents it in his film, the first time I recall seeing it done, and I remember thinking then that there is no other way to stage it. Our military adviser Richard Smedley, an ex-paratrooper, talked to us about the hundreds and hundreds of yards of running that is involved in getting into firing positions and advancing and retreating from them, all of this in the terrible palls of smoke and dust that hang in the air during a battle. So when the soldiers run in at the beginning of this scene we felt that they should hit the floor in utter exhaustion, unable to do any more. The problem with Henry's speech is that, though the soldiers may watch and listen to you intently, giving you all the energy they can, what they can actually say to help is absolutely nothing. So we decided to improvise the scene. It was great. One soldier flung down his gun, choking and throwing up as he refused to go back. Others began to respond to Henry's 'now attest / That those whom you call fathers did beget you' (III.i.22–3) by shouting 'Yea, come on' and flinging the 'bastards' charge at others. When I said

> And you, good yeomen,
> Whose limbs were made in England, show us here
> The mettle of your pasture
>
> (III.i.25–7)

one little group starting shouting at another 'They can't do it, they can't do it!' and the others shouted back. It was brilliant; we were energized, we were motivated and vocalized, and we spent the next couple of days of rehearsal working out a precise staging for the scene that preserved these energies and kept that conversation going. Indeed, that is exactly what 'Once more unto the breach' is: it's a conversation between Henry and his men in which you only hear Henry speak. That is how we got it onto the stage and I'm proud that we found a way of giving new reality to such famous lines.

For the threats to Harfleur a couple of scenes later we again depended on our military adviser, who said that we should use a microphone and loudspeakers. Although some audience members found this funny, the set-up we created was regarded as absolutely accurate by everyone from the military who came to see the production, with (they said) all the actors on stage looking and sounding like soldiers. After all, loudspeakers and microphones have been used to demoralize and threaten opposing armies since the Second World War. The same sense that what we were doing was accurate was shared by people connected to government who saw the production, and not just with regard to this scene, but to the cabinet meeting at the beginning and the way in which we switched in an instant from a public face for television to a private face with friends.

A television camera was used to record Henry's threats to Harfleur, but it was decided that I should signal for this to be cut as the threats get nastier. 'How yet resolves the Governor of the town?' (III.iii.1), Henry asks, and pauses for a reply. When none comes he continues, with the threat that Harfleur will 'in her ashes...lie burièd' (III.iii.9); and again he waits. When there is still no response the threats become more menacing and the politician in him starts to become uncomfortable with what he is having to do as a soldier, and he cuts the camera. The rapes and other atrocities committed by advancing armies, all well documented in modern warfare, are all here in Henry's threats, though my own view is that he is only trying to frighten the town. His conscience, and his stance towards God, make it inconceivable that he would stand by and let this happen, and though he threatens that he would not be able to prevent it, I believe he has the discipline of his army in absolute control.

That discipline was presented most vividly in our production, and perhaps most controversially, in the execution of Bardolph for robbing

17 Adrian Lester as King Henry V, *Henry V*, Act III, Scene i: 'Once more unto the breach, dear friends, once more.'

18 Adrian Lester as King Henry V, *Henry V*, Act III, Scene iii: 'Will you yield, and this avoid? / Or, guilty in defence, be thus destroyed?'

a church. In the text this takes place off stage and by the authority of Exeter, but many recent productions have chosen to show it on stage, often with Henry forced to confirm the order. Nick was keen that we should take this further, and in our production I shot Bardolph in the head with my own pistol. In the interests of creating a moment of shock and disbelief in performance, this obviously departs somewhat from the sort of standard army procedure we were elsewhere trying to emulate, though our military advisers were clear that execution might still be the ultimate fate, after all the charges and courts martial, of a soldier convicted of a serious crime. Here in the play, Henry knows that his former friend is certain to be executed, and rather than have him stood up in front of a wall, blindfolded, and shot, he takes on the responsibility himself and kills him instantaneously and painlessly. And he does it in front of his men, at a point where they are demoralized and weary and trying desperately to get away from the French army: 'You have robbed a church. Nobody in my army is going to do that. Bang!' It is an act of absolute political leadership, of cold-blooded, searing clarity. It is, for me, one of those moments that's on the end of the scale, and I feel that I really have to reach for it to make it believable. It also shows us another side of the multi-faceted character that Henry is. One by one he has to kill his friends because they betray the qualities of leadership and the elements of kingship that he must uphold in order to carry out his task.

Into the extraordinary mood created by the death of Bardolph comes, on his first visitation, the French herald Montjoy. After trying the usual rather chivalric way of doing this scene in rehearsal, we decided that Henry made rather a mess of this first encounter – something that I think his rather disjointed speech patterns reveal. He begins confidently enough, but then he starts to admit that 'my people are with sickness much enfeebled' and 'we would not seek a battle as we are' (III.vi.143, 162), then to correct himself, and then to go over it again, with his soldiers listening and wondering 'What the *hell* is wrong with you?'. About half way through the speech, at 'Go, therefore, tell thy master here I am' (III.vi.151), he seems to find a bit of a tack and runs with it for a few lines, but it soon peters out. He makes it to the end at last – 'So tell your master' (III.vi.164) – but he's floundering through most of the speech. Montjoy sees that, and his men see it; and Henry knows that they all see it. We decided, therefore, that the scene should end with me keeping my back to the soldiers and telling Gloucester to give the order to march; I simply cannot do it myself. When we discovered this route in rehearsal we decided it was the right one for us. Nearly everyone knows the play and knows that Henry V defeats the French, but Henry and his soldiers don't know that. Their absolute belief is that they are all going to die before Montjoy comes back. To play this line is to restore drama to the situation – as well as to send everyone out at the interval thinking to themselves that there's something very wrong here.

The absolute belief that he is going to die tomorrow is crucial to Henry's behaviour in the scenes before the battle. When he wanders out on his own, to a point from which he can see the French preparations, he is coming there to think about this, as are the other men he meets. He is very, very lonely at this point, painfully aware that, as king, he cannot be seen to question the leadership, or the cause, or to be worried about his own death or the deaths of his followers. Being muffled in the disguise of Erpingham's cloak allows him to be on his own and to be a normal man for a few moments. And in this state he meets Bates, Court, and Williams, who energetically reject his claim that the king is just a normal bloke, trying to do the right thing – reject it with mockery and derision. He doesn't respond to their questioning of his 'cause' (IV.i.128); he doesn't go into the rights and wrongs of the Salic Law with them, for they wouldn't listen if he did. But he does become intensely involved with their accusation that their deaths, and their sins, 'will be a black matter for the king that led them to it' (IV.i.140). So involved, indeed, does he become that in our production they leave him talking to himself as he goes on about 'God' and 'sin' (IV.i.164 ff.), until, perhaps a little grudgingly, they admit his conclusion that 'every subject's soul is his own' (IV.i.172). In reaching this conclusion Henry has listed some of the sins of which soldiers may die guilty: 'beguiling virgins', 'making the wars their bulwark' for 'pillage and robbery', 'premeditated murder' (IV.i.157–60). It is a remarkable fact that he is guilty of every one of them himself – even the last in the killing of Bardolph. He has completely cornered himself and the encounter with his soldiers ends in acrimony, very bitter and aggressive acrimony in our production.

However you do Shakespeare, Elizabethan or modern, if you do not have the presence of two things, death and God, firmly in mind, you will lose so much of the play. Henry comes out of this conversation firmly believing that he is guilty, before God, of leading his men to their deaths. As king, as leader, he is absolutely responsible; there can be no allowances, none. He has tried to worm his way out of it with his analogies of the servant miscarrying while on his master's errand, but it hasn't worked, and he gets angry at the people who force him to realize this. Then he gets angry at ceremony: 'What are you worth? You're worth nothing.'

Henry hates his job at this moment, but through the 'Upon the king' soliloquy (IV.i.223 ff.) – his only one – he arrives at a resolve, a resolve to be ready to die. It's not that he's positively prepared to die, but rather that he finds a quiet acceptance of its inevitability. For me, it's like someone going through therapy: when you get to the point of the problem there's a huge emotional surge from the patient. Henry resents the fact that the ordinary man can live his life as he wishes, and in our modern-dress production I found it appropriate to do this straight out to the audience; '*You* lot are far better off than me; you have it all so bloody easy.' And I tried to show that realization coming with all the bitterness that it would bring with it. Erpingham's little interruption is followed by the prayer, the prayer with the extraordinary surge of guilt – and tears, in our production – at his father's crime 'in compassing the crown' (IV.i.287). This seems to come from nowhere; no-one has mentioned his father, no-one, but this has apparently been churning away inside him. We all hope to achieve more than our fathers, and Henry has set enormous goals, for himself and for the country; and now he faces what he sees as certain death. The prayer has to be said before he dies; he has to get it off his chest before he is killed in tomorrow's battle. That is how it feels to me. And having done so, he is ready to accept his fate with no more worrying and no more forlorn hopes of escaping it. Accepting it makes him content with it, and in the 'Crispin, Crispian' speech he can share this new-found serenity with his men.

The Crispin's day speech comes, then, from this state of acceptance, this state of a kind of grace. He simply talks to his men and tells them that they are here to do a job, and that the job may go well for us, or it may not go well for us, but the point is the job and how we carry it out. He actually passes on to them at that moment something he believes himself about leadership, which is that your own needs don't matter; only the needs of the many matter. It's not (even though it's always thought of as such) a particularly rousing speech and I believe you may lose the reality of what's happening through it if you do it with bombast and a rising inflexion. It's the element of everyday conversation in it that I was anxious to find. Henry begins something in it that he finishes in the second encounter with Montjoy. This follows just after it, and returns to and develops many of its ideas. With his men at battle pitch (something every army commander needs to achieve – that fine line between getting the men worked up enough to kill or be killed but not tipping over into a frenzy that cannot be commanded), Henry now completely reverses his earlier failure to deal convincingly with Montjoy. Together he and his men confront the impudence of the herald's invitation that they should make 'a peaceful and a sweet retire' (IV.iii.86), with, in our modern-dress production, a recognizably soldierly response: 'Fuck off!'

Also made possible by our modern-dress production was our decision to stage the killing of the French prisoners. They were kneeling for mercy in front of the English soldiers, bags over their heads, not understanding anything that's being said, when Henry gives the order that 'every soldier kill his prisoners' (IV.vi.37). It's like a gang-land execution, and the soldiers refuse to do it – a situation that, according to our military advisers, happens quite often. There are so many wars happening around the world as you read this; without television cameras present, the rules of engagement are not always observed. The soldiers refuse to obey Henry's order and it is left to Llewellyn, fiercely supportive of the king, to carry it out on his own. This allowed Robert Blythe to take the presentation of Llewellyn a little further than usual and portray him as somebody who, cracking under the pressure of battle, becomes blindly patriotic.

Nick was very clear that he did not want my order to kill the prisoners to be an emotional reaction to the news of the deaths of York and Suffolk. It must be a different facet of Henry: he grieves for his lost companions in arms, completes that process, then he moves to dealing with the fact that 'The French have reinforced their scattered men' (IV.vi.36). He therefore needs to use the soldiers guarding the prisoners in active fighting and the order to kill is as cold and as logical as possible in the heat of battle. We felt that we needed to push the moment that far: the play is presenting both a national hero and an anti-war agenda, and the audience must see Henry in relation to the two extremes.

That is why we decided not to offer the usual response to Henry's reading out of the list of French dead, with his men doffing caps and bowing their heads in respect. We thought they should behave like real soldiers would on hearing that they had killed the people who had been trying to kill them, and had sardonically sent a herald to suggest their surrender; the people who had killed York and Suffolk, and, behind their backs, too scared to face them, slaughtered the boys guarding the luggage. The second reaction, of course, is 'O, no, we shouldn't smile', but the first, the gut reaction, is relief that you've killed those who would have killed you, and Nick decided to let the two develop together.

With the victory won, Henry comes, in military uniform, formally to accept the French surrender. It's not negotiation, which is why we chose the uniform rather than a suit; he has come to make sure that it all goes through without him having to give an inch. He is pushing them all the time to accept the terms, to end the miseries that Burgundy describes, but to do that they

> must buy that peace
> With full accord to all our just demands.
> (v.ii.70–1)

This even extends to the requirement that the French king, who, in our production, was in grief for the loss of his son, should call Henry 'son and heir', in both French and Latin, in all correspondence with him. Henry is utterly implacable here – and again manages to shift the blame: it's not him, but the French king's failure to give in to '*all* our just demands', that is holding up the agreement. And in the mean time the English 'peacemakers' are carving up the country and stripping its assets, solving those national financial problems that prompted the invasion in the first place. (History repeats itself.) Henry is so ruthless yet so slick here; it's in this scene that I feel he gets to be as oily a politician as anywhere in the play.

Then, suddenly, we get to see another facet of Henry – or, rather, several – in the wooing scene with Katherine. It is the only time in the play that he gets to speak to a woman and he needs to move through several of his facets before he finds the right key. It's a wonderful bonus of a scene: it enables you to play the rest of the piece as hard as you like, because you know that this scene of humour and comedy is coming at the end, when you get to stretch some very different acting muscles.

When we started looking for the heart of the scene in rehearsal the question we set ourselves was 'How would a modern princess behave if the leader of an invading army turned up and asked to marry her, in order truly to secure the peace?' This question gives the whole thing a much tougher mood. I think Henry understands French much better than he pretends to, but to conduct the scene in Kate's language would concede control of the conversation to her. He therefore has to cope instead with her inarticulate speech patterns, and frequently with her silence. She is polite, but unimpressed and resistant, and he jumps through all sorts of hoops trying to amuse her and to soften her a little. But it doesn't work. His patience is whittled down until he finally, brilliantly, comes into his own and states the basic facts of the situation: that the agreement has been made, and that even if it's not love, why don't they just strike a bargain and produce an heir. He tells her that he is an honest and honourable man and offers her a true heart that is worth more than a fad of love based on a pretty face. He tells her that he cannot gasp out his eloquence, and is extremely eloquent; that a speaker is only a prattler and then delivers a beautiful speech. Henry wants to create an empire, and he needs her agreement, and her loins, to produce the heir. He doesn't want a forced marriage and a pregnancy that is the result of a kind of rape; he wants her happily pregnant, for the good of the child. I don't believe he's genuinely in love with Kate for one moment; I believe he understands how bad she must feel and that he uses that to try to charm her into the honeymoon suite. He wants to make sure that his line continues and, consummate politician that he is, if he needs to be in love to get the job done, then be in love he will. He ends the play satisfied that he has achieved all that he set out to achieve. He will never know what his and Kate's child, the heir he so desperately wanted, King Henry VI, did with that achievement – but that's another story, and another play.

Joan of Arc in Part 1 of *Henry VI*, and Margaret of Anjou in Parts 1, 2, and 3 of *Henry VI* and in *Richard III*

FIONA BELL

FIONA BELL played Joan of Arc and Margaret of Anjou in Michael Boyd's productions of the three parts of *Henry VI* and of *Richard III* at the Swan Theatre in Stratford during the winter of 2000–2001. The productions were later seen at the Power Centre for the Performing Arts at Ann Arbor, Michigan, before they moved to London where they played at the Young Vic. These were Fiona Bell's first roles for the RSC. Her other theatre work includes *Macbeth*, *Oleanna*, *The Master Builder*, *Cyrano de Bergerac*, *Pride and Prejudice*, and *Medea*. Among her films are *Trainspotting*, *Gregory's Two Girls*, *Duck*, and *Between Dreams* and her extensive work in television includes *Soldier, Soldier*, *Truth or Dare*, and *Stand and Deliver*.

Before I played Joan of Arc and Margaret of Anjou, my experience of acting Shakespeare had been limited to Lady Macduff and a fairy in *A Midsummer Night's Dream*. My reaction was, on the one hand, delight at being offered such a chance and, on the other, feelings of complete inadequacy. I had, however, worked with Michael Boyd several times before in Glasgow, when he ran the Tron Theatre, and I tend to have a fairly Pavlovian response to Michael: he asks me to work for him; I say yes.

On a very basic level I had a lot of work to do: verse-speaking, speaking (and I'm not joking – I'd done mostly television for a couple of years and my voice was woeful), and sword-fighting (which had to be convincing, as I had to win). So the initial shaping of my performance was really informed by fear: I felt like a rabbit in the headlights. Fellow actors would later remark on how calm they thought I had been during rehearsals, although I later developed urticaria, a very unpleasant skin condition brought on by various things, including stress. It worked out all right, though I was put on large doses of steroids for a month or so – fantastic for the battle-scenes!

An early decision we made was that Joan would have a Scottish accent (my own) and that Margaret would have a 'Received Pronunciation' English accent. At Michael's behest I did try to play Joan too in 'RP' for the first few days, but I didn't think it worked. I felt like the principal boy in a pantomime. The Scottish accent seemed immediately to make her working- or peasant-class next to the aristocrats of the French and English courts. Besides that, I loved getting to roar from the battlements in my own accent:

> Advance our waving colours on the walls;
> Rescued is Orleans from the English.
> (Part One, I.vi.1–2)

I never even thought of playing Margaret with a French accent (which doesn't say much for my imagination) and by the time I heard that other actresses had successfully done so, it was a bit late to go down that road – though I think that a French accent on top of everything else would have finished me off for good.

Even a bad job is made more bearable if you have a nice frock. This was a good job and I had about seven or eight nice frocks, so costume-wise I was very happy. There was much more of an organic process in the costume design than I had ever known previously – more so for Joan, as Margaret's costumes were much more elaborate affairs and therefore had to be designed well in advance. I wanted to avoid any clichés when it came to Joan's outfit, and as I had read that there is no authenticated portrait or bust of her in existence I felt that there was a degree of freedom in our choices. Obviously I had to be practical, for there was so much running and jumping about, but I wanted her clothes to reflect both her past and her future. We ended up with a light-coloured, floor-length tunic which was quite ambiguous as it looked like an acolyte's habit but could also, at a pinch, be reminiscent of a shepherdess's clothes. When Joan went into battle we added knee-length boots, a breastplate, and a sword-belt over this tunic. Obviously the costume wasn't particularly feminine, but it did pronounce my shape, which I felt was important because of Joan's manipulative use of her sexuality.

The casting of the same actress as Joan and as Margaret has a significant bearing on the interpretation of the parts, especially that of Margaret. In this production Joan informed Margaret throughout. Michael had transposed two scenes (Part One, Act Five, Scenes Three and Four), which resulted in Margaret's first entrance coming directly on the heels of Joan's burning. I would appear, literally in a puff of smoke, as though emerging from the embers, a new, more advanced model of Joan. The metaphysical world is ever present in these plays, so the idea of a reincarnation is well within the bounds of 'reality'. But even if you do believe in such a thing, it is still physically impossible as the two women were contemporaries. It was the impression that this idea gave, however, rather than the actuality, that was important. It added another dimension to Margaret and reinforced the milieu of the plays, the under-carriage of which is a never-ending, nigh-on-apocalyptic struggle between good and evil.

This 'dual' casting was a feature of the productions: basically bad characters turned into other bad characters and good ones turned into good. Because the plays span such a long period of time and involve so many characters this obvious logic to the casting worked practically as well as thematically. So the same people were continually popping up to wreak havoc, albeit in another guise. It seemed to cast a net of predestination over the whole thing, with all the protagonists eventually wrestling helplessly with their individual lots, pawns in the greater scheme of events which hurtle them, England, and the audience into the devastation of *Richard III*.

The similarities between the two women are striking: they are both young French women, fiercely intelligent and precocious, desperate for power in a male-dominated society and prepared to do almost anything to achieve their goals. These similarities, along with the synchronicity of their departure and arrival, would seem to point to its being intentional that Margaret appears to take over where Joan leaves off. Michael's choice certainly emphasized this, and also carried over Joan's supernatural awareness into Margaret. (This is an idea that I didn't fully understand until we came to *Richard III*, so I'll come back to that later.)

Shakespeare's Joan of Arc is so far removed from the present-day image of her that I found it infuriating, and to an extent unhelpful, to read up on her. I almost had to forget that I was playing an historical character, as the alternative information in the history books ended up leading me in directions that were ultimately of no use. Having said that, however, there were certain things that I came across that did stick in my mind and help me imaginatively. One of these was her name, 'Joan la Pucelle'. This was the name that the real Joan chose for herself when she embarked on her adventures and it is the name that Shakespeare uses for her. It's an interesting choice on her part, for although it means 'virgin' it has paradoxical connotations of innocence and nubility. Marina Warner describes it as 'the equivalent of the Hebrew "alma", used of both the Virgin Mary and the dancing girls in Solomon's harem in the Bible. It denotes a passage of time, not a permanent condition. It is a word that looks forward to a change in state.' I found this concept very useful when trying to plot Joan's journey through the play, as the idea of her moving from one life or state into another gave me somewhere to hang her outsized ambitions. Because the received wisdom of the time among the English was that Joan was unquestionably evil, she is, I think, written to be fairly two-dimensional. There is very little in the text that gave me an insight into her beyond her supposed nationalism. There is only one scene that shows her in a more personal light. A poor shepherd enters, just as she is about to burn, claiming to be her father. She denies him:

> Decrepit miser! Base ignoble wretch!
> I am descended of a gentler blood;
> Thou art no father nor no friend of mine.
> (Part One, v.iv.7–9)

He in turn berates her and then utters the immortal 'O, burn her, burn her! Hanging is too good' (v.iv.33). Now I may be wrong, but I should think that even by fifteenth-century standards that's a bit rough, and certainly not the treatment one would expect from a loving father. I started to build a picture in my mind of a quite unhappy child. Her treatment of her father is either delusional or sadistic, and for whatever reason she has felt the need to turn her back on her family and reinvent herself in a completely different world. I was aware that the scene could be interpreted in another way: she may be telling the truth, and if so this is an attempt by the English further to discredit her before they murder her. Joan is such a convincing liar that it is a decision the director has to make, and in the end the shepherd was cut completely. It was more important to me, however, that I had at least some normal familial information that helped me to create a background for her and stopped me from playing her as purely 'bad'. To an extent, therefore, I saw her as a damaged teenager, certainly a bit more dangerous than your average adolescent, but only because she has magical powers; strip those away, and you are left with opportunism and precociousness. It was not unusual for young women of that time to claim divinity. It usually occurred around about puberty, when an arranged marriage would be looming. If they were believed it allowed them to circumnavigate the impending marriage and children, if only for a while, and gave them access to the public arena which otherwise would have been denied them completely.

Rehearsal time was spent plotting Joan's emotional and mental journey. I know that sounds very obvious as this is what any actor would do when rehearsing a role, but while Joan's physical journey through the play is very clear, I found her emotional one to be less so. I think this is partly due to the reasons I have already mentioned, but it is mainly to do with the secrecy in which she has surrounded herself because of her initial duplicity. Everything she says and does is based on a lie: she has not seen the Virgin Mary, but has instead been calling on evil spirits to help her. This isn't divulged in the text until the end of the play, so Michael clarified it by having her 'fiends' appear whenever she needed a show of physical or mental dexterity. The play isn't about whether Joan of Arc is good or not: as I have said, an Elizabethan audience would have expected her to be a villain. By objectifying her magic in the shape of the 'fiends', Michael relieved me of the burden of having to give a modern audience hints as to her true nature.

The first time Joan appears, at the beginning of Part One, she is putting on a pious act, feigning the sort of bold timidity of one who is driven by, and herself given over to, a higher power. Behind this façade she is undoubtedly self-possessed – she could hardly be otherwise, for this is an amazing feat to even think of pulling off. Her confidence, nonetheless, grows apace with her military successes and her ensuing martial and sexual power over the Dauphin. Shakespeare tends to the negative interpretation of 'Pucelle' by intimating that she and the Dauphin are sleeping with each other from early on in the play. It is truly damning of him to do this, as it would have been imperative to the real Joan that she was believed to be sexually naïve since this would have been a prerequisite of her credibility. It is thought that she may have had anorexic tendencies in order to stop her periods. Amenorrhea would have been the desired effect as, for her contemporaries, it would only have added to her holiness, meaning that she remained in an untainted state, free from corrupting sexual knowledge. Michael went one step further than Shakespeare and intimated that she was in fact sleeping with several members of the French court. This was not

19 Fiona Bell as Joan of Arc with Aidan McArdle as the Dauphin, *1 Henry VI*, Act I, Scene ii; 'And while I live, I'll ne'er fly from a man.'

a moral judgement or a comment on her sexual appetites, but rather showed just how expedient she was politically.

The turning point in Joan's fortunes comes after the recapture of Rouen by the English when she manipulates the Duke of Burgundy into turning back to the French. She is so certain of her powers that she informs the French leaders:

> Then thus it must be; this doth Joan devise:
> By fair persuasions, mixed with sugared words,
> We shall entice the Duke of Burgundy
> To leave the Talbot and to follow us.
> (Part One, III.iii.17–20)

She is at the height of her power, and also of her arrogance. She shows the French her true colours, using the same tactics as she did to convince Charles of her divinity at the beginning of the play, and gives a bravura performance in emotionally hi-jacking the duke. Michael added to this by having her also show them what is behind her power; showing off, she treats them to a bit of a magic act, conjuring up the English troops. Once the duke has capitulated, however, and been accepted back into the fold, she exclaims 'Done like a Frenchman...', and follows this with an aside to the audience: '...turn and turn again' (Part One, III.iii.85). These are hardly the words of a patriot. Up until now she has been given the benefit of the doubt that she has done everything for the national cause, but this is the real Joan talking. Like a lot of politicians, her 'cause' is a smoke-screen, hiding a simple thirst for power. If her journey is only about her blind pursuit of power, however, and not bedded in something more altruistic, then, once she has gained power, she will have nowhere left to go.

A few scenes later, when Talbot is killed at Bordeaux, the French come across his body and that of his son. Sir William Lucy enters to survey the bodies and begins to reel off all the titles that Talbot possessed. The other French leaders seem inclined to be respectful, but Joan instead lambasts him with

> Here's a silly stately style indeed!
> The Turk, that two and fifty kingdoms hath,
> Writes not so tedious a style as this.
> Him that thou magnifiest with all these titles
> Stinking and flyblown lies here at our feet.
> (Part One, IV.vii.72–6)

Apart from thus berating him, I ended up laughing at Lucy throughout the whole scene. He refuses to give in to her and continues to venerate the dead soldier, and they end up trying to outdo each other, her laughter becoming more and more deranged. I think it is very telling that the major cracks begin to show once Talbot is taken out of the equation. He has been her nemesis and represents all that the English purport to be – but aren't. He has been brave and courageous, unquestioningly performing his duties to the crown. He is the antithesis of Joan. Prior to Lucy's entrance she had been telling the other French leaders of her meeting on the battlefield with the young John Talbot:

> Once I encountered him and thus I said:
> 'Thou maiden youth, be vanquished by a maid.'
> But with a proud majestical high scorn
> He answered thus: 'Young Talbot was not born
> To be the pillage of a giglot wench.'
> So, rushing in the bowels of the French,
> He left me proudly, as unworthy fight.
>
> (Part One, IV.vii.37–43)

Something in Joan knows that she will never achieve the status she needs. She is put face to face with pure nobility, who can see her for what she is, or for what she feels herself to be. I think it crushes her, and the only way she can hide her fear is to laugh at Lucy, who in Joan's mind is being quintessentially English, with his pompous declarations. I think she knows that the end is in sight, so when the rest of the French commanders are all rejoicing that Paris is in revolt I wanted her to loathe them and their simplicity. She knows that they wouldn't have got anywhere without her, and now she thinks herself above and beyond them. And then they are surrounded. She calls on her 'fiends', who appear but refuse to help her. It's as if they have realized that she isn't the girl they thought she was; she's no longer up to the job and she is dismissed. She dies very badly and I think Shakespeare intends her to be seen as cowardly at the end. She jumps between claiming to be chaste and holy, having been sent by God, and telling them she is pregnant, in a bid to escape burning. Michael didn't want me to show a lot of fear in all these rantings; instead he wanted her to believe her lies, unconsciously moving between the opposing personalities of martyr and victim. Under this extreme pressure, her normal strategy of deception goes into overdrive and finally into disfunction.

The burning scene was directed to be very vicious. With the words 'And yet, forsooth, she is a virgin pure!' (Part One, v.iv.83) York would stab me in the genitals and show his hand with the blood on it, ironically suggesting that he has broken her hymen. Their cruelty helps set these Englishmen apart from the likes of Henry V and the two John Talbots, and shows they are no better than the young girl they are torturing. It also foreshadows York's death in Part Three when Margaret tortures and kills him. I think her final words are maybe all that we ever hear of the real Joan, free of any artifice or watchfulness. She knows she has no chance of surviving and she can at last give some rein to her vast resentment. She screams at her enemies:

> May never glorious sun reflex his beams
> Upon the country where you make abode;
> But darkness and the gloomy shade of death
> Environ you, till mischief and despair
> Drive you to break your necks or hang yourselves!
>
> (Part One, v.iv.87–91)

Michael's transposing of the burning scene and the Margaret/Suffolk wooing scene meant that I entered as Margaret literally thirty seconds after the last of Joan's executioners had left the stage. When we played the Swan in Stratford I used to have to descend on the stake into the trap and, as soon as I could jump off the ladder, dash up a few flights of stairs, outside and round the building to a tent that had been erected to mask the main double-doors entrance onto the stage. Once there, I had to change clothes, put on make-up, stop sweating, and get my breath back before entering onto the stage looking and behaving like a princess. I always got there on time, but was never very sure about the princess part.

At first I found the metamorphosis very confusing and it threw up a lot of questions which may sound a little stupid now. Was I just Margaret, or Joan in Margaret's body, or Margaret with a vague sense of Joan? And then I realized that it didn't matter: the effect that Michael wanted from the transformation was beyond my control; it created an 'otherness' about Margaret, but that was a by-product and could only affect the audience, not the actors involved. I had to play the two women as separate entities but at the same time had to allow them to be the same person when the production dictated. Michael used to tell me to keep the memory of the burning with me when I was playing Margaret, not as a conscious, front-of-the-brain thought, but tucked away at the back, subconsciously letting it fuel her hatred and ambitions.

So Margaret/Joan arrives in England, and this time round she has the right accent and trappings to get straight in at the top. Over the course of the next three plays she changes from an impetuous young woman to a warrior queen and finally to an outcast, hated, feared, and pitied by the new generation at court. Unlike Joan with her nationalistic cause, Margaret cannot, and does not, hide her desire for power. I felt that where Joan was consciously manipulative, Margaret just is – it is part of her make-up. She doesn't just want to be all-powerful, she fully expects to be so.

Although she uses her sexuality manipulatively, she doesn't seem to perceive her sex as a hindrance. The lords make it clear that they don't appreciate a woman being so forward with her opinions, but she never complains or thinks herself at a disadvantage because she is one. Sometimes when I was playing her I felt more like a phenomenon than a person. It felt as though she had no choice in her actions, but as if her body and mind were enslaved by the will of her spirit. I think it was Michael's intention that Margaret was, to an extent, a conduit for evil. Joan was alive and had crossed the Channel and until we encounter Richard III no-one can match her for badness.

Margaret's time of influence in the English court revolves round three men: Henry VI, the Duke of Suffolk, and her son Edward. Her relationship with Suffolk supersedes and dramatically takes precedence over her relationship with Henry. Their relationship is cemented in France, where she is married by proxy to the king. It always intrigued me that she would have gone through a wedding ceremony with Suffolk as the stand-in. We had decided that they would have started their affair before they arrived back in Britain. The idea that she has in a sense married Suffolk in France appealed to me, mainly because of the impact he has on her life, and also because he is already married. In a way it would be the only chance they would ever have of sanctifying their relationship, which although illicit was nonetheless heartfelt.

I had read accounts of other productions where it was made clear from the start of Part Two that Henry immediately disappoints Margaret on a physical level. Our Henry, however, was very attractive physically, so it wasn't really an option for us, and I think it led us to something quite interesting. Margaret and Suffolk are kindred spirits, so much so that they both think that they will manipulate the other to gain power within the court – but still carry on an intense love affair. But Henry and Margaret are polar opposites. Michael encouraged an almost perverse attraction between them, in that Margaret is drawn to the thing she knows she can never be and vice versa, with Henry ever hopeful that he can reform her. We decided that she should be having a sexual relationship with Henry as well as with Suffolk. I liked the idea that Margaret would be totally capable of separating and justifying her feelings for the two men, and in as much as Henry is being deceived, then so too is Suffolk. As our Henry was in no way the weakling that is often portrayed, it made his love for her more believable; and having a significant bond with Henry, who is, after all, the king, leaves her relationship with Suffolk open to other influences.

Margaret's dislike of the English court and her hatred of Gloucester and his wife seemed to me to stem more from an inferiority complex than from just her blind desire for power. Although their backgrounds are very different, it is another feature she shares with Joan, and like Joan it is the only real impetus, apart from her innate badness, that I could find to explain her initial resentment. It is common for characters throughout the trilogy to use her impoverished background as a means of insulting her. She herself refers to it only once, during her tirade to Suffolk against the Duchess of Gloucester:

> She sweeps it through the court with troops of ladies,
> More like an empress than Duke Humphrey's wife.
> Strangers in court do take her for the queen.
> She bears a duke's revenues on her back,
> And in her heart she scorns our poverty.
>
> (Part Two, i.iii.75–9)

I think her real self-image, like Joan's, is so slight and yet her ego so great that she can brook very little criticism. She dislikes Gloucester because of his influence with Henry and quickly realizes that he needs removing; but he also offends her personally. In the first scene he cannot hide his shock at finding out about the loss of Maine and Anjou to her father, in return for her hand. She is thus immediately at odds with Gloucester as he cannot hide this reaction and is so honest. In the later court scenes again Gloucester is the only one who openly defies her and tries to put her in her place. Gloucester's wife is cut from the same cloth as Margaret, and although her removal to the Isle of Man marks the beginning of the end for Gloucester, Margaret wants to be rid of

20 Fiona Bell as Queen Margaret with David Oyelowo as King Henry VI, *2 Henry VI*, Act I, Scene i: 'A world of earthly blessings to my soul, / If sympathy of love unite our thoughts.'

her for personal reasons also. It is this mixing of personal and public politics that gives the plays their richness and makes them such a joy to act. The court scenes proved very arduous to rehearse as there are always so many different stories going on at once, and the blocking, which ultimately looked so simple, was at first impossible to pin down, such was the complexity of everyone's objectives. Part Two really is Margaret's summer: she is in a position to exert real power, she has Suffolk as both her lover and her tutor in deception, and she has the problem of what to do with Gloucester as her new learning ground.

She cuts her teeth on the exile of the Duchess, which is mostly Suffolk's doing anyway, but she ends up taking charge of Gloucester's disposal. At the beginning of Act Three, Scene One she gives a Joan-like performance while trying to persuade the king of Gloucester's dishonesty – with obvious help from Suffolk; but at the end of the scene she breaks away and alone suggests that they murder Gloucester. She realizes, after Henry's damning speech, that the fair trial that Henry will give his uncle will probably not condemn him, so she takes the matter into her own hands:

> Believe me, lords, were none more wise than I –
> And yet herein I judge mine own wit good –
> This Gloucester should be quickly rid the world,
> To rid us from the fear we have of him.
>
> (Part Two, III.i.231–4)

It's a highly enjoyable scene to play, all these would-be murderers coming up with seemingly good and valid reasons why one of the best men in the kingdom should die, and pretending they are all doing it purely to ensure the safety of the king. Although they all feel their personal grievances so strongly, I sometimes felt that they weren't as aware of their actions as they thought: like all good liars, I think they partly believe their lies.

If Margaret takes charge in this scene, when she is pleading Suffolk's innocence in the aftermath of Gloucester's death, she has achieved fantastic confidence and is on flying form. When Henry points the finger at Suffolk for the murder, Suffolk is, for once, at a loss and it is Margaret who attempts to come to the rescue. Michael used to describe her speeches in Act Three, Scene Two as an aria. She makes a very astute choice very quickly: in defending Suffolk she makes herself the victim, saying that if Henry can condemn Suffolk then he must also be able to condemn her, as she was as true a friend to Gloucester as Suffolk was. Moreover, if he can care so much for Gloucester and so little for her pain at being dubbed a traitor, then it is obvious that he doesn't love her and their marriage is totally one-sided. Talk about changing the subject! The tension while playing this scene was excruciating, and as much as I enjoyed it I was always willing everyone to leave the stage so that I could get on with Suffolk's departure, where all the tension could be released in her upset.

In Suffolk's leaving scene Margaret has a speech that comes as close to a soliloquy as she ever gets. In the midst of her upset at Suffolk's banishment, Vaux enters and instead of letting him pass, she can't help questioning him about his destination. He tells her that her ally, Cardinal Beaufort, is on the point of death and that he's off to tell the king. It is here that she realizes that she doesn't need Suffolk as much as she thought she did. After Vaux's exit she says:

> Ay me! What is this world! What news are these!
> But wherefore grieve I at an hour's poor loss,
> Omitting Suffolk's exile, my soul's treasure?
> Why only, Suffolk, mourn I not for thee,
> And with the southern clouds contend in tears,
> Theirs for the earth's increase, mine for my sorrows?
> (Part Two, III.ii.380–5)

Instead of delivering this straight to Suffolk, I played it away from him, out, as though she is thinking aloud and it is therefore a revelation rather than a comment. Up until this point she has been trying to calm Suffolk down, telling him he must go but not being able to let him; but suddenly her resolve stiffens and she becomes adamant that he must go. He has also just broken down in front of her, in a way confessing that he cares more for her than for the power she gave him access to, and this is not the Suffolk that Margaret is used to, or necessarily likes. She realizes that she has the power and self-control to carry on the game-plan alone. Suffolk's final words to her are:

> A jewel, locked into the woefullest cask
> That ever did contain a thing of worth.
> Even as a spitted bark so sunder we;
> This way fall I to death.

And she completes his line with 'This way for me' (Part Two, III.ii. 409–12).

Even though it is very painful, she knows that she can carry on; 'this way' signifies the way back to the court and its politics. She knows that this is the world she was meant to inhabit. In the same instant that Suffolk's political life ends, she reaches political and emotional maturity. He has been her teacher in this new world, but she no longer needs him. I loved playing this scene, as it seemed pivotal to an understanding of Margaret, both of her past and future. We are given a glimpse of their relationship, away from the court, and witness that what has fuelled their ambitions has not just been their mutual lust for power and for each other, but also real affection. Their actions have still been despicable in that they planned and committed Gloucester's murder – I'm not letting them off the hook – but the fact that we are allowed to see their frailties makes them at once more human and more understandable, and therefore even more shocking. Up to this point Margaret's cleverness has been impetuous and nasty, but in this scene its tone is much wiser. She comes of age and is shrewd enough in her politics, personal and public, to accept it immediately, and act upon it.

A scene later Suffolk is murdered. Margaret goes temporarily mad with grief, holding and caressing his severed head, openly displaying her love for him in front of Henry. Henry finally acknowledges her with:

> How now, madam?
> Still lamenting and mourning for Suffolk's death?
> I fear me, love, if that I had been dead,
> Thou wouldst not have mourned so much for me.
> (Part Two, IV.iv.21–4)

Henry's and Margaret's relationship has entered a new phase. Michael used to describe Suffolk as Joan/Margaret's only friend. I had a marked reaction to this idea. It was Michael's way of bringing me back to the human being and in this instance, I think, the little girl. The only person that truly understood and liked her is taken away and the shock of it catapults Margaret into a new, very clear and harsh, reality. There is no need for deception any more. She knows that Henry loves her, and because of his Christian beliefs will never leave her. She has accepted that her place in the world is with Henry, so when she replies to her husband 'No, my love; I should not mourn, but die for thee' (Part Two, IV.iv.25) she is being wryly honest with him. Her double meaning is that she feels that part of her has died along with Suffolk, which she has allowed to happen. But she also means that she must stay with Henry until her death, because she is spiritually aware of the path her life must take. The next time we see her she has emerged from her cocoon of grief and undergone her dramatic transformation into the warrior-queen of Part Three. In the place of prettifying make-up I tried to harden her look. Michael wanted me to become gradually more and more physically androgynous. Gone were all the low-cut red numbers that I had worn up until this point, and instead I had a very severe, high-necked, black dress which I wore for all of Part Three, unless I was in battle dress. I thought it looked as though she was in continual mourning, either for Suffolk or for a part of herself. With Suffolk's death she eschews her overt sexuality and instead puts herself on a level playing-field with the men. She knows that she can be as ruthless and brutal as any of them and feels no need to hide it.

Chronologically the plays don't really add up. Part Two ends with the Yorkists about to chase Henry to London, there to claim the throne. Part Three starts with them entering the council chamber on their arrival. Meanwhile Margaret has produced a son and heir in Prince Edward, who is already about sixteen or seventeen. At no time in Part Two was there an opportunity for her to be pregnant and give birth, for the sequence of events happens so rapidly. We did try to plot it in near the beginning, in the petitioners' scene with Suffolk, but it would have been too ambiguous as we were playing the scene as if we were definitely sleeping together. Although historically there was some real-life speculation about Edward's parentage, there is no reference made to it in the play. And Part Three revolves so much around Henry's and Margaret's relationship with their son, that any doubt over his parentage would have been confusing and unplayable. So, at the beginning of the third play I was suddenly a mother, when a week previously I hadn't been.

Margaret dominates the relationship with her son Edward. For Margaret alone the production of an heir would have been highly desirable as it would have strengthened the Lancastrian claim to the throne and thereby prologued her own influence at court. For Margaret/Joan, Edward, as a man, embodies what they can never be, and in some way legitimizes their struggle with the world. The rage and hatred she displays on hearing that he has been disinherited is so monumental, and her subsequent torture and murder of York so sadistic, that I was glad of the added layer of Joan to give me some extra fuel. York's death was directed to be on a par with the burning of Joan in terms of physical cruelty. Where York mutilates Joan, Michael had Margaret's henchmen slashing at York with their knives throughout his speech. If Margaret eschewed her sensuality with Suffolk's death, I think it is replaced in Part Three with a visceral delight in the pain of her enemies. I thought she should be practically salivating when she is humiliating York and definitely be sexually aroused. She has complete power over her own, and Joan's, oldest enemy and in a sense has returned once more to the battlefield. When the worst crime of the tetralogy is replayed against her in the murder of Edward, she still has no remorse for Clifford's killing of Rutland and her emotional torture of York. I think her hatred of them is so strong and deeply rooted that she almost sees them as less than human and believes that the killing of a young child belonging to the York household is less offensive than the killing of her child. She is at the apex of her powers in this part of the plays. What was very liberating about playing Margaret was her complete lack of doubt or guilt. I know that she is morally reprehensible, but, that aside, her mental wiring is superb. She suffers a lot of hard knocks in this play, but she never gives in. It is only when they kill her son that she admits defeat. But even in that she shows incredible strength when she orders, and then begs, her enemies to kill her. Any mother would feel that she didn't want to outlive her children, the pain would be so great, but I felt that there should be a quality in Margaret's need to die that was very calm. After everything she's been through and endured, I wanted to give her a real clarity about this being the final straw and that she, as Joan and Margaret, just wants it all to stop now. But when death is denied her and she is forced to live, something in her gives way. When she laments over the absence of her great enemy Richard, the irony is just delicious:

> Hard-favoured Richard; Richard, where art thou?
> Thou art not here; murder is thy alms-deed;
> Petitioners for blood thou ne'er puttest back.
> (Part Three, v.v.78–80)

Once we got onto *Richard III*, I was able to realize the true extent of what her continued existence meant. Rather than its being insanity, Michael wanted her to have entered onto another plain of consciousness. He

kept telling me that she was now 'Old Testament', with all the physical and mental trappings she had acquired stripped away. I felt as if
her true spirit had been laid bare. She had come home, back to Joan,
back to the person who knows how to connect with elemental forces.
So where Joan had had a little bag of talismans – animal bones with
which to call up her spirit helpers – Margaret carried the bones of
her dead son, over which I delivered her prophetic curses. (Rehearsals
with the bones were very interesting, proving that most people don't
know a tibia from a fibula, and even in performance I would often have
his pelvis upside down, or his thigh-bone coming out of his shoulder
socket.)

Margaret is suddenly described by Richard as 'withered hag' and 'foul
wrinkled witch' (*Richard III*, I.iii.163,214), and although traditionally
this part is played by an older actress, there is nothing else to suggest
that she has aged significantly, apart from the stage direction 'Enter old
Queen Margaret' (*Richard III*, I.iii.108) – and that could well be the
doing of an overly descriptive stage-manager. Again it is hard to gauge
how much time is actually meant to have passed since Part Three, but
from the tender ages of the princes it seems safe to say roughly ten years.
Richard's comments could still be accurate, though: life has battered
her and she is far removed from the woman she once was, physically as
well as mentally. The clothes I wore were reminiscent of Joan's, with the
same style of tunic, but black, longer, and more bedraggled. My hair
was matted with dirt and I had rotten teeth, and on my back I carried
Edward's bones. What truly defines her, however, is her pain from the
loss of Edward, who Michael had significantly had tied to her with a
piece of rope. In her final scene, when she gives advice to Elizabeth on
how to hate her enemies, Michael had me hand over the bones to the
new queen. Elizabeth is now grief-stricken for the death of her sons,
and Margaret, somewhat arrogantly, is now 'officially' handing over
the mantle of queenship; and in order to be a queen she must learn
how to objectify her pain and use it as a weapon. Margaret begins this
scene still full of the bitterness we witnessed in Act One, Scene Three,
abusing the two women mercilessly. But when she turns her attention to
Elizabeth she trips herself up. When she reaches 'Who sues and kneels
and says "God save the Queen"?' (*Richard III*, IV.iv.94) I think she is
in real trouble, for she realizes that she is describing herself. Michael
helped this along by cutting the next section of the speech (it is just a
list and fairly repetitive) until:

21 Fiona Bell as Queen Margaret, *Richard III*, Act I, Scene iii: 'Witness my son, now in the shade of death, / Whose bright outshining beams thy cloudy wrath / Hath in eternal darkness folded up.'

Thus hath the course of justice wheeled about
And left thee but a very prey to time,
Having no more but thought of what thou wast,
To torture thee the more, being what thou art.
                                    (*Richard III*, IV.iv.105–8)

I played this as self-revelatory. It is the first and only time that Margaret admits that she has lost power and has no chance of retrieving it. Until this point I can almost imagine her having some game-plan that she erroneously believes will still help the lost Lancastrian cause. It takes the raw pain of the other women to make her crack and give in. She at last sees herself reflected in someone else and she has to admit defeat, just like Joan seeing herself in the eyes of the young John Talbot. I sometimes found her final speech quite unbearable to say. It is the only time she simply gives something back:

Forbear to sleep the nights, and fast the days;
Compare dead happiness with living woe;
Think that thy babes were sweeter than they were
And he that slew them fouler than he is.
Bettering thy loss makes the bad causer worse;
Revolving this will teach thee how to curse.
                                    (*Richard III*, IV.iv.118–23)

These women aren't about politics or the pursuit of power; they're just human beings in pain, and in pain for the same reasons she is. It's interesting that, apart from a tiny meeting with the Duchess of Gloucester in Part Two, Margaret only encounters other women in this final play and specifically in this scene. Her advice to Elizabeth, albeit a lesson on how to inflict pain on others, is an act of charity and marks her end, her capitulation. She will never experience any kind of normal life, but maybe ultimately she is saved from herself and reaches some kind of peace.

The four plays are so vast that while we were performing them I didn't always have as clear a picture as I do now of what Michael Boyd intended in his production. I think with any play an actor usually has revelations, well after the event, about what he or she should have done in certain scenes. Writing this has given me a lot of these moments. Performing these plays was one of the most enjoyable experiences I have ever had on a stage. The complexities they contain are astounding and I still marvel at Michael's understanding of them. It is, however, their humanity that affects me most deeply. The forces at work in Joan and Margaret are the stuff of the plays, and the expansiveness of that could sometimes be hard to handle, in that it was hard to allot these two women their normality. They may be by turns a warrior, a queen, a bereft mother, and even a witch, but beyond all that drama you have to be able to make the normal, mundane connexions that also allow them to be real and also fallible, as opposed to just 'bad'. Michael used and shaped both the text and my performance in such a way as to remind me always that first and foremost these women are only human.

Duke Humphrey in Parts 1 and 2 of *Henry VI*, and Buckingham in *Richard III*

RICHARD CORDERY

RICHARD CORDERY played Humphrey, Duke of Gloucester, and the Duke of Buckingham (as well as King Louis of France) in Michael Boyd's productions of the three parts of *Henry VI* and of *Richard III* at the Swan Theatre in 2000–2001. The productions were later seen at the Power Centre for the Performing Arts at Ann Arbour, Michigan, and thereafter at the Young Vic in London. Richard Cordery's earlier work for the RSC had included Brabantio, Friar Lawrence, Corvino in Jonson's *Volpone*, Wilbraham in Edward Bond's *In the Company of Men*, and Dr Warburton in T. S. Eliot's *The Family Reunion*; he returned to the RSC in 2002–3 to play Menenius and Falstaff in touring productions of *Coriolanus* and *The Merry Wives of Windsor*. His theatre work elsewhere includes *Macbeth*, *The Winter's Tale*, and *'Tis Pity She's a Whore* and among a wide range of television credits are *Will Shakespeare*, *Goodbye Mr Chips*, and *Plotlands*.

For me, one of the many delights of being with the RSC is the sheer variety of the work. I had spent a very busy but happy fifteen months performing every night in three plays – by Shakespeare, Ben Jonson, and T. S. Eliot – when Michael Boyd approached me about his 'project'. I read the *Henry VI* plays through and my heart sank at the prospect of a whole year charging round in leather and armour amidst the confusion of half-remembered 'O'-level history and *Beyond the Fringe* sketches: 'You are too hot, saucy Worcester'. I certainly could not see where Michael's enthusiasm came from. Then he added the role of Buckingham to the offer of Duke Humphrey and I accepted; surely I could endure all that armour, and all those lords, in those three seemingly dull plays, in return for the opportunity of tackling, in the fourth, the part of Buckingham, one of the great supporting roles in Shakespeare.

When we met up in the RSC's Clapham rehearsal rooms for the first day's rehearsal there was a strange hum of enthusiasm. It was a glorious summer's day and Michael had assembled a huge company: twenty-nine actors, five stage managers, Tom Piper the designer, Jimmy Jones the composer, Liz Ranken the choreographer, Fiona Walton the assistant director, Sarah Esdaile the associate director, and Gavin Marshall who would 'be in charge of rope-work' – whatever that might be. Michael opened a tatty A5 exercise book with pages taped together to form a three-foot-long pull-out chart and started outlining his ideas. Gradually we became aware that the cross-casting between the plays was not an arbitrary exercise based on expedience and what each actor's agent had fought for, but part of some greater plan that would link these plays together to form one whole drama. He described how characters grew and developed, formed allegiances, turned traitor, died, and reappeared as a similar character, or with a similar function, later in the plays. Thus Joan of Arc was burned at the stake but would reappear to continue tormenting England as Queen Margaret. Immediately we were conscious of the possibility of some logic making these impenetrable plays clearer.

Tom Piper then outlined his plans for the stage, which would take the theme of 'the body of England' literally. The Swan Theatre (surely every actor's favourite playing space) was to be revamped, the stage to be removed and replaced with audience seating, the floor plan redesigned in the shape of a corpse, and two huge metal doors installed at one end. The height of the playing area was also to be raised throughout the auditorium so that audience and actors were on the same level. This was rare stuff.

Every actor has his own way of working, developed through practice and custom. Some are less confident, others more. Some spend ages reading around the plays – and our rehearsal rooms were, indeed, full of historical accounts of the Wars of the Roses. Some acquire several editions of the plays and scour the notes for clues and understanding. Ten years ago a man called Patrick Tucker introduced me to the First Folio of Shakespeare's plays. He convinced me, through a series of practical workshops with experienced actors and with students, that the Folio is a treasure-trove of acting advice, available to all of us should we choose to look. I don't, of course, make a case for the Folio's being perfect, but it is nevertheless the closest link we have to Shakespeare's own hand, sadly lost to us. Seven years after Shakespeare's death two of his closest friends produced an edition of his plays as a tribute to his genius. They would have worked actively on those plays over the preceding decades and presumably overseen any changes from the original manuscripts. I imagine that those manuscripts would have been kept under lock and key by the book-keeper, as they were immensely valuable to the company. Any later edition has gone through various emendations – but not by actors or even by directors, but by people who 'read' the plays. But the plays were written to be acted. In the First Folio there are dozens of clues to help us speak them which have been 'cleaned up' by editors who don't require them. They have been made into literary documents with corrected spellings, corrected punctuation, regularized lineation and capitalization to make them 'better' to read. But I always return to the First Folio to see if it works for me, and if it does, why should I take a different choice? For the last ten years I have followed the same procedure with every Shakespeare play I have been in.

No-one knows the rehearsal room process followed by the original actors, but we have some evidence. We know that their work-load was immense. According to Philip Henslowe's records for 1595, his company did twenty-six performances in thirty days of sixteen different plays and introduced a new one into the repertoire every two weeks. When they performed Marlowe's *Dr Faustus* on 13 February 1596 it had been 140 days since they had last performed it and they had, in the meantime, given 107 performances of twenty-one different plays. All this makes the RSC's repertory system look a touch conservative. Astonishingly, however, the day before they staged *Dr Faustus* after that long gap, they gave their first performance of a brand-new play, *The Blind Beggar of Alexandria*. With only so many hours in the day, when did rehearsals as we know them occur? It is clear to me, and becomes clearer with every Shakespeare play I work on, that the 'direction' for the actors is offered in the way the script is prepared.

In a period when there was no copyright, the plays owned by Shakespeare's company were a valuable and a risky asset and the practice of offering only 'sides' (that is, the actor's part and his unattributed cues), which continued well into the nineteenth century, and in some repertory companies even into the twentieth, was a security measure. A careless actor leaving his script in a tavern would lose only his own ten pages or so and not jeopardize the whole company's assets. Besides, how expensive and time-consuming it would have been to copy out an entire play (which would be, of course, as yet untried) a dozen or fifteen times by hand: so much more sensible to give to each actor only his own role.

A question this raised for me was whether the original *Hamlet*, performed in such haste in a busy schedule without the luxury of weeks of rehearsal, was somehow less impressive than a modern version. And if it was less impressive, why did it survive? Did people know what we would one day make of it? – of course not. It had the impact then that it has had since. How did those actors do it? Patrick Tucker's view is that Shakespeare understood the actor's problems and so put mood, character, and even moves into the individual speeches. All that the actor needs to know about his character, *everything*, is in the lines, and the lines only. Modern actors sometimes raise the objection that this may produce inconsistencies in their performances: their character may appear to be courageous in the first scene and then be reported to be cowardly in the second, so surely they need the whole script in order to smooth out these irregularities. But what could be more life-like? How often does what people say about us differ from our own opinions? And who knew more about acting, character, and theatre than Shakespeare?

I prepare my script, therefore, by deleting the names of the other characters and all their lines, leaving only the three-word cue to my own lines. I omit all scenes that I am not in. I remove all stage directions that do not directly relate to my own character (for example, who comes on, who goes off, who stabs whom, etc.), and with this much-depleted script I now go to work. And this is where the excitement really starts.

Now of course this does not mean that I don't try objectively to review my characterizations in the pub, or wherever, afterwards: actors always want to talk about their characters. My point is simply that I have been trying (I hope successfully) to keep this process out of the rehearsal room and trying also not to bring it onto the stage from the dressing room. I attempt to react to the script, situation, and subsequent intercourse with other characters in the moment, to experience my character's relationship with others from day to day and evening to evening, responding in what I say to how they speak to me, not pursuing a conceptualized character-line or a pre-determined emotional journey. This leads me to be surprised sometimes, even after giving a hundred performances of a role, to see a character waiting in the wings who is to come on later, not for the part of the scene I am about to play. Though it obviously fades in the end, I am often surprised at the length of time the freshness produced by this non-objective approach, this attempt to be immediate, may last.

Because I am not sure in the early stages what each scene is about, or, indeed, what happens in it, I must concentrate fully on what I do have, which is language, lineation, parenthesis, and capitalization. For example, in Part Two (1.ii.17–18) Duke Humphrey addresses his wife thus (in the Folio reading):

> O *Nell*, sweet *Nell*, if thou dost love thy Lord,
> Banish the Canker of ambitious thoughts.

Now there was, in the rehearsal, some discussion as to their relationship: does he love her and she him, are you aware that this is his second marriage, do you know that she is nouveau riche, etc? But I think this is all redundant. There can be no doubt that his use of the diminutive 'Nell' (he calls her 'Eleanor' later in the scene (Part Two, 1.ii.41–2) when he chides her), with 'O' and 'sweet', shows his deep affection for her. It may be that she doesn't return that affection – indeed, later, behind his back, she criticizes his 'base and humble mind' (Part Two, 1.ii.62) – but this doesn't affect his love for her because he doesn't hear it. Indeed, how much more subtle is the effect when the actor playing Gloucester is unaware of what the audience knows. So I can play fully my love for my wife based purely on what the language offers and don't temper it with any restraint I might be tempted to show if I knew of her deception.

I find that as I learn my lines I begin to understand them and never resort to paraphrasing to make sense of them. Without the burden of the rest of the play I am amazed how much information my 'sides' offer me. Unless I can make sense of my role's language as it is, how can an audience hope to do so? But through constant repetition while learning (I always learn my lines outside on long walks) the sense invariably becomes clear. As I learn my lines, and as we begin to put the play on its feet, I rely entirely on my 'sides'. This makes me concentrate very hard on my own character's language and constructions and, because I don't know what other actors are going to say, it ensures that I listen very much more intently to their speeches in rehearsal. I pay particular attention to the forms of address, from the formal 'you' and informal 'thou' which give an immediate indication of status, to the various ways of addressing other characters. When Henry demotes Gloucester as Lord Protector, Humphrey refers to 'thy father Henry' (Part Two, II.iii.34), the only occasion that I could find when he uses the familiar 'thy' to the king other than at the end when he is taken away to be murdered.

This gives, it seems to me, a clear indication of the desperation he feels.

Gloucester calls the king at different times 'sweet prince' (Part One, III.i.154), 'your grace' (Part One, III.i.155), 'my lord' (Part One, v.v.26, Part Two, III.i.93, IV.i.65, etc.), 'my good lord' (Part One, v.i.8), 'gracious lord' (Part Two, I.i.52), 'your highness' (Part One, v.v.26), 'your majesty, my liege' (Part One, III.iv.15), 'the king' (Part One, III.i.120), 'good king' (Part Two, II.iii.37), and 'noble Henry' (Part Two, II.iii.32), each of which shows a subtle variation in his attitude towards the monarch. When all you can examine is your own lines, you tend to give these clues more weight than you might otherwise and you soon discover the particular attitude behind each, from the absurdly formal 'your majesty, my liege', to the implicit reprimand of 'my lord'. I know all actors make these discoveries; I find that doing it this way I make them more quickly than I used to.

Another aspect of the First Folio to which I attach huge importance is the capitalization of words. The following passage (Part Two, II.i.188–94) reads as follows in the Folio:

> Sorry I am to heare what I have heard.
> Noble shee is: but if shee have forgot
> Honor and Vertue, and convers't with such,
> As like to Pytch, defile Nobilitie;
> I banish her my Bed, and Companie,
> And give her as a Prey to Law and Shame,
> That hath dis-honored *Glosters* honest Name.

It seems to me that the work has been done for the actor here. I am not here advocating the 'emphasizing' of the capitalized words. Rather one selects those words with initial capital letters as the vital weigh-stations on the route through the speech and one thus finds that Gloucester's disgust, dignity, resolve, and nobility seem to be summed up perfectly. How many of us might have gone for 'honest' in the final line? But isn't that too obvious? Isn't it a given as far as Gloucester is concerned? 'Name' is the important word here, and to help the audience, and the actor, he rhymes it. This is not rocket science; the simplicity is what attracts me.

Elizabethans were brilliantly versed in rhetoric, and as modern actors we sometimes shy away from it. Repeated words can have wonderful weight, and give the speech terrific power when we are bold with them.

The following lines (Part Two, I.i.73–5) provide an example (again in the Folio reading):

> Brave Peers of England, Pillars of the State,
> To you Duke *Humfrey* must unload his greefe:
> Your greefe, the common greefe of all the Land.

The temptation to avoid the repeated 'grief' and select the qualifications and possessives is strong: '*his* grief: / *Your* grief, the *common* grief of all the land'. But when the word 'grief' itself is selected – 'his *grief*: / Your *grief*, the common *grief* of all the land' – it tolls like a bell through the lines and we experience Gloucester's political expertise, like a modern politician thumping the lectern.

Verse is extremely useful as a tool for helping to make clear the thought structure and development in a speech. This requires strict observation of the Folio punctuation – and three other guidelines that I always try to follow: (1) only breathe at the end of a line, never in the middle; (2) only complete the thought on a full stop, but if that occurs in mid-line, don't pause but continue; (3) at a colon keep the thought-process going; this makes some sentences quite long, but their sheer scope can be very exciting to an audience. In the Simpcox scene in Part Two (Act Two, Scene One) Gloucester makes a rare departure from verse and talks in prose. I tried to mark the change and to create a theatrical reason for it: in that particular scene I used the prose as a form of confidentiality with the scurrilous con-man, whispering to him 'Now, sirrah, if you mean to save yourself from whipping, leap me over this stool and run away' (II.1.139–40).

Concentrating on only your own lines as you learn them puts the verbal conceits, the alliteration, the assonances, the rhymes at the forefront of your work. Preconceptions about how the scene might go are left behind. In performance I am as a consequence much more in the moment, even after a hundred performances, than I used to be when I had the whole of the scene before me.

We began to rehearse Part One. One of the joys of this project was the feeling that we had all the time in the world: seventeen weeks to work before we need show the results to the public. It seemed like a long time, but in it we had to produce three full-length plays. (*Richard III* was to be rehearsed when we had the three parts of *Henry VI* in performance.) This gave our designer, Tom Piper, the chance to design around the performances and the actors had repeated consultations with him during this period. The process was slow at first as we experimented with sounds and movement, as well as watching characterizations emerging. Jimmy Jones brought in some recordings of eastern chants and we had long sessions of learning and adapting rhythmic patterns. Liz Ranken held movement sessions, which were later joined by Terry King the fight-director, to find a language of battle. Michael Boyd was adamant that he didn't want the typical 'strobe-and-smoke' effects and what we ended up with was a distillation of the combined invention of those participating.

We rehearsed Part One without reference to Part Two, though actors often read ahead. I remember arriving early on in rehearsal with a stick and being asked by all concerned what it was: 'My staff of office; as the Lord Protector I need it.' 'Why?' 'Because in Part Two Henry specifically asks me to "Give up thy staff. / Henry will to himself Protector be"' (Part Two, II.iii.23–4). So I carried the totem around, and soon felt uncomfortable rehearsing without it. As Protector I was armed with this 'political' weapon while everyone else had daggers, swords, and knives: it gave Humphrey – me – a certain authority. In Part Three, as King Louis of France, I was given, at the suggestion of the stage manager, a replica of this baton, in royal blue, as a sceptre; the idea underlined the continuity of casting throughout this project.

All acting is reacting – to the words, the situations, and to the other characters – and it is impossible for me to attempt to describe the process that I went through to arrive at Humphrey Duke of Gloucester without reference to David Oyelowo's performance as Henry VI. I had known and worked with David during the previous eighteen-month season. During the early rehearsals of the *Henry VI* plays I watched with fascination as this young man's courage, dignity, and integrity combined to produce a powerful and at times heart-rending depiction of the young king. I had huge admiration and affection for him and as his 'Protector' it was the easiest job to feel both the necessity and the desire to look after him. He played Henry as a committed individual who knows he is right, and I think he found Michael Boyd's warnings that he didn't want Henry to be a 'weak' king rather puzzling. He saw no reason for regarding Henry's deep Christian conviction as a weakness or failing, and in this was a large part of the success of the performance: another actor might have 'commented' on Henry's Christianity while playing it. My own method of working, too, of playing only what is written, staying in the moment, and avoiding subtext, meant that

22 Richard Cordery as Humphrey, Duke of Gloucester, with David Oyelowo as King Henry VI, *2 Henry VI*, Act I, Scene i: 'Some sudden qualm hath struck me to the heart / And dimmed mine eyes, that I can read no further.'

Gloucester wasn't forever stepping back and seeing the inevitability of the kingdom's destruction because of Henry's supposed political ineptitude. Only when Gloucester says 'France will be lost ere long' (Part Two, 1.i.144) is he operating in that way, and, there, he is quite self-consciously prophesying.

When we had completed Part One and moved on to rehearse Part Two, where the relationship between Henry and Gloucester is soured and eventually broken through the intervention of Margaret and Suffolk, Humphrey's grief was made all the more profound by the experiences of Part One. And this is where our project really paid dividends. We left the first part rehearsed and 'ticking over' to concentrate on the next play. The actors brought with them to this new endeavour their own experiences of Part One and, as we worked hard on the new play, relationships between characters were often already half formed. Michael Boyd then asked us to run Part One, and bringing to this play what we had now discovered in Part Two meant that those relationships became more sophisticated and less obvious. David Oyelowo and I had had quite a physical uncle/nephew relationship early on, with much hugging and overt, albeit robust, affection. When we revisited the first part this was simplified, and became more so: we no longer needed to demonstrate our relationship and that physicalization was replaced for the most part with an occasional look. On our return to Part Two that confidence developed further and there was a reciprocal growth in our understanding of each other. This process was repeated in dozens of ways each time we re-ran another part, a distillation and simplification of our story-telling.

After Duke Humphrey is put to death, the Bishop of Winchester 'sees' him on his death-bed in a vision (Part Two, Act Three, Scene Three). I was surprised to be called to these rehearsals, but the Celt in Michael Boyd was adamant that we would have 'ghosties'. But surely, I thought, we aren't terrified by such things nowadays, and we struggled for quite a while to rationalize (for me) what I might be doing there. Various ideas were tried which involved my helping Winchester (my arch-enemy) out of this world, but they all appeared spiteful and petty, and I complained to Michael about this. My own idea was that if I had to be a ghost I should retain my dignity and simply observe Winchester's demise, but Michael persisted. Eventually I said I thought Humphrey would be brutal, like a butcher, and hang the bishop on a meat-hook, but there was no chance of achieving that. Then, astonishingly, Tom Piper and Michael Boyd, with the help of the technicians, came up with an idea for making it possible; and every night a rope dropped from above to which I attached poor Chris Ettridge (who played Winchester) and, using a series of pulleys, hauled the poor chap up into the flies. This was quite some height at the Swan, but when we performed at Ann Arbor, Michigan it was a distance of forty feet. To add to the ghoulish effect, the sound designer, Andrea Cox, put a microphone in my boots so that my footsteps resounded around the auditorium as I made my entrance from the dark, and my face was made up to appear heavily bruised and swollen in accordance with the earlier description of Humphrey's corpse:

> But see, his face is black and full of blood,
> His eyeballs further out then when he lived,
> Staring full ghastly like a strangled man.
> (Part Two, III.i.168–70)

As I walked through the auditorium on my nightly journey to string the bishop up, audience members recoiled in twenty-first-century horror and stared in fascination at the sight of him disappearing upwards – as they did in the nightmarish Jack Cade scenes later, when I was joined by the headless body of Suffolk and other 'corpses'. My final ghostly appearance was during the king's granting of a pardon to the rioters. As the penitents retired Duke Humphrey was revealed in the shadows echoing their earlier 'God save the king' (Part Two, IV.ix.22), and as the king dashed towards the vast steel doors they slammed shut, leaving him alone in his court for ever.

Once all three plays were rehearsed and up and running, we turned to *Richard III*. As a company we were very used to each other by now, and a lot of time seemed to be spent rehearsing the children, who were new. Adopting the same approach as usual, I was struck by the urbane and courteous quality of the language that Buckingham uses. I had no conception of how long the scene was in which Margaret curses Richard, for it seemed so brief in my 'sides'. Throughout it, Buckingham is merely an observer, and in rehearsal, to underline this, I moved down the leg of the 'body' that was the playing area and leant against the Swan structure to watch from a distance. From then on I came to find this position useful for a character who refuses to push himself forward and is content to hitch his wagon to Richard's star. Watching the confrontation between Richard and Margaret night after night I found a certain mistrust of Richard creeping into Buckingham, though I think he is also excited by the sheer daring. When he says, though, that his 'hair doth stand on end to hear her curses' (I.iii.303) I believe he means it, and this, again, meant that I stayed in the moment, relieved of the need to question in the longer term the relationship with Richard, happily ignorant of the larger picture.

I had known Aidan McArdle, who played Richard, as long as David Oyelowo, and had a great affection for him too, which made our relationship on stage easy. When offered the earldom of Hereford as a future gift, I took Richard's hand to shake it as I said 'I'll claim that promise of your grace's hand' (III.i.197). Aidan McArdle, who is much shorter than I am, jokingly directed his hand down, so that I had to kneel. Smilingly I accepted the reduction in status and as I kissed his hand he laughed. As we walked off he slapped me on the back, suggesting close friendship and a shared joke. And it was as a joke that Buckingham saw it, a joke in which he joins heartily: I didn't know, or need to know, what Aidan's Richard was thinking. The joke makes Buckingham happy and, if he is wrong, it is better from the point of view of performing it that I (the actor) should buy into it wholeheartedly. The temptation to comment on the character you are playing is always to be avoided.

Here, as elsewhere, there are obvious parallels between the two relationships, Humphrey's with Henry VI and Buckingham's with Richard: the older man with respect, and admiration, for the younger and more powerful one, and with no desire to be number one. Buckingham can feel that Richard likes, needs, and respects him; he can also feel horribly betrayed and humiliated when he reminds Richard of his promise of the earldom of Hereford and is rejected. But in order for it to be shattered, the relationship must obviously exist without suspicion, or we aren't playing the shocks that the writer wrote. It doesn't seem to me to be at all fruitful to analyze the relationship in all its stages and then to inform the moment-to-moment choices one makes with this overall conception: nothing is to be gained by clever pre-empts. Is there a suggestion of mistrust of Richard in Buckingham's 'Give me some little breath, some pause, dear lord' (IV.ii.24)? I tried to play it quite simply as 'this is too fast, let me have a moment', which gives a vivid immediacy of contrast when he returns a few lines later demanding 'the gift, my due by promise' (IV.ii.87) – 'I want out, *now*, with what I've earned!'

I mentioned earlier that Shakespeare helps you with moves as well. When the young prince says 'I pray you, uncle, give me this dagger' (III.i.110), we discussed for some time what the blocking of the scene might be. It seemed obvious to me that the judicious use of 'this' rather than 'that' suggested that the boy is close to the dagger when he speaks. What else is the reason for this choice of word? Why would you say 'this dagger' if you are far across the stage? Such is the result of examining the language in isolation from the scene as a whole.

What I particularly enjoyed about playing Buckingham was the gradual increase in his involvement in the play, his growing confidence culminating in that astonishing series of speeches to the citizens when he pleads on their behalf to Richard to accept the throne (III.vii.95–218). Because we were performing the *Henry VI* plays on matinées as well as in the evenings, there was less time for rehearsals of *Richard III* than for the other three plays and I worked alone on that scene during my long walks through the fields around Stratford. Not having Richard's responses to hand, I was unaware of the cynical element in Buckingham's approach. This allowed me to practise it as a genuine plea and it was only when we came to put it together in rehearsal that it struck me what Buckingham was really achieving. This is important, for it meant

23 Richard Cordery as the Duke of Buckingham with Aidan McArdle as
King Richard III, *Richard III*, Act IV, Scene ii: 'Give me some little breath,
some pause, dear lord.'

that I could play it straight and leave the audience to judge his deceit
rather than try to play his duplicity.

After the first preview Michael Boyd suggested that I elicit the help
of the audience by raising the hand of an audience member on 'Refuse
not, mighty lord, this proffered love' (III.vii.201). I was appalled, but he
was persuasive and so I gave it a go. It certainly sent a frisson around the
audience, many of whom, I'm sure, gave thanks that I hadn't singled out
them. The knock-on effect of breaking through this imaginary fourth

wall and allying myself directly with the audience was that when I said (III.vii.238–9) – and to return for the final time to the Folio reading –

> Then I salute you with this Royall Title,
> Long live King *Richard*, Englands worthie King

it took very little encouragement to get the audience to chant the 'Amen'. Indeed, when we performed in Michigan, the fifteen hundred people in the auditorium raised the roof with their response, often giving themselves and Richard a huge round of celebratory applause. This certainly affected them when, a little later, Richard is crowned and rejects Buckingham: they were suddenly very conscious of their own involvement in his elevation and this sobering realization affected their response to the latter part of the play.

I was struck during the relatively brief rehearsal period that was allotted to *Richard III* how much was accomplished by a company of actors who knew each other's working methods so well. In July 2000 we had begun a project that was at last complete in February of the following year. We had come together as a disparate group of performers and specialists and through an intensive and exciting eight months we had grown into a company which had produced some of the work with which I am most proud to have been associated.

King Richard III

HENRY GOODMAN

HENRY GOODMAN played the title role in Sean Holmes's production of *Richard III* at the Royal Shakespeare Theatre in the summer season of 2003 (the first Stratford season in several decades from which most productions did not later move to London). The performance marked his return to the RSC after a long absence; earlier roles for the company had included Dromio of Ephesus, Kitely in *Every Man in his Humour*, Voltore in *Volpone*, and Harry in *The Time of Your Life*. A wide range of work for the National Theatre includes Shylock (for which he won the Olivier Award for Best Actor), Gower in *Pericles*, Shalimov in *Summerfolk*, Nathan Detroit in *Guys and Dolls*, and Roy Kohn in *Angels in America*, and among his many other theatre credits are *The Producers*, *Follies*, *Feelgood*, *Unfinished Business*, *Art*, *Chicago*, and *Tartuffe*. A long list of films includes *Notting Hill*, *The Saint*, *Mary Reilly*, and *Final Curtain*. He has also worked extensively in radio and among many television credits are *The Mayor of Casterbridge*, *Arabian Nights*, *Cold Lazarus*, *Broken Glass*, and *Maigret*.

Playing Richard III requires the peacock as well as the priest from the actor. Both facets, both poles, of the actor's persona are insisted upon, and both must be used, in revealing Richard's character, in establishing his stage presence, and in sharing his interior and exterior journey with the audience. I came to the role after a long time thinking that I would never get to play it. I was fifty-three – and had been since the most recent anniversary of Shakespeare's birth! – when the part was offered to me by Michael Boyd, soon after his appointment as Artistic Director of the RSC. We arranged to keep in touch about it until we agreed on a director who was free and with whom I might develop a rapport – and not very long afterwards I was in regular discussion with Sean Holmes about the play and the role.

To be cast as Richard III is inevitably to lay oneself open to what has been called 'the anxiety of influence'; legions of fine actors through history, from Burbage to Katherine Hunter, have played this part, and it seemed to me essential to resist all temptation to be different just for the sake of it. There is surely something dyspeptic, or just plain wrong, in undervaluing or trying to ignore what has gone before. What happened to being released, and inspired, by earlier work? I enjoyed enormously the splendour of physical presence, the idea of an athletic youthful survivor, that Antony Sher presented in the role. I was also much impressed by Ian McKellen's older, restrained military man, whose physical dexterity bespoke his scheming, watchful self-reliance, and by the speedy, volatile, vulnerable Richard that Simon Russell Beale revealed in the part. All of these, and what I knew, or read, of other important performances, needed to be embraced as guides, not resisted as threats, in playing the role; the shape of those exciting performances was released by the muse of the actors who created them and the same had to apply to my own responsibility in responding to this extraordinary part, to that dialogue with myself that had to happen while I was trying to undergo the experience of being Richard.

Before I ask the reader to take an interest in my approach to this part, or in my interaction with this play and the process of rehearsing it, some imperatives that are deeply rooted in my own working intentions as an actor may be worth sharing – and even listing:

(1) If the creation of significance out of the everyday is the overriding purpose of all art, it is especially demanding, imperative indeed, in the shaping of theatre. Amongst much else, such significance in the theatre may include audience identification, emotional insight, lucidity of thought, and the fresh understanding of past history; none of these precludes humour and all of them are relevant to *Richard III*.

(2) Acting is 'a promise to respond', and responding courageously to imperatives within oneself, as a person and as an actor, is a promise that must be kept.

(3) Live theatre must be alive, an experience unique to being in that auditorium, on that night, with those actors, in that world, listening to those words. Immediacy of present involvement has far-reaching implications for the acting of Shakespeare, not least for *Richard III*.

(4) The greatest challenge to the actor of Shakespeare is to be at ease in the heightened language of poetic drama. Poetic drama is uniquely able to get under the skin of its audiences, to tap into their

willingness and need to find meaning; that need and the actor's meet in the response to, the reaching up for, metaphor in dramatic poetry. The actor thus becomes a conduit for experience in the audience and their meeting creates a new level of connexion, a special theatre-enabled reality in which the stage is the meeting point for a heightened form of imaginative and sentient listening and seeing that makes us notice more lucidly than almost anything else the lives we lead and the experiences we go through.

Sean Holmes and I met several times while we were both busy with other projects on either side of the Atlantic. For some of this time I was playing Molière's Tartuffe, another wonderful icon of villainy, though in his religious hypocrisy perhaps rather more narrowly focused in his wickedness than Shakespeare's Richard. Sean and I communicated regularly during this period. He kept me updated about casting and about bringing together our company from all the complexities of the busy schedules of actors in other plays in the 2003 Stratford season and from the handful of new actors who would join for our production. I flooded him with my own thoughts and ideas about the play, well aware that they needed refining and fitting into his world and his thoughts for the production.

Among these early ideas of mine were a number that, interestingly, shared connexions with childhood, in particular that Richard should be attended by a page, a young boy in his own image, that there should be a rocking horse, and that Richard should have his own private space, a more disturbing version of the teenager's bedroom, perhaps, with its pictures on the wall. To these Sean later added a throne that looked curiously like a child's high-chair. The boy and the rocking horse, as well as the high chair, survived through into production, the boy a frequent, silent presence near Richard, his only companion. I shall return to him later. The rocking-horse became connected with the young Duke of York, Richard's namesake. He was seen pushing it for his sister at the beginning of Act Two, Scene Two, and at the end of that scene we decided that I should heave it into violent motion before my exit. First seen thus at Richard's mother's initial appearance in the play, it provided a link with Richard's own childhood, with his mother's reviling him – as she immediately does here, of course – and with the idea that, on a horse, even a rocking horse, he is freed of his deformity and becomes big and grown-up and cured of his illness; on a horse he can become a kind of centaur. And at the end, the rocking horse would reappear when the false back-wall of the set flew out and the ghosts were revealed, young York now riding it with terrible energy, and Richard's cry 'My kingdom for a horse' (v.iv.6) taking on a disturbing sense of the need to escape again to childhood innocence. The idea that Richard should have some sort of private space, maybe a small truck downstage, with photographs – but for Richard they would be of all the people he needs to destroy, so that it would become a psychopathic killer's lair – became transmuted during rehearsals into an actor's dressing-room and was then dropped altogether. Other such early ideas that got lost along the way were the notion of a set that would change as the moral environment of the play grew more corrupt, England's decay becoming palpable, even that the brick wall at the back of the set should split open to signify the cracks in the play's political universe – though the backcloth that had seemed so permanent did in the end fly out to reveal the supernatural realm behind Richard. Sean was very good at fielding all these ideas – some potentially exciting but unaffordable – knocking some out and refining others, rationalizing the compromises that the real world, and the repertoire system, make inevitable.

This process of early collaboration, particularly for a play in which all plots and subplots seem to emanate from the title-role, spinning out from Richard at the hub (as it were) of the wheel, inevitably brought out the director in me. I realized that I must make sure in rehearsal that I did not slip into trying to shape the staging around my own needs, into trying to co-direct the show. To try to be self-effacing and yet lead from the front in this vast and demanding role is a balancing act not unlike Richard's dissembling his hidden motives. Once rehearsals began, however, I quickly became obsessed with the huge amount of energy, mental and physical, that the part requires and in trying to cope with that was more than happy to let the director get on with controlling the overall issues.

At the same sort of stage as Sean and I were involved in these early discussions, he and our designer Anthony Lamble had found the idea of the great red curtain separating the two worlds of, on the one hand, 'theatre', the world of Richard's soliloquies to the audience in front of the curtain, and, on the other hand, 'action', the Victorian world in which, behind the curtain, the events of the play were to be set. Such contexts of costume and period immediately released social behaviour, while the raising of the red curtain meant that the empty space behind

it, with very little in the way of set, became a viable language in itself –
though I always had a slight sense that some of these decisions were also
convenient ways of sharing the same basic stage set with three other
shows at a very tough financial time for the RSC! Sean and Anthony
also had the lovely idea of suggesting, in front of a backcloth of the
London skyline, the River Thames at the back of the stage, offering
a metaphor of time always flowing onwards, as well as providing the
means of conveying Clarence, and the princes, to their deaths in the
Tower.

My link with Richard, from the first, was as a man rather than as
a king, a man – son, brother, husband – crucially isolated, alienated,
frustrated, and dysfunctional in all those areas of his life. It seemed to
me that what really interested Shakespeare was the way Richard goes
about getting what he wants in spite of rejection by his brother, his
mother, his family, his society, and his God. As ever, I did a good
deal of preliminary reading, both on Richard and on the historical
background of the period. Among psychological studies of Richard,
I found Adler interesting on the concept of organ inferiority, with the
idea that bodily defectiveness leads to devaluation of self, which in turn
leads to compensatory striving. Freud's ideas on the personality ruined
by success, crumbling when it has succeeded in achieving its objective, were also illuminating and attractive in thinking about Richard,
who does indeed become erratic and guilt-ridden and fearful once he
has achieved the throne. What really struck me, though, was Freud's
attempt to explain Richard's first soliloquy. He suggests that the audience is deeply attracted to Richard because in him they see a person
behaving in a rebellious, neurotic, antisocial way because he believes
himself to be exceptional. The frivolous surface of the soliloquy contains only a hint of his true motivation, which the audience is left to
supply; when the frivolity vanishes, we, the audience, realize that we
too have hidden motivations and feel that we are exceptional, and realize that we might become like Richard. Though Freud is rather out of
fashion, I was very taken with these ideas, which made me eager to
explore the relationship with the audience as fully as possible.

Freud's further suggestion that Richard's will to power derives from
his frustrated will to sexual power, seemed to me too simplistic. Murray
Krieger's notion (in his book *The Play and the Place of Criticism*) that
Richard's will to power is a perversion of his sexual need for power I
found more convincing. Krieger argues that Richard not only pursues

power as he might pursue a mistress, but that he pursues it in order that he may coerce a mistress and force her, regardless of the revulsion she feels for him, to play the game of treating him as a lover; thus he can feel that he too has been 'framed in the prodigality of nature' (I.ii.243). Krieger also argues that women accept Richard because, like everyone else in this play, they are hypocrites, needing to lie in order to live. This accords with my own sense that, though Richard may be the personification of evil, he is, after all, only a fox among foxes. Unlike the men and women around him, the cheerfully deluded Hastings, the canny Derby, the 'deep-revolving witty Buckingham' (IV.ii.42), Catesby, Elizabeth, Dorset, Rivers, Grey, hypocrites one and all who 'smooth, deceive, and cog' (I.iii.48) but are shown to have feet of clay, Richard is at least self-conscious and consistent – honest, indeed – about his own duplicity.

If one thinks about the play in these terms, all the curses and false oaths with which it abounds are seen to be a terrible indictment of England, not just of Richard. The play in this sense is directly connected with the drama of lust and blood and nemesis with which western tragedy began, the Greek plays of feuding families having to be cleansed by the gods, transmuted here, in this Elizabethan manifestation of the theme, into cleansing by God. This way of thinking about Richard's perversion of his sexual needs into a need for power seemed to me perhaps relevant to the fact that he never openly admits that need: 'another secret close intent' (I.i.158) is as close as he ever gets to speaking of it, even to his own accomplices, the audience. That desire to control others which power, professional or political, brings with it, is frequently a means of compensating for a sense of inadequacy (sexual or in other aspects of self-esteem), and as an actor playing Richard the idea of wanting to control those around me by undermining their control of themselves felt useful and relevant. Richard wants also to expose them all, to destroy legality and beauty because they are built on deception and malignity every bit as ugly as his own appearance – but to these ideas I shall return later.

The psychological insights that came from this preliminary reading, then, were very useful in developing the role, for the sense of Richard's self-awareness that they provoked is, I'm sure, important. Whereas in life we are mostly unaware of the operation of such psychological forces within ourselves, Richard's wilfulness is never anything but self-aware; his is an entirely conscious use of his own skills, and ills. The actor is forced to notice himself performing the role, because that is part of the character he is portraying; naturalism is not enough.

My historical reading, unlike these psychological explorations, was mostly of background relevance. To learn that it was Richard who brought William Caxton back with him from the Low Countries and that the first books published in England were published for Richard doesn't exactly inform one's performance, though I find it liberating to know that Richard's world was literate as well as troubled. Some of my reading in history, though, was certainly of direct use in creating the role, not least a sense of the play's time-scheme. Richard tells us that it is only 'three months' (I.ii.240) since he killed Prince Edward at the Battle of Tewkesbury. That battle took place in 1471 when Richard was a young man of nineteen. By the time of the Battle of Bosworth at the end of the play we are in 1485 and Richard is in his early thirties. This fourteen-year span had never struck me when I had seen the play. There appear to be four time-gaps – after Act One, Scene Two; after Act Two, Scene Three; after Act Four, Scene Five; and after Act Five, Scene One – but the action seems to be taking place on eleven, or perhaps twelve, days over a period of a few weeks or months. In rehearsal I tried to explore the youthfulness of Richard at the beginning as a petulant, rather messed up nineteen-year-old and to suggest a journey through experience to his death at Bosworth as a psychologically awakened, wilfully self-aware, hell-bent-for-death soldier of the devil.

Reading about the childhood and adolescence of Richard also fed, indirectly at least, into my preparation. At the age of eight his mother showed him the heads of his father, the Duke of York, and of his teenage brother Rutland, impaled on spikes above the gates of York by the victorious Lancastrians, and imposed on him the duty of avenging their deaths. His childhood was spent in fear, in hiding and in exile from the dangers of civil war, in the Low Countries and in France, with his mother, a frightened, embittered fighter on his father's behalf. He was seven before he met his elder brothers Edward and George, ten and eight years his seniors, who were already energetic soldiers for the Yorkist cause; by the age of twelve Richard was himself recruiting soldiers in northern England, and by his teenage years he too was commanding armies. His young life was shaped by the constant awareness of the presence of enemies around every corner, by memory of the shame of his father's head displayed as a traitor, by the sense that he ought to be with his brothers, fighting to restore the family's honour.

His passionate, loyal support of his elder brother and of the York family – his personal motto was 'Loyalty binds me' – is certainly a powerful motivating force as the play opens, but it is now distorted by his fierce resentment of the Woodvilles, the parvenu family into which Edward has married, throwing away, it seems to Richard, almost as soon as it has been won, all the years of fraternal struggle to regain the honour of the House of York and to get Edward onto the throne. Mixed in with all Richard's psychological motivations to destroy, then, is the terrible English tradition of class, the hatred that old blood feels for new money. The Victorian setting chosen for our production worked well for this aspect of the play, providing a social world where superficial civil behaviour and seeming religious observance could hide corruption and seething sexuality, where verbiage – 'these fair well-spoken days' (I.i.29) – conceals venality (Edward's rampant womanizing, for example, with syphilis almost certainly the cause of his death). Cynicism has at all times been suicidal for the ruling classes; in his biography of Voltaire, André Maurois writes of 'a critical, ironic bourgeoisie' appearing from 'the ruin of a collapsed nobility', and here in *Richard III* one observes a society where people who can 'flatter and look fair . . . smooth, deceive and cog' (I.iii.47–8) rise to the top, where the merchant classes, the relations and allies of the queen, are infiltrating the aristocracy and achieving, through her, positions and offices normally in the exclusive gift of the king. The deep resentment that this causes among the older nobility – the only modern analogy I can think of is the reaction there might have been a few years ago if Margaret Thatcher had been made queen! – is something that Richard can harness and exploit, as well as share: 'We are the queen's abjects, and must obey' (I.i.106); ''tis the queen and her allies / That stir the king against my brother' (I.iii.329–30); and, of Elizabeth and Jane Shore, these 'mighty gossips in this monarchy' (I.i.83).

And here one comes back to thinking about Richard's psychology, and more particularly to his hatred of women. For there is a real misogyny about Richard as he fantasizes about love but is incapable of giving or receiving it. In his deformity he reasons – and his thinking is made 'crooked' by hell, as he puts it near the end of *Henry VI* (Part Three, v.vi.79) – that love is something he will never receive because of the world's love of beauty. I had a strong image in my mind of the historical Richard, as a boy, growing up, as he did, with Lady Anne Neville and falling in love with her, but being unable to express it because of the threat he sensed from his handsome, upright older brothers exacerbating his consciousness of his own deformity. There is, it seems to me, a great deal of genuine passion for her, mental and sexual, in the wooing scene. All these feelings too, then, become part of the destructive fury and contempt that are seething in Richard as the play begins and that lie behind the first soliloquy.

Before turning to that soliloquy I should say a word about the presentation of Richard's physical disability, for it is something that every actor of the role must deal with. We decided early on that Richard had had polio, and we spent a lot of time through rehearsals in working out how to present the resultant deformity. I wanted it to be disturbing – nothing at all like the exhilarating leaping about on his crutches that Antony Sher had presented – and we decided that the whole of the left side of Richard's body had been distorted by the polio. I felt that I could portray this physically, without the aid of expensive prosthetics, but frequent exercise is essential if you are constantly to put weight on one side of your body only and to dwindle and distort it, so in the wings between scenes Richard was often to be seen demonstrating a remarkable compensatory athletic energy! In keeping with the idea of making Richard's physical appearance disturbing, we used false teeth to distort the face, and an ugly dark birthmark down one cheek. And this was the figure that would be presented to the audience in the opening soliloquy.

Not presented quite at the beginning, however, for another of our early ideas that survived through to production was of a physical transformation in Richard during this first speech, which I shall come to in a moment. Our production's division of the play into two clearly differentiated worlds – the 'front cloth' world of the soliloquies, and the Victorian domestic world of the court behind the red curtain – meant that the curtain actually descended to mark the beginning of our production. Richard is the central character and the spine of this play and in his first appearance he is eager to tell the audience 'This is about me. Watch me.' Richard is the only Shakespearian villain who starts his own play and then guides the audience through it – 'it's about *me*, in *their* world, with *your* help' – and he becomes their hero and villain all in one. The actor must beware of ingratiating promiscuity in making friends with the audience in this first soliloquy, but he must also make sure to get them on his side, to get them to like him and to care about him. The proper use of charm in this contract with the audience is

24 Henry Goodman as King Richard III, *Richard III*, Act I, Scene i: 'Now is the winter of our discontent / Made glorious summer by this sun of York.'

essential: so, for instance, I learned quickly in the playing of it that he must not feel sorry for himself here, or this will alienate the audience; his ability to turn around his deformity, to take delight in it and make opportunities from it, is what endears him, ennobles him even, from these first moments of the play. And this enticing charm of Richard is symbiotically connected to his entrapping challenge; it is the means by which his malevolent morality is set to work.

In the play's very first line, the actor must decide to whom '*our* discontent' refers. Is it Richard's, in the royal plural sense; is he already taking a kingly viewpoint though he is not yet king? Or is it 'ours' – that is yours, the audience's, and mine, together here in this theatre tonight? Or is it 'ours' – those of us up here in this onstage world, excluding you, the audience? The contract here being made is the springboard for so much else that evolves in his relationship with the audience, and in theirs to the play, that I believe it works best when it feels as though it's 'ours' in the sense of all of us here tonight. But that puts demands on the setting and staging of the show to differentiate between the play's two worlds, one of Richard and the audience overseeing, and by implication conspiring, together, as accomplices in the acts (in every sense) that are to follow; and the other of the audience separated from their guide, their MC, their link-man, their very reason for watching, and reduced to voyeurs and terrified witnesses. This is, I think, an early attempt by Shakespeare at a kind of alienation as a means of inducing learning in the audience. It was this duality that we tried to reflect in our production.

It is not for nothing that the word *now* recurs so often in this opening speech. It is not just the 'now' of the play's period setting; more importantly, for me, it invites Richard's knowing connexion to this audience, on this night, in this theatre – *now*! This opens up all sorts of exciting possibilities for the audience to move in and out of empathy with and for Richard. With this sense of immediacy in mind, for example, the lines

> I am determined to prove a villain
> And hate the idle pleasures of these days
>
> (i.i.30–1)

work, unavoidably, on both levels: first, that of the onstage action that the audience is invited to watch and be complicit in as Richard, through duplicitous dissembling, endeavours to get his revenge on the world and on God; second, that of the crucial private bond between Richard and the audience, with 'the idle pleasures of these days' an enticement to them not to be idle but to work with him, in active and exciting participation, in exposing and undermining the world behind him.

This is why, in previews and right up to press night, I tried going off stage amongst the audience during this opening soliloquy and ripping up someone's programme – 'Hey, I gave three pounds for that!' I would open it and see Shakespeare's picture inside and with a disgusted 'Ha!' rip him into pieces to make tangible my hatred of him for so maligning me in this play. This idea was dropped, however, as had been the earlier notion of the play starting with a great Covent-Garden-like regal swag across the red tabs saying 'Royal Shakespeare Company', which I would deface by spraying, graffiti-fashion, the word 'Richard's' over the word 'Royal': so now it's *my* company, not the king's – and sod royalty anyway! Then I would scrub out the word 'Shakespeare' – a bolder version of the same instinct that led to the programme-ripping idea – and finally destroy also the word 'Company', thus unleashing, immediately, an anti-social, theatre-hating, petulant actor of a Richard. For me, at the

Royal Shakespeare Theatre in Stratford-upon-Avon, Richard's hatred of 'the idle pleasures of these days'(i.i.31) seemed like the actor, in private with his accomplices the audience, declaring his hatred of this theatre, of the RSC itself, of that bloody Shakespeare (my author, who wronged me – a Pirandellian truth!), and of the whole world of spin. All my research had made me rootedly aware of the wrong done to this king by all the accounts – Holinshed, Hall, More, Polydore Vergil – that Shakespeare had probably read, and of the consequent problem of choosing between playing the history or playing the play. I was excited by this tension, and it seemed for a time that our 'front-cloth' staging of the soliloquies might make it possible to explore it in this way and, in a rather post-modern sense, to put Shakespeare on the stage and challenge him. But we couldn't quite seem to make it work and in the end I was persuaded away from it, as I was from the idea of ripping down the red curtain before my coronation scene, and making myself a huge trailing robe from it, marking the end of that separate theatre world that Richard had shared with the audience.

The early idea of mine that did survive, however, and that Sean was excited by, was Richard's physical transformation during the first soliloquy. I wanted to make it absolutely clear that Richard has had to dress up for this new summer of opportunity, this summer of content, and that it sickens him. He grew up in war: war is part of his mentality; he was formed and shaped by it. But the war is now over and I wanted to find a way, very quickly, of illustrating the contrast between past and present. One idea was to raise the curtain to reveal people playing croquet, the gentility of the pastime contrasting with Richard in his messed-up physical and mental state. In the end, however, this seemed unnecessary and we kept only Richard's transformation, from the apparently debonair presenter who first appears in top hat and tails, who has had to dress up in these clothes and try to dance, but who cannot do so because it hurts too much, to the deformed and twisted figure who hates it all, who refuses to 'entertain these fair well-spoken days' and who is determined instead 'to prove a villain' (i.i.29–30). In early performances I began with a deftness, a cockiness perhaps, that meant that the moment was misread as a vaudeville turn, or as an actor stripping off his finery in order to play Richard – for if we had been wanting to explore the idea of Richard as actor we would have continued the concept through the play; what we settled on finally was a Richard, still in top hat and tails, who was certainly dressed up for the party but who was, from the first, clearly incapable, physically and mentally, of taking part in it, his walk already a discernible limp and his face distorted by pain.

Once this opening to the play is achieved, however, an invisible, umbilical partnership with the audience is created, and worked, by Richard (and by the actor playing him), and that partnership remains, even when the actor doesn't break out of the onstage world to nod or wink or connive with the audience – which I was determined not to do (not wanting to make it seem like vaudeville), but which is hard to resist in a few places. (O, the tyranny of taste, whether my own, the director's, or Shakespeare's!) I set myself the challenge, however, not to indulge this connexion with the audience in a too knowing or too artful way, and this yields sweet fruits later when, fascinatingly, Richard stops talking to the audience, his secret collaborators, and does not resume until his world starts to collapse, after his coronation, and he needs them again.

Richard believes that he is going to show us what is going to happen to him, but events then take on a life of their own and seem to suck him in. To offer a humble analogy, he is like the guide with the microphone on the tour bus who stops talking to the passengers when the journey takes directions he wasn't expecting and cannot control. His planned destination is the throne and, predictably, the fun is in the early stages of the journey; when he gets there he falls to pieces and the audience watch him in a tragic battle – the play is called a 'tragedy' in both the quarto and folio printings – with himself, with political events, and with fate in the guise of divine providence. That sense of him falling to pieces is clear in the wooing scene with Queen Elizabeth, where his desperation to hang onto the throne through marriage to his niece makes him blind to its incestuousness. There is something deranged about him here, and about the clear, terrifying, mad logic of his proposal to her that because her sons are dead she has no future and that she should therefore give him her daughter so that, by begetting children upon that daughter, he may give back to Elizabeth her future. Faced with this and all the other evidence of his world imploding, Richard's co-conspirators in the auditorium, guilty by association, feel the need to try to stop him. They cannot do so, and are only cleansed and relieved of their guilt when he is finally brought low by Richmond, that Goody Two-Shoes representative of providence provided by Shakespeare's Tudor historians. At the simplest level that is the shape of the play.

25 Henry Goodman as King Richard III, with Maureen Beattie as Queen Elizabeth, *Richard III*, Act IV, Scene iv: 'Be the attorney of my love to her.'

The start of Richard's fall, unnoticed by him but quite clear to the audience, comes when he is at the very top of his fortune's wheel, as he becomes king. The play is an early Shakespearian essay in gradual deterioration and its straightforward rise-and-fall structure means that the actor needs to find the animating force that propels the upward drive and the countervailing decaying force within and outside Richard that makes his downfall inevitable, and thus to lead the audience on a similar journey. That is why I feel that the fascist dictator overlay on the play, however effective it can be theatrically, doesn't really help, for it diminishes the possibility of the audience becoming complicit with him. Having had the pleasure of watching his evil with impunity, the audience has to experience the pity and terror, and the justice, of his downfall and the deep inner debate that at last affirms their need to stop the evil they have supported. Their journey is from relaxed encouragement, to guilty complicity, to disgusted observation of the appalling events that they have unleashed. That is the spine of the play, the backbone from which hangs the social and political muscle. Two worlds must thus be created (our production did it with the help of the curtain), one which brings the audience within Richard's world, actor and watchers able to acknowledge and enjoy each other; the other which leaves them outside it, watching and needing to stop Richard (in whose mind they are), but unable to do so.

Richard's primary motivation as the play opens is (to put it simply) revenge – revenge for the unfair way that the world has treated him, exacerbated as the play is beginning by loathing for the post-war world of sham and hypocrisy, and by contempt for the Woodvilles who exploit it. He makes clear his rejection of God, of nature, of the court, of love, and of his family, and offers himself instead to the audience, convincing them, by being honest with them, that it is perfectly reasonable to behave as he does. And the audience goes along with his assessment of fate's cruelty to him, with his view that since God has treated him so unfairly then it is fair that he should insult God; they go along with his appallingly logical dismissal of lives and of love, with the psychopathic reasonableness of his explanation of his need to kill. They understand his need to be self-sufficient, to be independent of God; they understand his rejection of mother and brothers, of the women who recoil from him; they understand his need to prove that he needs no-one, no deity. Deep down, and until it is too late, Richard sees himself as beyond God's will and moral code; at war, indeed, with God, his world merely a battleground upon which to act out that war. The audience in the early stages of the play have to be dazzled by him, to admire him, to understand the logic of his reasons for being the intelligent, witty, hubristic sinner that he is. They have to understand his need to defeat God. Even becoming king, they realize, is enjoyable primarily to prove everyone wrong, to spit in the face of conformity, to become God's scourge.

But as God's scourge, in the middle reaches of the play, he is, of course, being made use of by that very same God whom he himself had used as an excuse for his own evil deeds. He thinks he is showing God, with impunity, that he can treat the world, and the people around him, duplicitously and sinfully. He wants to disrupt and overturn the unfairness of the so-called righteous order of things, the order that has belittled and branded him, and that sense (as I want to consider in a moment) remains with him to the end.

Five words overwhelmingly enforced themselves on my mind in rehearsing, and in playing, the role. They are: 'myself', 'love', 'dissemble', 'conscience' and 'God'; a number of further words – 'heaven', 'nature', 'justice', 'oath', 'curse', 'swear'– are significantly connected with them. Each of these five words reveals for me the axis of the play, and without a real sense of ownership of these words one cannot fully realize the role. If a 'sentence' on Richard's life were to be created using an amalgam of these words it might read like this: 'I cannot be fully myself, or happy, in these times, and love a God who dissembles, without myself dissembling to God and to all around me; so I will curse God by making the people who believe in him, and curse me, lose faith in him and curse him. This will give me equality and justice; and thus I shall have no moral doubt and my conscience will be clear.' For the actor these words reveal the lived experience; they are the shapers, the animus, of Richard's development, and of the play's, and any production that is to be more than a surface exploration must creatively connect the forces implied in these words, inside and outside Richard. It may be useful to look at each of these five words in turn.

Myself The word involves the way Richard – 'I' – the way *I* have to judge myself by others' standards, my discovery of myself, the world of *me*, in relation to *you*, the audience, and in relation to the world I operate in – in our production, the Victorian setting, with its politenesses and its politics. I am an outsider, alienated, a rebel by force of circumstance – and maybe innately too. It is by means of successful lying, conning, and killing that Richard learns, literally, to value himself.

Dissemble This concerns the way I have to hide my real feelings, the way I have to overcome my disabilities, my deformity, and to hide my bitterness with seeming kindness. It is about the way the church, and God, dissemble, and cheat me. Not only do I hide my feelings, but I pretend to feel what I don't feel, and can even make myself feel the opposite of my real feelings. My God, I am an actor!

Love This is about the way the people around me show their so-called love; about the rejection of my ugliness by the beautiful; about the lack of respect for my love as it has been shown in loyalty and courage for my family. I hate love, above all for the loneliness of not having it and for the impossibility of giving it when no-one finds you attractive. My mother's love is savage and dysfunctional. Queen Elizabeth's love for my brother is at my expense and our family's. Anne, my wife-to-be, has a weak sort of love, distraught and destroyed. By the time I tell Queen Elizabeth that I will 'love' her daughter 'everlastingly' (IV.iv.349) I know that my loving someone will inevitably mean that I kill them, and at the end I realize that 'no creature loves me' and that after my death 'no soul will pity me' (v.iii.201–2). My young boy is the only loyal person who loves me, and I need that love. To reinforce this idea, and inspired by the many even more radical textual alterations of earlier actors and directors – O, the liberation of influence! – I took six lines from *Henry VI* and added them to the first soliloquy:

> Then since the heavens have shaped my body so,
> Let hell make crooked my mind to answer it.
> I have no brother, I am like no brother;
> And this word 'love', which greybeards call divine,
> Be resident in men like one another
> And not in me; I am myself alone.
>
> (Part Three, v.vi.78–83)

In extremis, therefore, I can only trust, possibly only love, that young boy, for it was as a young boy that I suffered the traumatic exposure to family destruction and death that has shaped my mind. He alone understands me.

Conscience This implies living under a moral code that makes sense: good and bad make conscience viable. In their absence, conscience is merely weakness – 'a word that cowards use . . . to keep the strong in awe' (v.iii.310–11) – and to possess strength is to kill all moral scruples. Misanthropy and misogyny thus become perfectly valid ways to think and live.

God With 'heaven', 'nature', 'justice' (and 'curses') the word encompasses the forces that oppose Richard. 'Shine out, fair sun', he says, that I may see my shadow' (1.ii.262–3), and the idea of being shone upon, or frowned upon – 'loured upon' (1.i.3) – by God, in his active presence, rewarding and rebuking mankind, is vital to the play. Without a sense of divine providence, without a moral code, *Richard III* is just facile melodrama; with that code clearly sensed, it becomes, if not the equal of some of Shakespeare's later tragedies, still a real tragedy of a real man, and not just of a medieval villain-king. A world of justice and divine providence underpins the entire structure of the play and the actors and the audience need to feel that structure if the play is to be more than facile. This does not mean that it has to be presented in a medieval, Christian setting, but the world that Richard operates against must imply a spiritual dimension that he has defied and defiled. The production must offer some tangible experience of this for the audience to believe in, of hope for retribution against wrong, of moral balance and of a set of just values in the world. This binds together all the feuding of the families and the factions, the unanswered suffering of the women, the wrongs committed and rebuked, the retribution, and the salvation finally earned – all of them the subjects of Richard's twisted will, the victims of his cheating and his fatal charm (on both sides of the 'curtain' in our production, the complicit audience in front of him and, behind him, his contemporaries in the world of the play collapsing around him).

I want to conclude this essay by applying some of these ideas to that crucial moment in Richard's tragic arc through the play as he awakens from his dream on the eve of Bosworth:

> What do I fear? Myself? There's none else by.
> Richard loves Richard: that is, I am I.
> (v.iii.183–4).

The words mark a turning point, a crisis of deep personal realization, an ontological awakening akin to Albert Camus's idea of a moment of 'absurd lucidity' – and the play has a profound link with this battle of the individual in revolt against the meaningless world. One's choices in speaking the lines are therefore limited, for if this is a moment of self-discovery there can only be one choice that makes sense; the moral universe upon which the play floats will thus dictate, or creatively limit, the actor's discovery of these lines. To be specific: one might have wanted 'What do I fear?' to mean 'nothing scares me', and thus stress *I*; or one might have wanted it to mean 'what exactly is it that's getting to me?', and thus stress *What*; or one might have wanted it to mean 'I feel many things, but not fear', and thus stress *fear*. Clearly, however, I must choose according to my belief that this is 'lucidity', a new self-knowledge about to be awakened: stressing the last two syllables is thus the only choice that makes sense, and mainly the word *I* itself. The discovery of his new 'I-ness', his humanity, his vulnerability, his ability to be scared and to dream the dreams from which he has just woken, is the door from this emotional fulcrum to the end of the play.

The way he faces this new-found fear, and with it the God he has rejected, and cheated so cleverly (and charismatically), marks a sudden, violent fall in the wheel of his fortune. That is why I say that one cannot act his immediately following discovery that he does have a conscience, and that it has 'a thousand several tongues' (v.iii.194) that all accuse him, forcing him to accept that his past deeds were sins, without a sense of a moral universe, a universe that is difficult to make alive in today's post-Nietschian world; for if God is dead, then so too is this play. Conscience cannot exist without a sense of good and bad, and good and bad cannot exist in the play without God – and the devil. Richard here discovers self-awareness in a way that is almost taken for granted in some of Shakespeare's later plays – *Hamlet* and *Macbeth*, for example. But *Richard III*, more than any other Shakespeare play, surely, depends crucially on the idea of divine retribution, making Richard's revelatory experience of conscience here vital: in this speech, it seems to me, he ceases to be a morality vice figure and becomes a human being – 'Shakespeare and the invention of the human', indeed!

This means that although the audience has been enjoying him, with impunity, as the essence of evil, they are now forced to share in his self-discovery, to feel guilt for having sat there taking pleasure in his performance, encouraging his evil; they must, in short, take responsibility for what has been happening in the play. This is why (as I said earlier) it is so important that Richard should not be sorry for himself at the beginning of the play, for the audience must go through the experience with him, working towards this moment of discovery; the Richard at the beginning of the play (fourteen years earlier, it is worth remembering), self-justifying in his anger and destructiveness, youthful and petulant, is a long way from the depth and vulnerability of the figure that is here revealed. This battle with himself and the ghosts of his past will determine the outcome of the Battle of Bosworth. 'It is now dead midnight' (v.iii.181) – and *now* it surely must be, taking us back to the play's first word, not the 'not' that one of the quartos presents and that some editors, astonishingly, adopt; it is the moment of discovery, of old day becoming new day and old ways new ways; it is, in short, judgement time.

What will he do? Will he, or will he not, be human? That is the exciting question that the audience senses in this scene. Shakespeare, cleverly, postpones an answer by taking Richard off, in his new-found fragility, to check on what support he has in his army – are they too against him now, like God? We then see him trying to put on a brave front while dealing with all the bad omens – the striking clock, the lack of sunshine, the frowning, cloudy heavens, the note found on Norfolk's tent, and the rest – and then comes the decision:

> Let not our babbling dreams affright our souls;
> Conscience is but a word that cowards use,
> Devised at first to keep the strong in awe.
> Our strong arms be our conscience, swords our law!
> March on, join bravely, let us to't pell-mell,
> If not to heaven, then hand in hand to hell.
>
> (v.iii.309–14)

He will go down as a rebel, continuing to spit at God, whose rejection of him he saw at the beginning, and continues to see now, as giving him mastery over his own fate. So he will embrace hell with open arms; and the audience must respect his bravery and insolence, as well as feel relief that, when he dies, there is a returning sense that some justice still prevails in the world.

If explored in this way the live theatre experience of the end of the play can, I believe, be a modern and rewarding one, not just an attempt to perpetuate the Tudor myth that with Richard's death all is suddenly well in the land – a myth that self-evidently has little meaning today, especially when the play is done, as it usually is, on its own and not as part of a 'Wars of the Roses' sequence. In playing Richard I am, for the audience, the archon of the arc of his tragedy; I must lead them into temptation, and, interestingly, I must lead them out of it through the way I deal with the opportunity of salvation, making them feel the need for divine retribution, reaffirming their sense of moral order in the play's movement from chaos to calm. I must show them that a life devoted to 'I am I' (v.iii.184) is wrong and that no man is an island unto himself. In this way the play can work as much more than a chronicle of civil war and become a cycle of rehabilitation and even, like *The Winter's Tale*, of redemption.

I feel strongly that Shakespeare wanted the audience to feel the need for divine retribution to exist. That is why, although he is here still a comparatively young writer yet to evolve the sensitivities of self-revelation of the later tragedies, he so surely grasps the Senecan tradition of the *individual* at the fierce, hot centre of the play. Richard knows all the tricks in the book; the speed of his wit is demonstrated in the quick riposte of the stichomythia episodes with Anne and Queen Elizabeth; he has an astute knowledge of other people's weaknesses; he knows how to work people, where their vanities lie, and how to turn those vanities against them – which explains the speed of his judgement on Hastings, or Buckingham, as 'simple gulls' (I.iii.327) who believe his dissembling. He has an apparently endless ability to find the right way through, to change tack, to put on a performance – a performance, for example, after all the earlier repartee, of the deeply wounded lover, hurt by Lady Anne's hatred of him – or to see a way of getting the better of the 'deep-revolving witty Buckingham' (IV.ii.42). Nothing, it seems, can stop him, and this allows the audience to wonder whether he might even defeat God. The change in all this at the end means that they are brought to pity his demise: no pity, no tragedy – and this is a tragedy. As the play progresses, the audience becomes increasingly frightened and appalled as the number of murders spirals out of control while Richard rises to unmitigated power, and so terror begins to enter the emotional equation of their response to him: no terror, no tragedy – and this *is* a tragedy. From thrilling enjoyment of his intelligence, audacity, and courage (however Machiavellian), by way of surprise, to shock and horror, and then through fear of what he may do next to terror when he does it, the audience should move from admiration to a sense of pity at the waste of such phenomenal energy and so ardent a life-force.

Richard, it seems to me, gets sucked into the engrossing demands of actually being king and becomes less self-aware and less aware of that other world (in front of the curtain, in our staging of it) of his relationship with the audience. He forgets about them, and stops talking to them as events press in upon him and he is forced to deal with those events from a state of stress within himself. In the end, it is his own actions that pull him down to self-destruction. Shakespeare seems to have wanted the audience to see divine retribution as the cause of Richard's downfall, to accept that a single human being alone against fate will always lose; but modern productions perhaps work most effectively when divine retribution becomes a kind of poison that Richard administers to himself. In the last decade of the sixteenth century such an idea would obviously have been regarded as blasphemous, but for the modern actor playing Richard the duality begs to be realized and the question he needs to be asking himself, and the audience, in these extraordinary final stages of the play, is whether it is forces within himself, or forces beyond himself, that hurl Richard to destruction.

Production credits

Productions are listed in the order of essays in this volume. Dates are those of the first preview performance, with the press night usually a week or so later, though the British press night of Michael Boyd's 2001 production of *Richard III* was delayed until 25 April 2001. Five of the productions (*King John*, *Edward III*, *Richard II*, 1 and 2 *Henry IV*, and the 2003 *Richard III*) were part of their respective RSC summer seasons in Stratford, playing there in repertoire before moving briefly to Newcastle-upon-Tyne and thence (with the exception of *Richard III*) to London, *King John* and *Richard II* to the Pit Theatre at the Barbican, *Edward III* to the Gielgud Theatre, and 1 and 2 *Henry IV* to the Barbican Theatre. (*Richard III*, along with nearly all the rest of the 2003 Stratford season, was, for reasons made clear in the introduction, not seen in London.) *Henry V* played a spring to autumn season at the National Theatre's Olivier auditorium. 1, 2, and 3 *Henry VI* and the 2001 production of *Richard III* (which formed, with *Richard II*, 1 and 2 *Henry IV*, and a production of *Henry V* not here represented, the RSC's 'This England' millennium project of all eight history plays of the first and second tetralogies) played at the Swan Theatre in Stratford during the winter season of 2000–1, then moved to the Power Centre for the Performing Arts at Ann Arbor, Michigan, and later joined the four histories of the second tetralogy in London, with the first tetralogy playing at the Young Vic while the second tetralogy was at the two Barbican theatres. For two weeks in May 2001 it was possible to see the complete cycle of all eight plays in sequence.

KING JOHN
Swan Theatre, 21 March 2001
Director: Gregory Doran
Designer: Stephen Brimson Lewis
Lighting: Tim Mitchell
Music: Corin Buckeridge
Movement: Jack Murphy
Sound: Martin Slavin

EDWARD III
Swan Theatre: 10 April 2002
Director: Anthony Clark
Designer: Patrick Connellan
Lighting: Wayne Dowdeswell
Music: Conor Linehan
Movement: Ian Spink
Fights: Terry King
Sound: Martin Slavin

RICHARD II
The Other Place: 20 March 2000
Director: Steven Pimlott
Designer (environment): David Fielding
Costumes: Sue Willmington
Lighting: Simon Kemp
Music: Jason Carr
Fights: Terry King
Sound: Andrea J. Cox
Dramaturg: Simon Reade

1 AND 2 HENRY IV
Swan Theatre: 10 April and 21 June 2000
Director: Michael Attenborough
Designer (set): Es Devlin
Costumes: Kandis Cook
Lighting: Tim Mitchell
Music: Paddy Cunneen
Fights: Terry King
Sound: Scott Myers

HENRY V
Olivier Theatre (National Theatre): 13 May 2003
Director: Nicholas Hytner
Designer: Tim Hatley
Lighting: Mark Henderson
Music: Simon Webb
Fights: Terry King
Military Adviser: Richard Smedley
Sound: Paul Groothuis

1, 2, AND 3 HENRY VI AND RICHARD III (2001)
Swan Theatre: 23 November, 28 November, 2 December 2000, and 14 February 2001
Director: Michael Boyd
Associate Director: Sarah Esdaile
Designer: Tom Piper
Lighting: Heather Carson
Music: James Jones
Movement: Liz Ranken
Fights: Terry King
Rope-work: Gavin Marshall
Sound: Andrea J. Cox

RICHARD III (2003)
Royal Shakespeare Theatre: 11 July 2003
Director: Sean Holmes
Designer: Anthony Lamble
Lighting: Tim Mitchell
Music: Adrian Lee
Fights: Terry King
Sound: Martin Slavin